# TWENTY-FIRST CENTURY
# CHICAGO

EDITED BY DICK SIMPSON AND CONSTANCE A. MIXON

*UNIVERSITY OF ILLINOIS AT CHICAGO AND ELMHURST COLLEGE*

cognella™
San Diego, CA

Bassim Hamadeh, CEO and Publisher

Christopher Foster, General Vice President

Michael Simpson, Vice President of Acquisitions

Jessica Knott, Managing Editor

Kevin Fahey, Cognella Marketing Manager

Jamie Giganti, Project Editor

Luiz Ferreira, Licensing Associate

Printed in the United States of America

ISBN: 978-1-60927-767-3 (pbk)/ 978-1-60927-387-3 (br)

www.cognella.com  800.200.3908

# Contents

# Part III: Chicago Politics

# Part IV: Chicago Government

# Part V: Global Chicago

## Part VI: Metropolitan Chicago

## Part VII: The New Chicago

*To the next generation of Chicagoans who will create a better future*

# Acknowledgments

This book is completely new but draws upon the work of the writers and editors of the earlier ***Chicago's Future in a Time of Change*** books published since 1976 by Stipes Publishing. With this book we build upon that foundation.

We were aided by the efforts of Cori Smith in scanning original documents for us. And the book would not have been so well done except for the work of Missy Zmuda who not only scanned documents, but helped us in all the many editing and correction processes which greatly improved the manuscript.

We are also grateful for Bettye Mixon's assistance in retyping and editing many portions of the manuscript. And Dorothy Storck who helped to polish our words in the introductions.

Finally, Cognella's staff Al Grisanti, Senior Field Acquisitions Editor, Jamie Giganti and Jessica Knott, Project Editors, and Amy Wiltbank, Graphic Designer made the book you hold in your hands possible.

# Part I

## Chicago in the 21st Century

# Choosing Chicago's Future

C hicago was born more than one hundred and fifty years ago. Some of our suburbs are over a century old. As the third largest city in the United States, we have a population of just under three million people. Eight and a half million live in the Chicago metropolitan region; so we are larger in population and have greater wealth than most nations in the world.

During the last several decades, Chicago has been transformed into a "global city." At the same time population, jobs, and housing stock have declined for the first time in the history of the city since the Great Chicago Fire of 1871. We are also enduring the "Great Recession," which began in 2008.

The "political machine" that has governed the city since the Chicago Fire and, more firmly since its reorganization in 1931, was transformed under Mayor Richard M. Daley even as it was challenged by independent reform political forces. His twenty-two-year reign brought Chicago into the global economy and reoriented political power.

The mayoral and aldermanic elections of 2011 were watershed elections just as Mayor Washington's 1983 and Mayor Daley's 1989 elections were. We are at a point of transformation once again as Mayor Rahm Emanuel and a new city council face a billion and a half dollar structural deficit.

The governing structures in the Chicago metropolitan region today remain antiquated and misaligned for any meaningful form of regional governance. Meanwhile racial minorities such as African Americans and Latinos have become the majority in the city and in a number of suburbs. They will soon play an ever more important role.

In this book, we explore many of the fundamental conditions of Chicago metropolitan life. While some of the articles in the book will stress the region's shortcomings, we want to emphasize that Chicago has many possibilities for a positive future. We have some of the best businesses on the planet. We have a population that represents nearly every segment of the world and speaks nearly all of its languages. We have a positive history of reform efforts (as well as a history of scandals and rogues). By our decisions and our actions, we will collectively determine the future of Chicago in the twenty-first century.

Throughout the 1970s and early 1980s, the city of Chicago lost jobs at a rate of 25,000 a year, for a total loss of more than 250,000 manufacturing jobs. Of course, some of these jobs were regained in other economic sectors and some of these manufacturing jobs moved to the suburbs. But even suburbs in our metropolitan region are now losing manufacturing jobs. The suburb of Harvard for example, lost thousands of jobs when Motorola executives made the decision to close its 1.5 million square foot cellular manufacturing and distribution facility and move overseas.

Due in part to the job losses of the 1970s, the city of Chicago also lost an average of 12,500 units of housing and 60,000 residents a year. Our total city population dropped from 3.6 million in 1950 to less than 2.8 million today. That is a loss in the city itself of nearly a million people—despite the pretty new buildings in the South and West Loop and new condos popping up in the neighborhoods. Without our gain in Latino population over the last several decades, the population loss in Chicago would have been much greater. Today, the older manufacturing base of Chicago's regional economy has mostly been replaced—first by the service economy, and now by the global economy.

While manufacturing jobs in Chicago once paid the equivalent of at least $50,000 a year, plus full health benefits and good pensions, many of today's jobs are at the bottom of a two-tiered service economy. Low end service jobs in Chicago are typically part time positions with few benefits and an average salary of $15,000 a year.

Since moving toward a service economy in the 1990s, Chicago has become a global city. In fact, Chicago has become the Midwest regional capital of the global economy. This means that Chicago's fate is now directly connected to the fate of the international economy of which it is a part. We saw this dramatically in the economic downturn after the terrorist attacks of September 11, 2001. We saw this again after the 2008 "Great Recession."

The September 11, 2001 terrorist attacks and the recession that followed produced the following changes for Chicagoland: 1) The private sector declined; 2) Tourism and conventions, which had been a major source of revenue for both the private sector and city government, also declined and only recovered to their previous levels in 2005; 3) State government has had a continuing multi-billion-dollar deficit since 2003. State cutbacks in education and human services were particularly severe; and 4) Between 2001 and 2005, Chicago city government revenue declined before recovering—there were virtually no new funds for government expenses. After the economy recovered by 2005, it went into a similar downturn in the current recession which began in 2008. Hopefully, we will experience the same recovery.

This earlier recession led to a city government budget cut of about $300 million and the elimination of 1,500 city employees. This pattern is happening again with the 2008 recession, which was caused by the collapse of the mortgage industry and housing sector. The city of Chicago faced a $400 million deficit in 2009, which it partially closed by selling off the city's parking meters to a private firm. It faced an additional $654.5 million deficit in the 2011 budget, which led to more employee furloughs and to cutting more city jobs. The Chicago Public Schools and the public transportation system (CTA and RTA) faced an even greater funding crisis in 2011.

In 2002, cutbacks in federal funds to the city of Chicago resulted in a 10% loss in funds for social service agencies that provided food, shelter, and community services for the poorest Chicago metropolitan citizens. The situation became much worse in 2010 with cuts in state funds becoming so great that some social service agencies failed and others reduced services drastically. These economic recessions and loss of intergovernmental funds affected not only the city of Chicago but many Chicago suburban governments as well.

As part of the global economy, international conditions and the role of transnational corporations directly affect our region in ways we no longer control. Decisions like the merger of our banks, the closure of factories like Motorola, collapse of major service companies like Arthur Andersen, and bankruptcies of major companies like United Airlines and the Chicago Tribune all occur without input from city, suburban, or state governments. Local corporations and certainly local communities have little to no voice in determining what will be done. These decisions are made elsewhere in a global economy. There are few restraints on global businesses.

During recessions and economic upturns like those in the 1990s or from 2005–2008, a large homeless population in the tens of thousands in Chicago and suburbs remained. While the overall regional unemployment rate in 2010 was about 9.5% (which was much higher than in previous years), unemployment has been as high as 40% of households in the poorest Chicago communities and southern Chicago suburbs.

As the articles in this book will detail, the major economic change in the Chicago metropolitan region over the last four decades has been the loss of factories and manufacturing jobs. We switched first to the service and now to the global economy. With this new global economy we face the problem of making sure that the benefits do not create a new richer class and leave a much poorer, more desperate class behind. We must find a way to have a more equitable distribution of the wealth generated by the new global economy.

## Social Conditions

From 2000 to 2010, the city of Chicago lost over 200,000 residents while suburban Cook County gained 18,000. At the same time, the metropolitan statistical area as a whole, which includes the far suburban regions, gained almost 363,000 residents. This continues population trends that have existed for decades in Chicagoland and throughout U.S. metropolitan areas.

In this ever-larger metropolitan region, our principal social problem is not found in any one system that doesn't work, such as the public schools, the healthcare system, or the criminal justice system. The major social problem in our metropolitan region is the connection between race and poverty, which has created a permanent underclass.

Metropolitan Chicago remains one of the most segregated regions in North America. It has a segregation index of about 81%. This means that for each Chicago neighborhood and suburb to have a racial mix equal to the metropolitan region as a whole, 81% of the people would have to move. Approximately 81% of us currently live in segregated neighborhoods.

The City of Chicago is now about 33% black, 34% white, 27% Latino, and 6% Asian and other. The 2010 census reports a continued reduction in African American and white populations and a growth of the Latino population. From 2000–2010, 72 census tracts in the metropolitan region of 1,821 census tracts have switched from white to Hispanic, and 22 from white to black. The clearest change is that whites are no longer the majority in the city, where they have been dominant since its founding in 1833. While whites remain the majority in the metropolitan region, population changes are occurring rapidly in every part of the region. Most suburbs remain racially segregated just like the city neighborhoods, although Latinos and Asians have made substantial inroads in some previously all-white suburbs.

Many minorities, especially African Americans, live in our poorest communities—race and poverty go together in Chicagoland. Yet, to paraphrase President Abraham Lincoln, we know that Chicago cannot exist half slave and half free, half black and half white, half poor and half rich. Being black and poor must no longer be synonymous. Neither should being Asian or Latino.

Unfortunately, there is a racial or "color gap" in metropolitan Chicago. Income inequality has continued to rise since the 1960s, despite national policies such as Civil Rights laws and the "War on Poverty" that attempted to eliminate discrimination and poverty.

The concentration of misery and high crime in the racial ghettos of Chicago and Chicago's segregated suburbs is unjust. The same division of poverty and wealth that occurs so obviously in the city occurs in the entire metropolitan region. Suburbs like Harvey and Markham are black and poor, communities like Oak Park and Evanston are managing to handle their racial and economic disparities, while many communities on the North Shore and in DuPage County, remain all white, segregated, very wealthy, and very smug.

The most telling study of the segregation was originally done in 1965 by demographer Pierre de Vise. He examined 250 Chicago community areas with more than 2,500 people in them. He measured median family income, medium value of homes, and assessed real estate valuations per resident or median rent and ranked each community from 1–250. The ten richest communities were then, and remain now in the suburbs. They are nearly all white, mostly far north or west of the city. Examples include suburbs like Kenilworth, Winnetka, and Hinsdale. The ten poorest communities remain on the south and west sides of Chicago, and are nearly all black. Later studies up to the present day have only confirmed this same basic pattern of geographical and racial segregation.

In an effort to solve the ghetto problem of Chicago, the city and the federal government have torn down high-rise public housing projects like Cabrini-Green and Robert Taylor Homes. The original plan was to scatter residents in newly built mixed-income housing. But the new housing, for which CHA residents qualify, was not built as fast as the buildings came down. The Chicagoland region has too little affordable housing for poor and working class families. As a result, racial and economic segregation persists.

One of the problems of residential segregation is that poor minority communities also have the worst schools, the highest level of crime, the fewest jobs, and the fewest ways out of poverty. It leads to a permanent underclass in which families are trapped in poverty for generations.

## Political Conditions

A governing elite of business people, politicians, and heads of major institutions have ruled the city of Chicago for the last hundred and fifty years. Most suburbs are similarly run by a governing elite of local businessmen and women along with local suburban politicians.

Political machines were created in the city after the Great Chicago Fire of 1871. The first political boss was Michael Cassius McDonald, a gambler-saloonkeeper who noticed the common bonds between criminals and politicians and introduced them to each other. The first machines served the rapidly growing ethnic communities in Chicago during the last part of the nineteenth and the first part of the twentieth century.

The machines of Chicagoland have been both Republican and Democratic, suburban and urban. To understand them, we need to define our terms. As political scientists, we use the term "political machine" to mean a permanent political organization or political party that is characterized by patronage, favoritism, loyalty, and precinct work. They spawn patronage, corruption, and inefficient costly governments.

Machines provide certain pay-offs for supporters at all levels. They provide patronage jobs for precinct workers, local government services as favors to those voting for the party slate of candidates, and lucrative, over-priced contracts for business people who give large campaign contributions.

In the suburbs of Chicago, Republican machines are being challenged by ever-more successful Democratic candidates such as former Congresswoman Melissa Bean and former Congressman Bill Foster. Although both lost reelection in 2010, it does not change the overall pattern of greater penetration by Democrats into previously controlled Republican areas of the metropolitan region. DuPage County, once the most Republican county in the United States, voted Democratic for President in 2008. This was the first time a Democratic candidate had carried DuPage County since 1852. In the 2010 primary elections, nearly 55 percent of all DuPage voters pulled Democratic ballots. The Republican advantage in counties like DuPage rested on the assumption that new suburban growth centers were filling up with prosperous middle-class professionals who care most about low taxes and being left alone to raise their kids. This is changing.

At the same time political change is occurring in the suburbs, the Chicago political system is also evolving. The Richard M. Daley regime, which combined the remnants of the old machine and elements of a new political machine, ended in 2011. We have now entered the post-Daley era in Chicago political history.

The old machine tradition of Chicago politics has continued with patronage and corruption in city contracts. Mayor Richard M. Daley enhanced the previous model of machine politics with contributions from corporations and individuals involved in the global economy—banks, law firms, insurance companies, and stock and commodity traders. Their millions of dollars in campaign contributions bought the best political consultants, direct mail, and TV ads. These contributions, along with old-fashioned precinct work, elected and reelected Richard M. Daley (and many of the candidates he has supported) for over two decades. In return, he delivered the policies and amenities favored by the owners and white-collar workers of the global economy. Examples include: Navy Pier; the ever-expanding McCormick Place; Cellular Field; Millennium Park; flowers in the parkways; wrought iron fences; and a lost bid for the 2016 Olympics. The inevitable side effects of machine politics, even new machine politics, however is corruption, scandals, and inefficient government service delivery.

The chief political problem of the metropolitan region has been the continued dominance by old party machines and the new pro-growth money-media machine developed under Richard M. Daley. But we are entering a new political era. It remains to be seen whether Mayor Rahm Emanuel will attempt to continue the modern machine politics of Mayor Daley, or if Chicago politics will be reformed.

## Governmental Conditions

Chicago and Cook County governments, and governments throughout the metropolitan region, are characterized by fragmentation. They are a nineteenth century set of governments trying to cope with twenty-first century problems.

In Cook County there are 540 separate units of government with the power to tax. There are 1,200 separate units of government dispersed throughout the metropolitan region. Chicagoans pay property taxes to seven governments, while suburbanites pay property taxes to as many as seventeen separate government agencies. Strong political machines and strong bosses like former Mayor Richard J. Daley who reigned from 1955-1976 were needed to make this cumbersome governmental machinery work at all. Today's plethora of governments continues to inhibit accountability, efficiency, effectiveness, and coordination.

The legislative branch of Chicago city government, the Chicago City Council, remains a "rubber stamp," although there have been sparks of independence in the last few years. In the 2011 election, nine aldermen retired and one was elected Cook County Board President. Altogether, eighteen new aldermen were elected as more than 350 candidates filed to run for the 50 seats. With a new city council in place, it is again time to consider city council reforms in which the council becomes a genuine check and balance to the mayor and the public has the opportunity to affect public policy more directly.

Many suburbs also need to improve and reform their local town and village councils. Many suburban town councils vote unanimously on all legislation without any meaningful dissent. In almost none of the of the 540 governments within Cook County does a strong and vital legislative branch exist. This must change if local governments in the metropolitan region are to work well and democratically in the twenty-first century.

The 540 governments within Cook County include: the county itself, which is the 19th largest government in the United States; 129 municipalities; 30 townships; and 380 special districts such as the school, park, and library districts. Other districts include large regional districts like the Metropolitan Water Reclamation District of Greater Chicago and the Regional Transportation Authority.

Cook County government under the previous Cook County Board President, Todd Stroger, was even more ineffective and more corrupt than Chicago city government. The lines were stark between supporters and opponents of Stroger on the county board over budgets, ordinances, and new taxes. On most issues, Stroger had only a bare majority. A sales tax repeal vote resulted in thirteen of the seventeen commissioners voting against Stroger. With the 2011 election of Cook County Board President, Toni Preckwinkle, and a turnover of some of the County Commissioners, Cook County government may be reformed in the years ahead—but this remains a daunting task. To plug a $487 million county deficit, President Preckwinkle laid off hundreds of county employees, cut travel expenses, and raised court fees in 2011.

In addition to rampant political corruption, patronage, and waste, the crazy quilt of taxing authority governments within Cook County creates duplication and inefficiency. It is a fractured, multi-layered government that has grown up haphazardly over the last 150 years and is unprepared to meet the needs of the twenty-first century. Overlapping governments in Cook County lack the scope needed for comprehensive metropolitan planning and governing. Any proposal to improve Cook County government by creating a metropolitan government fails because there are almost no "metropolitan citizens" who identify with the metropolitan region. Proposals for metropolitan government are blocked by powerful political interests, racial tensions, and the suburban fear of being governed by the Chicago Machine.

One small improvement has been made in regional governance. NIPC (Northeast Illinois Planning Commission) and CATS (Chicago Area Transportation System) have been merged into a single regional agency with a single staff, authority, and a larger budget. The new agency is called CMAP, the Chicago Metropolitan Agency for Planning. However, this new agency has too few powers to compel compliance with its plans by all the separate governments. Without real money or power it is not very effective in constructing a system of governance in the metropolitan region.

The relatively new regional Mayor's Caucus has allowed for some coordination and cooperation between Chicago and suburban towns. But, it is forced to avoid contentious issues like expansion of O'Hare field or a new third regional airport. Like CMAP, the Mayor's

Caucus depends on voluntary cooperation between multiple separate units of government that jealously guard their powers.

The major governmental problem in the Chicago metropolitan region is that governments are fragmented, inefficient, and inequitable in their delivery of services to citizens.

## Conclusion

In the new global economy and changing society, we face many challenges. For us to have a more positive future, we must begin by understanding our past and collectively adopting a plan to implement our vision of the future. As we enter the new post-Daley era, we do have a choice. We can choose a more positive future for our metropolitan region.

# State of Chicago, 2000–2010

## By Richard M. Daley

*Once a year, the Mayor of the City of Chicago gives a "State of the City" address, highlighting the achievements of the past year and sets forth an agenda for future years. Originally hosted by the League of Women Voters, these addresses are now given before audiences of various not-for-profit social service agencies and are regularly covered by the media.*

*Examined over time, these addresses provide an encompassing picture of the City of Chicago and its hopes for the future. A content analysis of Mayor Richard M. Daley's speeches by Deidre Ferron of the University of Chicago from 1989-1999 found three key themes: 1) civic pride; 2) redevelopment and revitalization; and 3) governmental efficiency and reform. The three speeches excerpted here continue those themes but also emphasize safety concerns and budget constraints.*

## February 19, 2000

I begin this new year determined not to rest on our achievements, but to build on them.

We can't be satisfied because our schools are better today than they were five years ago....We can't simply take comfort in the fact that our crime rates are down eight years in a row....We can't point to the lowest national unemployment rate in 30 years and presume that everyone in Chicago is doing fine....

I view the year 2000 less as a milestone of achievement for Chicago than a new reference point from which we will continue to build a better and brighter future....

We've invested more than $5 billion on tangible, visible, and meaningful new projects and developments in neighborhoods all across Chicago....

In November, the Council approved the Neighborhoods Alive Program, an $800 million effort over the next four years to invest in our community anchors.

By the time this effort is complete, all 25 police stations in the city will be new or fully rehabbed. Up to 20 new state-of-the art firehouses will be built. Every branch library in the city will be new or improved.

We'll also reach our goal of building 100 school campus parks in communities throughout the city....

...[T]he Park District has launched a record $101 million capital program this year, continuing our commitment to make parks and green space a vital part of every community....

Thanks to the strong economy and our ongoing efforts, we're starting to make progress. In the past two years, we've attracted or retained over 32,000 jobs just in our neighborhoods....

We are united by a mission to make our neighborhood quality of life and schools second to none, and we have demonstrated the willingness – year after year – to make the commitments required to meet this goal...

## February 8, 2005

*The recession which followed the terrorist attacks on September 11, 2001 impacted Chicago, as it did cities across the country. Mayor Richard M. Daley cut city government jobs and many projects were put on the back burner. Millennium Park, was not completed until 2004, four years behind schedule and with a $450 million cost overrun. In 2005, despite being in the midst of court cases and allegations that his administration had given out corrupt contracts and existed on patronage, Mayor Daley began to pick up on many of the themes found in earlier State of the City addresses.*

[During the fifteen years since I became mayor] many things have changed, but one has not. Chicago is still the world's greatest city—better, stronger and more inclusive today than when I first reported to you.

Working together on behalf of all the people of our city, we have confronted our major challenges head-on and improved the quality of life....We have rebuilt our neighborhoods—with new parks, libraries, police and fire stations as well as new streets, alleys and sidewalks. We have rebuilt downtown—as a family and tourist definition....

But with all these strides, we haven't yet realized the vision for Chicago that all of us share:

A city in which every family can afford housing in a safe and clean neighborhood;

A city in which every child receives the education he or she deserves;

A city in which a good job with a future is available to anyone who wants to work;

And a city where people who are frail or vulnerable can get the support and care they need to make the most of their lives....

Let me make this very clear. Anyone who believes that my interest in public life in is enriching my family, friends or political supporters doesn't know or understand me at all.... [A]nyone who games the system or cheats the City of Chicago is undermining everything I'm trying to achieve, tarnishing our city and a record I have worked a lifetime to build.... Anyone who violates the rules and regulations governing contracts or any other aspect of city business deserves the harshest possible punishment....

And I'm determined to ensure that, with all our successes, these failures are not my legacy as mayor....

Soon I will sign an executive order banning anyone who does business with the city from contributing to my political campaign....Tomorrow, I will introduce an ordinance in the City Council to strengthen the city's ethics ordinance and enhance the penalties for any city employee who improperly solicits political contributions....I will also introduce...an ordinance strengthening local penalties for fraud in the women and minority business programs....

Each person here today should be proud that our progress over the last fifteen years has been unmatched by any other major city in the nation....

Despite ongoing budget challenges, next year we will continue to invest in our neighborhoods...

So, in closing today, I want to restate the commitments I made to you almost 16 years ago that continue to guide me:

- to keep Chicago working together and in partnership...
- to improve neighborhood quality of life...
- to maintain a government that people trust and believe in...
- And, to make our city work fairly on behalf of everyone...

# August 4, 2010

*By 2010, in the midst of a recession which had begun in 2008 and showed no sign of ending, the tone of the Mayor's speech was different, but many consistent themes and promises remained. In this speech, fighting violence is highlighted. Mayor Richard M. Daley also pledges not to increase property taxes but to make extensive budget cuts instead.*

It is an understatement to say that we are living in complex and difficult times.

Far too many people in Chicago and across our nation continue to feel the pain of the nation's worst recession in seventy years.

People are still struggling to get by.

And even though statistics show that violence on Chicago's streets is far less than a decade ago, unfortunately it continues, leaving pain and suffering in its wake.

Revenues for most cities and states are slow or declining, and businesses have been tentative in hiring new employees, if they're hiring at all….

Even though these challenges are great, I know we can overcome them. And that every Chicagoan—especially those who were forced to put their dreams on hold because of the recession—can again realize their dreams for the future….

[My] commitment is seen in our long term efforts to transform our economy, turn around our schools, control costs and spending in government and take many other steps that are fundamental to better quality of life and the creation of economic opportunity across our city….

It is because—together—we had the foresight to invest in new schools, police and fire stations, parks, green spaces, housing, libraries and senior centers, along with streets, alleys sidewalks, water mains, bridges and medians—that our neighborhoods are stronger today.

Without these neighborhood improvements Chicago would be far behind—without the foundation for creating new opportunity as we emerge from the recession….

During good times and bad, we've done more with less in City government. We've cut spending by $2.6 billion and implemented management improvements including best practices….

We've protected our property taxpayers by limiting property tax increases and raising them as a last resort….

We have also taken many steps to prevent corruption and wrongdoing by implementing fundamental reforms in areas such as hiring and in the way contractors do business with the City.

I've appointed independent Inspector Generals and given that office more authority. We often work proactively with them to uncover and punish misconduct.

In general, we've made government more transparent, accountable and accessible….

I want to address the most immediate and pressing problem we face as a city—violence in our streets, in our homes, in our communities….Like every Chicagoan, I'm not satisfied that the numbers show that homicides today are far fewer than a decade ago. Numbers don't provide much consolation if you've lost a family member or friend to violence or feel vulnerable to its awful grip….

I truly believe that with strong policing, greater resident involvement—parents, churches, block club leaders—strong gun laws and better coordination at the local, state and federal levels that we can turn the tide of violence….

We're putting more officers on street duty and collecting more guns. Since 2006, our "gun turn-in" programs have collected almost 23,000 illegal guns. At my direction, the Department has transferred 268 officers from behind desks to street patrol in the last year and retained them for their new duties. And, as I've announced, in next year's budget, despite our financial challenges, we will fund the hiring of 100 new police officers to patrol our neighborhoods. This is essential and it is our priority….

The fundamentals of Chicago's economy, which we put in place long before the national recession began, have helped us get through these tough economic times....

[But] in America—and Chicago—we must take a long term view, like China does, when they look 20 or 25 years down the road in planning their economy and making major investments to support jobs and growth....

We will continue to invest in new community anchors. In 2010, we will have opened a new library, two new beach houses, a new park district field house and a new police station, with more scheduled to open next year.

By the end of 2011, we will have opened eight new schools and completed four major additions and four major renovations.

Also in 2011 we will open three new libraries, one fire house and another new field house.

Even during these austere budget times we've kept investing as much as we can afford in our neighborhoods....

As you know next year we're facing a budget deficit of $655 million. To get ahead of our budget deficit, we've consistently cut spending and taken steps to control costs. I'm leading by example. I'm taking a $20,000 pay cut. In addition, this year we've cut non-personnel, non-safety spending across the board by another 6 percent and implemented other cost cutting efficiencies. We're working with vendors to reshape their contracts and cut their costs by 10 percent. In the last two-and-a-half years we've cut nearly $400 million in spending....

I can't rule out that to balance next year's budget we'll be forced to put many things on hold or reduce or cut some services—permanently or for a year or two....

And, of course, we have to make sure that government is affordable for people. That is why we will not raise property taxes in next year's budget. People are still hurting and I don't want to add to their burden....

[W]e will move beyond the dark days of the recession and emerge stronger....[B]etter days, a bright future and greater opportunity for everyone lies ahead.

# Mayor-Elect of Chicago Acceptance Speech

## By Rahm Emanuel

*The following excerpts are from the Acceptance Speech of Chicago Mayor-Elect Rahm Emanuel. This speech was delivered the evening of February 22, 2011 after Emanuel received over 55% of votes cast on Election Day. Rahm Emanuel officially became the 46th Mayor of Chicago on May 16, 2011. His inaugural speech echoed many of the themes of his acceptance speech.*

February 22, 2011

What makes this victory most gratifying is that it was built on votes from every corner of the city, from people who believe that a common set of challenges must be met with a common purpose. It's a victory for all those who believe that we can overcome the old divisions and the old ways that have held Chicago back. It is easy to find differences, but we can never allow them to become divisions. Tonight we are moving forward in the only way we truly can. Together. As one city, with one future. And after five months, campaigning across this city and talking to thousands of Chicagoans from every community and every walk of life.

\* \* \*

We did [this election] for our city. We did it for the place we call home. I am more convinced than ever that we can meet the great challenges before us. I can say that because for all its beauty and bounty, the key to Chicago's greatness, it is what it's always been since my grandfather came here in 1917. It's you. It's the hard-working, plain-speaking folks who share a love for their city and a determination to keep it strong and to make it a place their children one day can call home. I share that love and I am determined with your help to meet our challenges head on and to make a great city even greater.

* * *

My sense, and I know it's your sense, we have not won anything until a kid can go to school thinking of their studies and not their safety. Until that child can go to school thinking of their studies and not their safety, we haven't won anything. Or until the parent of that child is thinking about their work and not where they're going to find work, we have not won anything. The real work of building a better future begins tonight. And I intend to enlist every living one of you, every one of you in our city, because the plural pronoun "we" is how we're going to meet the challenges of tomorrow. We need safer streets in all our communities, because I do not want to see another child's name on a memorial killed by gun violence. We need stronger neighborhood schools. We need our parents involved in their kids' education and off the sidelines and involved with them, because our teachers cannot do it without the partner in that home. The most important door a child walks through is the front door to that home for education. That is where they learn right from wrong and the value of education. And our teachers in the classroom deserve that partner. We need to attract and grow good jobs today and tomorrow. And we need to confront the budget deficit that threatens our future, not by burdening Chicagoans and Chicago families with more taxes they cannot afford, but by reinventing city government so city government works for the taxpayers. These are the challenges we need to set Chicago on the right course for the future. With a budget that is balanced and a playing field that is fair. I'm proud that we have never hidden the truth in this campaign. We said it's time for tough choices because denial in the face of challenge is no strategy for success. But we also told Chicagoans that our fate, our future, is in our hands.

* * *

We know we face serious new challenges and overcoming them will not be easy. It requires new ideas, cooperation and sacrifice from everyone involved. As we move forward to address the great challenges before us, we must make sure every community in Chicago is heard and included and has a chance to participate in that future. I look forward to working with tens and thousands of dedicated public servants. Those like my uncle Les, who patrol our streets, who teach our children and fulfill so many vital functions to meet our current challenges and to do it in a way that is fair to them and fair to the taxpayers who pay all of us. And while not all the contests are settled, I want to reach out tonight to the members of the next City Council. We have a chance for a new partnership that will serve our city and its taxpayers well. So thank you, Chicago, for this vote of confidence in our future.

Now I want you to remember, let's continue to work together to make sure Chicago remains the greatest city on earth.

# Part II

## Race and Class

# Race and Class

C lass and racial discrimination and stratification are found in most of our nation's metropolitan areas. Chicago is no exception. As discussed in this section's articles, race and class are intertwined. Although no longer the most segregated city in the United States, ten of Chicago's poorest fifteen neighborhoods are at least 94% African American.[1]

Residential segregation, all too common throughout the Chicagoland area, leaves citizens, mostly minorities, confined to ghettos with underperforming schools and few job opportunities. As early as the 1960s, demographer Pierre de Vise and sociologist William Julius Wilson studied the connection between the race and poverty. De Vise found that the ten poorest communities in the 1960s were all in the inner city and all black. The ten richest were all suburban, mostly north suburban and all white communities. Two decades later, in 1980, sociologist William Julius Wilson found that the patterns of poverty in Chicago had remained unchanged. Updating Wilson's work to the 2010 censuses finds that poverty is moving further south and west from the original ghettos and becoming slightly less concentrated. Still today, the basic patterns of poverty and wealth in the city of Chicago remain essentially the same as when de Vise and Wilson studied them.

This spatial racism was addressed by Chicago's Archbishop Cardinal Francis George in 2001, who argued that,

> *The face of racism looks different today than it did thirty years ago. Overt racism is easily condemned, but the sin is often with us in more subtle forms....Spatial racism refers to patterns of metropolitan development in which some affluent whites create racially and economically segregated suburbs or gentrified areas of cities, leaving the poor—mainly African Americans, Hispanics and some newly arrived immigrants—isolated in deteriorating areas of the cities and older suburbs.*[2]

The racial and economic disparities found in Chicago limit access to opportunity. This has been compounded by the recent recession that hit the poor, the young, the uneducated, and ethnic minorities the hardest. In 2009, 21.6% of Chicagoans had incomes below the federal poverty level; 10.1% were considered to be living in "deep poverty," with over 30% of Chicago's children living in poverty.[3] Even more troublesome is that poverty levels in Chicago for minorities have been estimated to be as high as three to four times the official poverty rates.

No longer simply a white and black city, one of the biggest changes in recent decades has been the increasing Latino and Asian population in Chicago. While their increasing presence has transformed the Chicago metropolitan region into a more multi-cultural, multi-racial, and multi-ethnic city, it has not been an easy transformation. Rather, as discussed in the articles that follow, it has been hampered by polarized political debate centered on immigration status.

## Notes

1. *Segregation in Chicago 2006*, Center for Urban Research and Learning at Loyola University Chicago Loyola University. Chicago, IL. http://www.luc.edu/curl/cfm40/data/minisynthesis.pdf.
2. George, Cardinal Francis, "Dwell in My Love: A Pastoral Letter on Racism," April 4, 2001.
3. "Poverty Rate Data: Information about Poor and Low Income Residents." U.S. Census, 2009. http://www.city-data.com/poverty/poverty-Chicago-Illinois.html#ixzz1BFpArK8f.

# Two Who Stood Up Against Racial Segregation in Chicago

## By Kenan Heise

*Racial segregation has existed in Chicago since its founding in the 19th century. But as long as it has existed, there have been Chicagoans who have fought to end it. This article is based on a conversation between Leon Despres, a white former alderman and life long civil rights advocate, and his friend Timuel Black, an African-American civil rights leader who unsuccessfully campaigned against the Chicago political machine on many occasions. Despres, age 99, and Black, age 88, discuss their experience with racism and segregation and how it has changed throughout the years.*

Timuel Black at 88 years old and Leon Despres at 99 years of age have witnessed enormous racial changes during their generational spans in Chicago. Over these years, they also personally attacked the mired-in-prejudice status quo and worked for change.

The two sat down to lunch recently in a Hyde Park restaurant. Leon is white, the former alderman of the neighborhood and a long-time civil rights activist. Tim is African-American, a professor, a four-time political candidate and an oral historian of Chicago's black community. They could not have eaten here together when they were young. The restaurant's predecessor at that time did not serve "coloreds."

Times have changed. Many around them wore dashikis and other Western African garb that proudly proclaimed their heritage.

Leon's life has spanned ten decades in the city long known as "the most segregated in the North." Tim's has done so for almost nine decades. Each man had found a unique and significant way to respond to segregation and racial bias.

This writer took notes on their conversation as it focused on what had occurred during their lifetimes, is happening today and yet can and needs to change in the future.

Tim has compiled the first two volumes of a three-volume Chicago African-American oral history, *Bridges of Memory: Chicago's First Wave of Black Migration* (Northwestern University Press, 2007).

On four separate occasions, he [Timuel Black] ran for political office in Chicago against patronage-laden candidates backed by the late Mayor Richard J. Daley. He lost each time.

Tim understood the system that he was up against and coined the term, "plantation politics" to describe a political environment in which African-American office holders were and still often are beholden to a white political boss and machine.

As alderman of the 5th Ward from 1955 to 1975, Leon earned a reputation as the city's unrelenting conscience on civil rights. Although he is white, a December 1966 Negro Digest article called him: "the lone Negro spokesman in the Chicago city council." There were, at the time, six black Chicago aldermen.

The Negro Digest's description of him echoed one by noted black novelist Ronald Fair. Both Fair and the article's author maintained that no African-American alderman deserved the title of "Negro spokesman." Each was too occupied with refusing to speak out or act on the deep rooted racial issues affecting not only the black community but also themselves and their own families. These aldermen's allegiances, the two writers maintained, were not to their constituents but rather to Mayor [Richard J.] Daley. They argued this fact clearly demonstrated that the black aldermen took their stances because they were not beholden to the voters but to political patronage and the various favors Daley dispensed. Leon and Tim took the occasion of their luncheon to share memories of the past and to look to the future.

Leon recalled the shock he had felt in 1930 when *The Chicago Defender's* founder, Robert Abbott, told him what he believed would happen if he, as a black man, walked into the Palmer House, attempted to get on an elevator and the man operating it shot him dead. The operator, Abbott said, would be neither convicted nor even arrested.

"He said it with certainty and I believed him," Leon recalled. "But I was stunned."

Tim responded that like any other African-American growing up in Chicago, he had experienced far too many instances of blatant prejudice to be able to record them. He spoke about early in his career being assigned to teach at a Chicago public high school. Once the principal saw the color of his skin, the young teacher was told that the position had been filled.

He added stories from his oral history volumes, citing one in which a man felt he had to put down "American" under the category "race" in order to get hired.

Things are far better now, especially legally, the two agreed. "At my age, I rejoice that Chicago has come as far as it has in regard to race," Leon said. "But people are still imprisoned by racial segregation in this city. Often—as in the past—it is an imprisonment based on where they are forced to live—in neighborhoods where there are no jobs, few opportunities, no good schools, no health facilities, no stores, no decent housing, no personal safety and limited public transportation." The dominant group here continues to use prejudice to label a people inferior. As a result, the segregationist himself pays a big price for his attitude in terms of the problems in his community that his actions and his mentality helped create. The victims, however, have to pay an even higher price.

"It is all more subtle now than it was in the past," Tim added. "It no longer seems as deliberate and as visible as it was, but it is very visible when you see where people live, many involuntarily." Both men agreed involuntary segregation continues to be an enormous problem for Chicago because it inevitably leads to an inequality of resources and opportunity. Among their combined suggestions:

1. Get the establishment to confront the problem in its entirety.
2. End housing segregation by race and class.
3. Find ways to help people with poor educational backgrounds get training to help their children learn.
4. Do something about the problem facing the black community of youth going to jail for drug-related offenses and then being released into the community with the consequent crippling effects.

"We need a massive effort in which people are given voices with which to speak and the tools with which to live," Leon added. "We especially must see people with prestige, influence and standing assume an active role against segregation, period. We need them to be forthright champions of racial equality, raise questions and speak up.

"By such people, I start with Mayor Richard M. Daley. You never hear him speak directly about segregation in Chicago. If you asked him if he is against it, he would say, 'Oh, yes.' But he must bring up the question. We all need to hear him do it. Neither do we hear the governor [Rod Blagojevich] or the president [George W. Bush] speak to segregation in this state or country. They have lines in their speeches, but that is a far different thing than speaking up for change.

"Segregation is deep-seated in our society and in our city. People who have influence have to contribute to the opposition to it." Tim added that real change can come if the different ethnic and racial groups—especially African-Americans, Latinos and Asian Americans—get together to see their common needs and unite around them.

"We need alliances, coalitions of these groups to work together, especially through their schools, churches and organizations. They need to map out what they can do socially as well as economically to bring about real change."

These comments are not the words of Sunday morning talk show guests. Rather, these were two community elders speaking about what they had fought for and intend to continue to fight for even when they have become what people consider "very, very old."

# Racial Segregation in Metropolitan Chicago Housing

### By Tyrone Forman and Maria Krysan

*Residential segregation, defined as the degree of physical separation between racial and ethnic groups, has declined slightly since 1970 in Chicago, but still remains high. The authors of this article discuss possible explanations behind this continuing segregation and their implications for public policy.*

The United States is experiencing rapid demographic changes that are altering its racial and ethnic landscape, particularly in urban centers. According to the 2000 census, 56 percent of residents of the 100 largest U.S. cities are nonwhite. Moreover, there is diversity in the composition of this nonwhite population. For instance, Chicago, historically a black and white city, is now 36 percent black, 31 percent white, and 28 percent Latino, with the remaining 5 percent mainly being Asian. Growing racial and ethnic diversity has not always meant increasing racial integration in the nation's major metropolitan areas. The Chicago metro area ranks as the fifth, sixth, and ninth most residentially segregated metropolitan area in the United States for blacks, Latinos, and Asians, respectively.[1] Residentially seg-regated neighborhoods in our urban centers like Chicago remain among the most salient reminders of our nation's history of racial injustice.

Extreme housing segregation is connected to persistent racial discrepancies in quality of health care, education, jobs, and other public and private sector services. Studies investigat-ing the effects of residential segregation for young African Americans have concluded that the elimination of residential segregation would lead to the disappearance of black-white differences in earnings, high school graduation rates, and unemployment.[2]

Tyrone Forman & Maria Krysan, "Racial Segregation in Metropolitan Chicago Housing," *Policy Forum*, vol. 20, no. 3, pp. 1-5. Copyright © 2008 by the Institute of Government and Public Affairs at the University of Illinois. Reprinted with permission.

Why does residential segregation in Chicago persist 40 years after the passage of the Fair Housing Act of 1968? Effective policies to counteract segregation require a clear understanding of why it persists. We address this question using survey data collected in Cook County in 2005 and the 2000 Census.

## Measuring Segregation in Chicago

Residential segregation is the degree of physical separation between groups (e.g. racial and ethnic) in terms of where they live. One popular measure is the dissimilarity index, which gauges how evenly or unevenly different groups in a metropolitan area are dispersed across neighborhoods. A value of 100 indicates total segregation of two groups, as when, for instance, all neighborhoods are either 100 percent Latino or 100 percent white. A value of zero (complete integration) means every neighborhood has the same percentage of whites and Latinos as there are in the metropolitan area. The City of Chicago would score zero on the Latino dissimilarity index if every neighborhood were 28 percent Latino. Values above 60 indicate a very high level of segregation; values between 30 and 59 indicate moderate segregation, and values of less than 30 indicate low segregation. In the City of Chicago, black-white separation has been high for decades, with the dissimilarity index peaking at 92 in 1970 and remaining as high as 81 in 2000. Values for Latinos and Asians are lower, but still moderately high, roughly 60 and 45, respectively, in recent decades.

## Explanations for Racial/Ethnic Residential Segregation

The three most common explanations for racial residential segregation are: 1) in-group preferences; 2) economic status; and 3) discrimination. Residential segregation could persist because most members of most racial and ethnic groups feel more comfortable living with their own kind. One elaboration on this theory posits that white reluctance to live with blacks is rooted, not in racial antipathy, but in fear of economic liability, as whites associate integrated neighborhoods with higher crime and diminished property values.[3] The research evidence on this point is inconclusive. A second elaboration posits that black segregation comes from a strong and unchanging African American preference for densely black neighborhoods. However, no studies have found many blacks preferring totally black neighborhoods; more typical is a preference for 50 percent black/50 percent white neighborhoods.[4]

A second possible explanation for residential segregation is economic. Racial/ethnic minorities might not live near whites, generally, because they have fewer financial resources and thus cannot afford to live in the same areas. Are the high levels of residential segregation in Chicago income-based? For blacks, no; for others, yes, in part. According to Figure 1, black-white dissimilarity indices within income groups in the Chicago metropolitan area barely change as income rises: the most affluent blacks are nearly as segregated as their

**Figure 1. Average Segregation Levels of Blacks, Latinos, and Asians from Non-Latino Whites by Income, Chicago Metropolitan Area, 2000.**

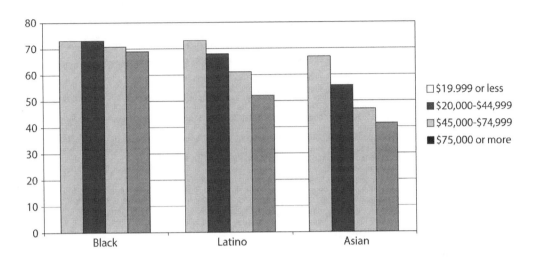

poorest counterparts. In contrast, dissimilarity indices for Latinos and Asians fall by about one-third when comparing those with higher incomes to those with lower.

A third explanation for racial segregation is persistent discrimination against racial/ethnic minorities within the housing market. Even as explicitly racial covenants have vanished, it could be that subtle steering and marketing practices take their place. Social scientists typically measure differences in the treatment of white, black, and Latino home seekers by means of a housing audit. White-black or white-Latino auditors are matched on social background characteristics, and then sent to randomly selected landlords/real estate agents to rent an apartment or purchase a home. The best available nationwide housing audit data indicate that minorities encounter unlawful discrimination approximately one out of every five times they inquire about renting or purchasing a home.[5]

## Data and Findings

The survey data reported here were collected by the University of Illinois at Chicago's Survey Research Laboratory (SRL) between August 2004 and August 2005. SRL conducted face-to-face interviews with 789 randomly selected black, Latino, and white Cook County householders aged 21 and older. The interviews were conducted in English or Spanish depending on respondent preference.

We know from audit studies that housing discrimination remains a problem nationally. However, while audit studies measure subtle aspects of housing discrimination that might not otherwise be revealed, they fail to measure a range of other aspects of housing bias. In our survey, we asked if, based on their race or ethnicity, respondents felt that they had experienced a landlord/real estate agent not renting or selling to them, racial steering, bias in the mortgage industry, or neighbors who made life difficult for them. Four in 10 blacks (41 percent), one-third of Latinos (32 percent), and just one in five (18 percent) whites report experiencing at least one form of housing discrimination based on their race/ethnicity. We also asked our respondents if they were aware of a friend or relative who had experienced at least one of these forms of housing discrimination. The results closely matched the first-hand reports: almost half of African Americans (44 percent), approximately one-third of Latinos (30 percent), and a little more than one in 10 whites (13 percent) responded affirmatively. In short, racial/ethnic discrimination in housing appears to be an ongoing reality in the lives of African American and Latino Chicagoans.

We now turn to neighborhood preferences. What are the preferences of Chicagoans? To answer this question we asked Cook County residents to imagine their ideal neighborhood (where they would feel most comfortable) and describe the racial and ethnic mix of it. In general, it appears that Chicago blacks, Latinos, and whites report a similar commitment to living in racially and ethnically diverse neighborhoods. First, all three groups choose a racial/ethnic mix that includes a substantial proportion of other racial/ethnic groups. For example, whites put equal numbers of blacks (13 percent), Latinos (12 percent), and Asians (12 percent) in their ideal neighborhood. Second, blacks, Latinos, and whites in Cook County want their own group to be largest in their ideal neighborhood. Yet, whites are the only group that prefers that their racial group be in the majority (56 percent).

Although these data about "ideal neighborhoods" shed light on the environs people say they prefer, we know very little about how these preferences play out in the real world. The data just reported are based on a hypothetical neighborhood, and in many cases the neighborhoods people describe are simply not available in the metropolitan area. So, what happens if we ask about real-life communities? We can learn about neighborhood preferences by examining the racial composition of the communities in which Cook County residents have actually searched for housing.

We showed our survey respondents a map that identified 41 communities in the Chicago metropolitan area that differed in important ways with respect to racial composition, social class characteristics, and geographical location. Blacks, Latinos, and whites were asked, among other things, whether they had searched for housing in any of these communities in the past 10 years. We sought to answer the question, "What are the racial/ethnic characteristics of the communities in which white, black, and Latino Cook County residents have actually searched for a place to live?"

The communities named by respondents according to whether they have majorities of the respondent's own race, some other race, are a mix of those two types, or were not among the communities on our map. A number of important contrasts emerge. First, 45 percent of whites have searched only in communities where whites are in the majority (that is, constitute more than 50 percent of the population); and just 4 percent have searched where any other group is in the majority. Second, approximately one in four whites have looked in both neighborhoods where they are the majority and where they are the minority. (The remaining one-fourth of white respondents have either not searched for housing in the last 10 years, or have searched in communities that were not identified on our map, whose racial composition we do not know.) For blacks and Latinos in Cook County, house hunting is a very different experience. Just 8 percent of blacks have looked only in majority (more than 50 percent) black communities. Moreover, one in five blacks has searched exclusively in communities where blacks are in the minority. Mostly, then, blacks have searched in both kinds of communities—those where they are in the majority and those where they are in the minority. Indeed, 81 percent of blacks included in their search locations a community where they are in the minority. These results severely challenge the view that blacks prefer to self-segregate in majority-black neighborhoods.

Latinos show a similar pattern. Fully 35 percent of Latinos searched only in communities where another group was in the majority. An additional 37 percent of Latinos searched in both communities where they were in the majority and ones in which they were in the minority.

## Conclusion and Policy Implications

Our analysis reveals several things. First, money is not the powerful explanation that conventional wisdom might suggest. Although segregation levels are reduced for Asians and Latinos with greater financial means, the same is not true for African Americans.

Second, our results demonstrate the complexity of the preference explanation. While Cook County residents of all three racial/ethnic groups included in the study profess an interest in diverse neighborhoods in principle, when we examine the expression of those preferences in the form of actual search locations, we discover far less evidence of a commitment to diversity on the part of whites. African Americans and Latinos seek out many different community types, even though, given patterns of segregation, we know they end up in communities that are highly segregated (especially blacks). This disjuncture between blacks' and Latinos' preferences and their actual neighborhoods probably originates, at least in part, in barriers presented by discriminatory treatment, in the form of exclusion, steering, and unfriendliness.

Third, our analysis indicates that 42 years after the most ambitious effort to end housing discrimination in Chicago (i.e., the Chicago Freedom Movement led by Martin Luther King Jr. and Al Raby), African Americans and Latinos in Cook County continue to report substantial levels of unfair—and illegal—treatment in the housing industry.

What are the policy implications of these findings? First, our survey data reveal a need for increased federal and state resources for the vigorous enforcement of anti-discrimination laws in housing (i.e., Title VIII of the Civil Rights Act of 1968). Discrimination still occurs, and enforcement is necessary.

Second, given the limited financial capacity of blacks and Latinos as compared to whites (in Chicago in 2000, median household incomes for blacks, Latinos, and whites were $29,000, $37,000, and $49,000, respectively), we need land-use policies which reverse decades of exclusionary zoning laws that set minimum floor space and lot size requirements and maximum density limitations. While usually appearing racially neutral, these policies often restrict suburban housing opportunities for racial and ethnic minorities by limiting affordable housing in these areas. Illinois has adopted inclusive legislation (e.g., 2003 Affordable Housing Planning and Appeal Act), but more is needed. One example is Montgomery County, Maryland's ordinance requiring that in developments of 50 or more units, 15 percent of the units must be affordable to households below 65 percent of the median income. A policy prescribing mandatory set-asides in communities lacking affordable housing may lead to more racially/ ethnically and economically diverse communities.

Third, altering preferences that work against integration is a far more complicated policy goal. However, according to our data, members of all three racial/ethnic groups report, in the abstract, a desire for greater levels of integration than presently exist. The challenge is to create situations where those abstract preferences can be translated into behavior. The affirmative marketing component of fair housing legislation is consistent with this need. Affirmative marketing refers to the active promotion of racially diverse, majority black, and majority Latino neighborhoods to whites and the encouraging of Asians, blacks, and Latinos to consider moving into majority-white neighborhoods. Organizations and entities that make individuals of all races and ethnicities aware of housing opportunities that are pro-integrative, and that help break down the barriers to integrated housing decisions, should be promoted and funded aggressively. In sum, dismantling the rigid housing color line that exists in Chicago will take concerted effort by residents, real estate agents, developers, community leaders, and legislators.

## Notes

1. Iceland, John, Daniel H. Weinberg, and Erika Steinmetz. 2002. *Racial and Ethnic Residential Segregation in the United States, 1980–2000*. U.S. Census Bureau, Special Report Series, CENSR-3. Washington, DC: U.S. Government Printing Office.

2. Cutler, David and Edward Glaeser. 1997. "Are Ghettos Good or Bad?" *The Quarterly Journal of Economics* 112: 827–872.

3. Harris, David R. 2001. "Why are Whites and Blacks Averse to Black Neighbors?" *Social Science Research* 30: 100-116.

4. Farley, Reynolds et al. 1994. "Stereotypes and Segregation: Neighborhoods in the Detroit Area." *American Journal of Sociology* 100: 750-780. Also see Krysan, Maria and Reynolds Farley. 2002. "The Residential Preferences of Blacks: Do They Explain Persistent Segregation?" *Social Forces* 80: 937–980.

5. Ross, Stephen and Margaret Austin Turner. 2005. "Housing Discrimination in Metropolitan America: Explaining Changes between 1989 and 2000." *Social Problems* 52: 152–180.

# The Halsted Street Saga

By Jane Addams, Florence Scala, Studs Terkel, and Dick Simpson

*The saga of the Halsted Street neighborhood was started a hundred years ago with Jane Addams' Hull House trying to offer an alternative to the cycles of immigrant poverty. It continues with the story of how the present day university has now gobbled up the old neighborhood. In between, Florence Scala tells us how it happened that a neighborhood, rich in tradition and heritage, was replaced by a university with an urban mission.*

*The three vignettes presented here trace a hundred years of struggle as neighborhoods are destroyed and rebuilt in a different 21ˢᵗ century city.*

## 1900–1920 by Jane Addams

*J*ane Addams and the settlement house she founded early in the twentieth century were *major forces in American history. She was an important leader in the settlement house movement, the progressive movement in American politics, the fight by suffragettes for women's right to vote, and the peace movement. She and her colleagues at the Hull House Settlement helped to expose many of the problems of the inner-city poor of her day and to pass laws and to change government policies in ways that benefited the poor. This is her description of the neighborhood in which she worked and lived in the early decades of the twentieth century.*

Halsted street has grown so familiar during 20 years of residence that it is difficult to recall its gradual changes—the withdrawal of the more prosperous Irish and Germans, and the slow substitution of Russian Jews, Italians and Greeks.

Halsted street is 32 miles long, and one of the great thoroughfares of Chicago; Polk Street crosses it midway between the stockyards to the south and the shipbuilding yards on the north branch of the Chicago River. For the six miles between these two industries the street is lined with shops of butchers and grocers, with dingy and gorgeous saloons, and pretentious establishments for the sale of ready-made clothing....

Hull House once stood in the suburbs, but the city has steadily grown up around it and its site now has corners on three or four foreign colonies. Between Halsted street and the [Chicago River] live about ten thousand Italians—Neapolitans, Sicilians, and Calabrians, with an occasional Lombard or Venetion. To the south on Twelfth Street are many Germans, and side streets are given over almost entirely to Polish and Russian Jews. Still farther south, these Jewish colonies merge into a huge Bohemian colony, so vast that Chicago ranks as the third Bohemian city in the world. To the northwest are many Canadian-French, clannish in spite of their long residence in America, and to the north are Irish and first-generation Americans. On the streets directly west and farther north are well-to-do English-speaking families, many of whom own their houses and have lived in the neighborhood for years; one man is still living in his old farmhouse.

The policy of the public authorities of never taking an initiative, and always waiting to be urged to do their duty, is obviously fatal in a neighborhood where there is little initiative among the citizens. The idea underlying our self government breaks down in such a ward. The streets are inexpressibly dirty, the number of schools inadequate, sanitary legislation is unenforced, the street lighting is bad, the paving miserable and altogether lacking in the alleys and smaller streets, and the stables foul beyond description. Hundreds of houses are unconnected with the street sewer. The older and richer inhabitants seem anxious to move away as rapidly as they can afford it. They make room for the newly arrived immigrants who are densely ignorant of civic duties. The substitution of the older inhabitants is accomplished industrially also, in the south and east quarters of the ward. The Jews and Italians for the finishing of the great clothing manufacturers, formerly done by American, Irish, and Germans, who refused to submit to the extremely low prices to which the sweating system, has reduced their successors. As the design of the sweating system is the elimination of rent from the manufacture of clothing, the "outside work" is begun after the clothing leaves the cutter. An unscrupulous contractor regards no basement as too dark, no stable loft too foul, no rear shanty too provisional, no tenement room too small for his workroom, as these conditions imply low rental. Hence these shops abound in the worst of the foreign districts where the sweater easily finds his cheap basement and his home finishers.

The houses of the ward, for the most part wooden, were originally built for one family and are now occupied by several. They are after the type of the inconvenient frame cottages found in the poorer suburbs twenty years ago. Many of them were built where they now stand; others were brought thither on rollers, because their previous sites had been taken for factories. The fewer brick tenement buildings which are three or four stories high are comparatively new, and there are few large tenements. The little wooden houses have a temporary aspect, and for this reason, perhaps, the tenement-house legislation in Chicago is totally inadequate. Rear tenements flourish; many houses have no water supply save the faucet in the back yard, there are no fire escapes, the garbage and ashes are placed in wooden boxes which are fastened to the street pavements.

One of the most discouraging features about the present system of tenement houses is that many are owned by sordid and ignorant immigrants. The theory that wealth brings responsibility, that possession entails at length education and refinement, in these cases fails utterly. The children of an Italian immigrant owner may "shine" shoes in the streets and his wife may pick rags from the street gutter, laboriously sorting them in a dingy court. Wealth may do something for her self-complacency and feeling of consequence; it certainly does nothing for her comfort or her children's improvement nor for the cleanliness of anyone concerned. Another thing that prevents better houses in Chicago is the tentative attitude of the real estate men. Many unsavory conditions are allowed to continue which would be regarded with horror if they were considered permanent. Meanwhile, the wretched conditions persist until at least two generations of children have been born and raised in them.

In every neighborhood where poorer people live, because rents are supposed to be cheaper, there is an element which, although uncertain in the individual, in the aggregate can be counted upon. It is composed of people of former education and opportunity who have cherished ambitions and prospects but who are caricatures of what they meant to be —"hollow ghosts which blame the living men." There are times in many lives when there is a cessation of energy and loss of power. Men and women of education and refinement come to live in a cheaper neighborhood because they lack the ability to make money, because of ill health, because of an unfortunate marriage, or for other reasons which do not imply criminality or stupidity. Among them are those who in spite of untoward circumstances, keep up some sort of an intellectual life; those who are "Great for books," as their neighbors say. To such the Settlement may be a genuine refuge. . . .

From the first it seemed understood that we were ready to perform the humblest neighborhood services: We were asked to wash the newborn babies, and prepare the dead for burial, to nurse the sick, and to "mind the children." Occasionally these neighborly offices unexpectedly uncovered ugly human traits. For six weeks after an operation we kept in one of our three bedrooms a forlorn little baby who, because he was born with a cleft palate, was most unwelcome to his mother, and we were horrified when he died of neglect a week after he was returned to his home; a little Italian bride of fifteen sought shelter with us one November evening, to escape her husband who had beaten her every night for a week when he returned home from work, because she had lost her wedding ring; two of us had officiated quite alone at the birth of an illegitimate child because the doctor was late in arriving, and none of the Irish matrons would "touch the likes of her"; we ministered at the deathbed of a young man who during a long illness of tuberculosis had received so many bottles of whisky through the mistaken kindness of his friends, that the cumulative effect produced wild periods of exultation, in one of which he died.

We were also early impressed with the curious isolation of many of the immigrants; an Italian woman once expressed her pleasure in the red roses that she saw at one of our receptions in surprise that they had been "brought all the way from Italy." She would not believe for an instant that they had been grown in America. She said that she had lived in Chicago for six years and had never seen any roses, whereas in Italy she had seen them every summer in great profusion. During all that time, of course, the woman had lived within ten blocks of a florist's window; she had not been more than a five-cent car ride away from public parks; but she had never dreamed of faring forth herself, and no one had taken her. Her conception of America had been the untidy street in which she lived and had made her long struggle to adapt herself to American ways. . . .

The Settlement, then is an experimental effort to aid in the solution of the social and industrial problems which are engendered by the modem conditions of life in a great city. It insists that these problems are not confined to any portion of a city. It is an attempt to relieve, at the same time, the overaccumulation at one end of society and the destitution at the other; but it assumes that this overaccumulation and destitution is most sorely felt in the things that pertain to social and educational privileges. From its very nature it can stand for no political or social propaganda. It must, in a sense, give the warm welcome of an inn to all such propaganda, if perchance one of them be found an angel. The one thing to be dreaded in the Settlement is that it loses its flexibility, its power of quick adaptation, its readiness to change its methods as its environment may demand. It must be open to conviction and must have a deep and abiding sense of tolerance. It must be hospitable and ready for experiment. It should demand from its residents a scientific patience in the accumulation of facts and the steady holding of their sympathies as one of the best instruments for that accumulation. It must be grounded in a philosophy whose foundation is on the solidarity of the human race, a philosophy which will not waver when the race happens to be represented by a drunken woman or an idiot boy. Its residents must be emptied of all conceit of opinion and self-assertion, and ready to arouse and interpret the public opinion of their neighborhood. They must be content to live quietly side by side with their neighbors, until they grow into a sense of relationship and mutual interests. Their neighbors are held apart by differences of race and language which the residents can more easily overcome. They are bound to see the needs of their neighborhood as a whole, to furnish data for legislation, and to use their influence to secure it. In short, residents are pledged to devote themselves to the duties of good citizenship and to the arousing of the social energies which too largely lie dormant in every neighborhood given over to industrialism. They are bound to regard the entire life of their city as organic, to make an effort to unify it, and to protest against its overdifferentiation.

*Decades after Jane Addams founded Hull House, Florence Scala, an Italian house wife and later businesswoman and aldermanic candidate, describes the fight between the Halsted/Maxwell Street neighborhood and city hall. It is a fight the neighborhood, like many urban neighborhoods, lost. Even the Hull House board of directors betrayed the neighborhood.*

I was born in Chicago, and I've always loved the city. I'm not sure any more. I love it and I hate it every day. What I hate is that so much of it is ugly, you see? And you really can't do very much about it. I hate the fact that so much of it is inhuman in the way we don't pay attention to each other. And we can do very little about making it human ourselves.

What I love is the excitement of the city. There are things happening in the city every day that make you feel dependent on your neighbor. But there's detachment, too. You don't really feel part of Chicago today, 1965. Any more, I don't feel any [attachment].

I grew up around Hull House, one of the oldest sections of the city. In those early days I wore blinders. I wasn't hurt by anything very much. When you become involved, you begin to feel the hurt, the anger. You begin to think of people like Jane Addams and Jessie Binford and you realize why they were able to live on. They understood how weak we really are and how we could strive for something better if we understood the way.

My father was a tailor, and we were just getting along in a very poor neighborhood. He never had money to send us to school; but we were not impoverished. When one of the teachers suggested that our mother send us to Hull House, life began to open up. At the time, the neighborhood was dominated by gangsters and hoodlums. They were men from the old country, who lorded it over the people in the area. It was the day of moonshine. The influence of Hull House saved the neighborhood. It never really purified it, you know what I mean? I don't think Hull House intended to do that. But it gave us. . . well, for the first time my mother left that damn old shop to attend Mother's Club once a week. She was very shy, I remember. Hull House gave you a little insight into another world. There was something else to life besides sewing and pressing. . . .

I always remember the neighborhood as a place that was alive. I wouldn't want to see it back again, but I'd like to retain the being together that we felt in those days.

There were Negroes living in the neighborhood even then, but there was not the tension. I've read about those riots in Chicago in the twenties - the race riots. But in our neighborhood it never did come to any kind of crisis. We used to treat each other as neighbors then. Now we look at each other differently. I think it's good and bad in a way. What we're doing is not understanding, some of us, what it was like then. I think that the American-born—the first generation, the second generation—has not hung on to what his mother and father had. Accepting someone naturally as a man. We don't do that today.

I think that the man who came over from Europe, the southern European especially, who was poor, could understand and see the same kind of struggle and have immediate sympathy for it. He accepted the Negro in the community as a man who is just trying to make a way for himself, to make a living. He didn't look upon him as a threat. I think it was the understanding that both were striving. Not out of some great cause, but just in a human way. I'm convinced that the first and second generation hasn't any concern about the other person's situation. I think money and position are hard to come by today and mean an awful lot, and now they see the Negro as a threat. Though they may say he's inferior, they know damn well he's not. He's as clever as we are and does many things better than we can. The American-born won't accept this, the first and second generation family, especially among the Italians and Poles, and the Irish, too. . . .

Through my teens I had been a volunteer at Hull House. After the War, Eri Hulbert, Jane Addams's nephew, told me of a dream he had. The Near West Side, our area, could become the kind of place people would *want* to live in, close to the city. Did I think this was possible? I said no, people didn't care enough about the neighborhood to rebuild it. But he introduced me to the idea of city planning. He felt the only hope for big cities, in these communities that were in danger of being bulldozed, was to sit down and look and say we have a responsibility here. He convinced me that you could have a tree on the West Side, see?

That's where my life changed. I became involved with a real idea and talking to people like the banker, the social worker, and the Board of Trustees at Hull House. But I suddenly realized my inadequacy. I simply couldn't understand their language, you know? I had to go back to school.

This is where I began to lose the feeling of idolatry you have about people. I think that's bad. I idolized the people that were involved in Hull House. I thought they could never make a mistake. I was later to find out they were the ones who could hurt me the most. I feel that people have to be prepared always for imperfections in everyone, and we have to feel equal, really, to everyone. This is one of the things lots of slum kids, people who came out of poor areas, don't have. Not to be afraid to say something even though it may be way off base. I did this many times and I'd be embarrassed, realizing I had said something that had nothing to do with what they were talking about. But Eri Hulbert kept saying it makes no difference, just keep at it. You're as good as they are ....

In those days it was a new idea. You had to fight the politician who saw clearance and change as a threat to his power, his clout. He likes the kind of situation now around Maxwell Street, full of policy and hot goods being sold on the market and this kind of stuff that could go on and on without too much interference from authority because it's so oppressed. The rotten housing and no enforcement of codes and all that business. We had a tough time selling the Catholic Church, too. From '47 to '56 were rough years. It was tough selling people on the idea that they could do it for themselves, that it was the only way it could be done. Their immediate reaction was: You're crazy, you know? Do you really think this neighborhood is worth saving?

All the meetings we had were so much frustration. Eri Hulbert was trying to lead us in a democratic way of doing something about our city. The misunderstandings never came from the neighborhood people. It arose out of the Hull House Board's unwillingness to understand. He couldn't get his point across.

Eri Hulbert committed suicide before our plan was accepted by the city. His death, more than anything else, opened a door which I never dreamed could open. You know, there's a real kind of ugliness among nice people. You know, the dirty stuff that you think only hoodlums pull off. They can really destroy you, the nice people. I think this is what happened to Eri, the way he was deserted by his own. I think it really broke his heart. What disturbs me is that I was a grown woman, close to thirty, before I could see. Sometimes I want to defend the rotten politicians in my neighborhood. I sometimes want to defend even gangsters. They don't pretend to be anything but what they are. You can see what they are. They're not fooling anybody, see? But nice people fool you.

I'm talking about the [Hull House] Board of Trustees, the people who control the money. Downtown bankers, factory owners, architects, people in the stock market. The jet set, too. The young people, grandchildren of old-timers on the Board, who were not really like their elders, if you know what I mean. They were not with us. There were also some very good people, those from the old days. But they didn't count so much any more. This new crowd, this new tough kind of board members, who didn't mind being on such a board for the prestige it gave them, dominated. These were the people closely aligned to the city government, in real estate and planning. And some very fine families, old Chicago families. (Laughs.) The nicest people in Chicago.

\* \* \*

In the early Sixties, the city realized it had to have a campus, a Chicago branch of the University of Illinois. (There was a makeshift one at the pier out on the lake.) There were several excellent areas to choose from, where people were not living: a railroad site, an industrial island near the river, an airport used by businessmen, a park, a golf course. But there was no give. The mayor [Richard J. Daley] looked for advice. One of his advisors suggested our neighborhood as the ideal site for the campus. We were dispensable. [This advisor] was a member of the Hull House Board. It was a strange thing, a very strange thing. Our alderman, he's not what I'd call a good man—even he tried to convince the Mayor this was wrong. But the Mayor was hearing other voices. The nice people.

The alderman alerted us to the danger. Nobody believed it. The priest himself didn't believe it. They had just opened the parish, a new church, a new school. Late in the summer of 1960 the community could have been touched off. But the people were in the dark. When the announcement came in 1961, it was a bombshell. What shocked us was the amount of land they decided to take. They were out to demolish the entire community.

I didn't react in any belligerent way until little kids came knocking at the door, asking me to attend a meeting. That's where the thing got off the ground. It was exciting to see that meeting, the way people felt and the way they talked and the way—they hurt—to hear our Italian priest, who had just become an American. This was in February, we had just celebrated Lincoln's birthday. He had just become a citizen, he couldn't understand.

Though we called the Mayor our enemy, we didn't know he was serving others. It was a faceless thing. I think he'd just as soon have had the university elsewhere. But the pressures were on. We felt it as soon as our protests began....

I shall never forget one board meeting. It hurt Miss Binford [a colleague of Jane Addams who had lived and worked at Hull House from 1906 until its destruction in 1965] more than all the others. That afternoon, we came with a committee, five of us, and with a plea. We reminded them of the past, what we meant to each other. From the moment we entered the room to the time we left, not one board member said a word to us. No one got up to greet Miss Binford nor to speak to her. No one asked her a question. The chairman came forward, he was a gentleman, and showed us where to sit.

Miss Binford was in her late eighties, you know. Small birdlike in appearance. She sat there listening to our plea and then she reminded them of what Hull House meant. She went back and talked, not in a sentimental way, about principles that must never waver. No one answered her. Or acknowledged her. Or in any way showed any recognition of what she was talking about. It's as though we were talking to a stone wall, a mountain.

It was pouring rain and we walked out of the room the way people walk out who feel defeat. I mean we walked out trying to appear secure, but we didn't have much to say to each other. Miss Binford could hardly speak at all. The shock of not being able to have any conversation with the board members never really left her. She felt completely rejected. She knew then there would be no help anywhere. In the past, whenever there was a serious problem in the juvenile courts, she could walk into the Mayor's office and have a talk with him, whoever he was. Kelly, for instance, or Kennelly, or Cermak. And never fail to get a commitment from him. Never. But she knew after this meeting, she'd never find that kind of response again. And sure enough, to test herself, she made the rounds. Of all the people who had any influence in town, with whom she had real contact, not one responded. They expressed sympathy, but it was hands off. Something was crushed inside her. The Chicago she knew had died.

I don't think we realized the stakes involved in this whole urban renewal system. The money it brings in, the clout necessary to condemn land ... a new Catholic Church was demolished, too. It had opened in '59, built near Hull House with the city's approval. The Church was encouraged to go ahead and build, so as to form the nucleus for the new environment, see? It cost the people of the area a half million dollars. The Archdiocese lends the parish money, but the parish has to repay. It's a real business arrangement.

Now the people of the area have learned a good deal, but it was a bitter education. The politicians' actions didn't bother us as much. We hated it, we argued about it, we screamed about it out loud. Daley gave the orders and the alderman followed it. This kind of thing we could understand. But we could never understand the silence of the others. A group wanted to picket the Archdiocese, but I felt it was wrong, because we were put into a position of fighting education, the University being built, you know....

In an area like ours, the uprooting is of another kind. I lived on the same block for over forty-five years; my father was there before me. It takes away a kind of stability big cities need. Lots of the people have moved into housing no better than the kind they lived in. Some have moved into public housing. The old people have really had it worse: Some have moved into "nicer" neighborhoods, but they're terribly unhappy, those I've spoken with. Here, downtown in the Loop, everything is clearing and building and going up. And the social workers in this town, boy! I can hardly look at them with respect any more. The way they've knuckled down to the system themselves, because everybody wants a Federal grant or something. They don't want to be counted out. I'm sick of the whole mess and I don't know which way to go.

There are the little blessings that come out of struggle. I never knew Jessie Binford as a kid at Hull House. I used to see her walking through the rooms. She had such dignity, she just strode through the rooms and we were all kind of scared of her. In the past four or five years, we became close friends. I really knew the woman. It meant something to her, too. She began to know the people in the way she knew them when she first came to Hull House as a young girl. It really gave her life, this fight. It made clear to her that all the things she really believed in, she believed in all the more. Honor among people and honor between government and people. All that the teacher tells the kids in school. And beauty.

There was a Japanese elm in the courtyard that came up to Miss Binford's window. It used to blossom in the springtime. They were destroying that tree, the wrecking crew. We saw it together. She asked the man whether it could be saved. No, he had a job to do and was doing it. I screamed and cried out. The old janitor, Joe, was standing out there crying to himself. Those trees were beautiful trees that had shaded the courtyard and sheltered the birds. At night the sparrows used to roost in those trees and it was something to hear, the singing of those sparrows. All that was soft and beautiful was destroyed. You saw no meaning in anything any more.

There's a college campus on the site now. It will perform a needed function in our life. Yet there is nothing quite beautiful about the thing. They'll plant trees there, sure, but it's walled off from the community. You can't get in. The kids, the students, will have to make a big effort to leave the campus and walk down the streets of the area. Another kind of walling off....

To keep us out. To keep the kids out who might be vandals. I don't see that as such a problem, you know. It wasn't the way Jane Addams saw it, either. She believed in a neighborhood with all kinds of people, who lived together with some little hostility, sure, but nevertheless lived together. In peace. She wondered if this couldn't be extended to the world. Either Jane Addams brought something to Chicago and the world or she didn't.

*The story of the Halsted Street neighborhood didn't end with the creation of the University of Illinois at Chicago in the 1960s. It continued in the twenty-first century when university expansion, with the help of Chicago city government, destroyed the commercial market place and the last of the neighborhood's history. Some call the new student housing and private market upscale condominiums progress. Others decry the wanton destruction of neighborhoods in the constant rebuilding of the city.*

The University of Illinois at Chicago has torn down the remaining buildings of the old Halsted/Maxwell Market. Yes, a couple of buildings like the police station—which served as the set for the Hill Street Blues television program—survived the wrecking ball. Yes, some building facades (with the silhouettes of people drawn in the windows) are glued to new structures like the mammoth parking garage. And a few more statues of children playing ball have been erected. And yes, in one old building there may be a museum open to document a past that not only doesn't exist, but which my university helped destroy.

Some call this progress. Others say it's inevitable. The cynical say it is just the way for real estate developers with political connections to make a buck on the backs of the poor. New housing and upscale shops have been built. The university has expanded its facilities to house more students and to provide better facilities for some departments. There is a new "Forum" building to hold local and international conferences and more university faculty and young couples now live in the new condos.

Certainly teaching the students of Chicago, the suburbs, and the world is a good service that we at the university provide. No one can be against better education. But the university, the mayor, and local politicians have conspired to expand university facilities in the worst way possible.

Today's policy of destruction began nearly 40 years ago when the university began at its Halsted site. At the time Florence Scala, who led the fight against destroying the Italian/Greek neighborhood which had been on the near West Side for more than 100 years.

Now more than 40 years later, the collusion between the local ward politicians, the university, and Mayor Richard M. Daley is even more blatant. The former 1st Ward Alderman and the city's department of Streets and Sanitation cut off city services to the Halsted/Maxwell Street Market. Rather than reorganize the old market with vendor licenses and fees and having the city clean up after each Sunday open-air market, they let the filth accumulate. A cleaned up and sealed off Maxwell Street Market has been moved a few blocks east to make way for more university expansion. Many fewer Chicagoans go there now. Many more visited the Maxwell Street Market of the last century. This Mayor Daley, like his father, readily agreed to the closing of the market and the university's expansion plan because it would get rid of this historic eyesore for him and the developers.

Once the Mayor decided to ram the plan through, all creative alternatives and efforts at compromise with the vendors, the preservationists, and the university were crushed. The fix was in: this was now a done deal.

So we will get a prettier Halsted/Maxwell area. The market has already been moved and downscaled. It probably will be completely eradicated over time. What is being lost? Bluesman Jimmie Lee Robinson, who like so many other Bluesmen and women, learned the Blues and perfected their craft performing on Maxwell street, puts it this way in his guest column in *Streetwise*: "Maxwell Street was a holy place. It was sanctified by the Jewish people and many Blues and Gospel musicians and preachers of every religion....[T]hese old buildings remaining on Maxwell and on Halsted Street are the temples of the Souls of Chicago Past. The aura of the past is still in these buildings."

Poor people aren't able to buy cheap goods at the market any more. Street peddlers who have risen to business prominence from humble Maxwell Street beginnings will not do so in the bright new twenty-first century. And a university which claims to value its urban mission has managed to kill yet another urban institution rather than creatively revitalizing it.

There is always in a city, a tearing down to build up. A new University Village has been born. New residents have moved in and are attempting to build a new neighborhood. But the neighborhood of Addams, Scala, and new immigrants is forever gone. The destruction which the university and the city began over 40 years ago is completed. Shame on us. We failed our urban mission. Florence Scala was right. You expect Chicago politicians to sell the people out—but at least they are honest about what they do. It's the good people you have to watch out for.

# Transforming Public Housing

By Larry Bennett

*By 2011, most of the old high-rise family housing structures, which have dominated public housing for more than four decades in Chicago, have been torn down. But much of the promised lower density, mixed income public housing replacement units have yet to be built. Larry Bennett, in this article, discusses the transformation of public housing in Chicago while suggesting ways to transform the Chicago Housing Authority from public bureaucracy pariah into an effective tool to reform public housing.*

During the glory days of Richard J. Daley's mayoralty, his admirers characterized Chicago as "the city that works." The expression carried a double meaning. As late as the mid 1960s, Chicago's economic might and reputation for sustaining a well-tended social fabric remained unquestioned propositions. And, more pragmatically, Chicago's municipal government was presumed to provide basic services—garbage collection, street cleaning, and the like—of a quality that was unmatched by other American metropolises.

Political Scientist Ester Fuchs, in her analysis of fiscal politics in New York City and Chicago, *"Mayors and Money,"* offers this observation regarding political leadership and governmental structure in Chicago: "Chicago mayors…effectively remove special district services from citywide policy debates, politically isolating their constituencies. Political accountability is weak in this type of system, but fiscal control is enhanced because interest groups simply have less influence over the budget."[1] By the 1970s, Richard J. Daley's stewardship of municipal finances was aided immeasurably by the fact of local jurisdictional fragmentation. Chicago's public schools were overseen by an appointed Board of Education and superintendent, who managed a budget separate from the city government's and derived from independent taxing authority. Similar arrangements also structured the operations of the city's mass transit system, the Chicago Transit Authority (CTA), as well as its huge public housing program, administered by the Chicago Housing Authority (CHA).

At the end of the Richard J. Daley era, Chicago—"the city that works"—with the possible exception of the municipal government, was empty rhetoric. The city's public schools were racially segregated and on the brink of financial crisis. The CTA was the proprietor of a badly decayed transportation infrastructure and capable of providing, at best, erratic service. But of these three independent agencies providing crucial city services, the CHA's circumstances were the most harrowing. Extreme racial segregation was the order of the day in developments such as the Cabrini-Green, Henry Horner, and Robert Taylor Homes, and across the CHA's properties, buildings and grounds were starved of basic maintenance expenditures. For Richard J. Daley's successors, the CHA's state of affairs produced a striking paradox. Conditions at CHA developments were too inhumane to be ignored, but for any public official possessing a grain of career ambition, wading into the CHA mess looked like a shortcut to political retirement.

Since the late 1980s, the CHA has experienced a kaleidoscopic sequence of policy realignments. In part, these have reflected the sheer scale of the policy challenge involved in bringing CHA housing back to reasonable standards of habitability. But in addition, as a new national policy consensus has emerged with regard to New Deal-era initiatives such as welfare and public housing, and as Chicago's municipal and civic leadership has worked to recast the city's position in the global economy, transforming the CHA has become a key element in forging a new Chicago.

## From Progressive Social Engineering to Hyper-Segregation

The Chicago Housing Authority was the product of state legislation passed in response to Congressional authorization of the public housing program in 1937.[2] During its first decade, the CHA built residential developments in various sections of Chicago, while also taking over the management of a few complexes that had been previously built by the federal Public Works Administration.[3] During this period, many CHA apartments were occupied by the families of workers engaged in war-related production.

The CHA was headed by Elizabeth Wood, a social progressive who supported the racial integration of the agency's properties. At the grassroots level, this policy encountered stiff resistance—and occasionally, physical violence—from the white population of residential areas adjoining CHA developments.[4] By the end of the 1940s, public esteem for the CHA had dropped to the point that, when the Illinois General Assembly drafted legislation to enable local implementation of the 1949 federal urban redevelopment legislation, the CHA was bypassed as the local governmental entity in charge of this new program. Elizabeth Wood was removed as CHA executive director in 1954, and the CHA's new leadership reached an accommodation with the Chicago City Council permitting individual aldermen to block the siting of public housing within their wards. From the mid 1950s until the mid 1960s, the CHA embarked on a mammoth building program, with nearly all of its construction in African American neighborhoods on the city's South and West Sides. By the late 1960s, the population of the CHA's "family developments" (multiple-bedroom apartment complexes) was almost entirely African American.

In 1966, a group of African American public housing residents sued the CHA for using project siting and tenant selection procedures intended to segregate its largely minority residential population. Three years later, U.S. District Court Judge Richard Austin ruled in favor of the Gautreaux plaintiffs, directing the CHA to target areas away from the segregated South and West Sides for new public housing.[5] The CHA's response was to stop building public housing. A subsequent ruling in the Gautreaux proceedings yielded the Gautreaux Assisted Housing Program, an effort to relocate public housing-eligible families, via Section 8 vouchers, to outlying city and suburban communities. The Gautreaux Assisted Housing Program was managed by a non-profit organization with no direct ties to the CHA.[6] For its part, the CHA moved so slowly in building scattered site public housing, another Gautreaux mandate, that during the 1980s a judicially appointed private "receiver" took over the construction of small pubic housing developments across the city.[7]

Apart from the CHA's use as a tool in the campaign to maintain Chicago's residential color line, the agency's internal operating capacity was also compromised. The CHA's inability to adequately maintain its properties derived, in part, from the approach to project development adopted during the 1940s. Facing widespread resistance to public housing, and seeking to acquire land cheaply and build rapidly, the CHA concentrated large numbers of apartments in individual developments (for example, at Robert Taylor Homes, 4,415 residential units), typically in high-rise structures. By the mid 1960s, the CHA estimated that 20,000 children lived at Robert Taylor Homes, a number that simply overwhelmed the development's physical infrastructure:

> Elevators, stairwells, lobbies, hallways, parking lots and alleyways, garbage cans, and laundry rooms became veritable playgrounds. Each possessed a particular set of hazards, which could add to their enjoyment. Parking lots were strewn with broken glass…hallways and stairwells were the domain of gambler and drinkers.

Once the agency began to experience fiscal pressure during the early 1970s, it never again was able even to begin to address the physical deterioration of its properties. And, as the foregoing description also reveals, substantial resident disorder, in turn, was becoming a fact of public housing life in Chicago.

"The CHA became a pariah bureaucracy. Deindustrialization swept Chicago's South and West Sides, eliminating many thousands of jobs and accelerating the impoverishment of public housing residents. For both newly unemployed adults and teenagers without mainstream economic prospects, the allure of the underground economy was substantial. Violent lawlessness caused by the burgeoning drug trade further undermined the quality of life in various developments. At Cabrini-Green on Chicago's North Side, the embattled residents were convinced that police officers simply pulled out, calculating that crime control was most readily achieved by allowing competing gangs to kill one another off."[9]

One of the most bizarre incidents in CHA history occurred in March 1981, when Mayor Jane Byrne—accompanied by a battalion of journalists—briefly settled in an apartment at Cabrini-Green. Byrne, whose upset election in 1979 had been fueled by African American voter discontent, claimed that she was trying to bring attention to the plight of public housing residents. Most political observers offered a less generous assessment, perceiving the media-conscious mayor's actions as a desperate effort to win back the support of a constituency discomfited by her pattern of deal making with the entrenched local Democratic Party leadership. In any event, even progressive African American Mayor Harold Washington distanced himself from the CHA during the mid 1980s. In 1986, the U.S. Department of Housing and Urban Development (HUD)—citing its "national reputation for mismanagement and patronage"—added the CHA to its list of "severely troubled" local public housing agencies.[10]

## The Winding Road to CHA Transformation

Following Mayor Washington's death in late 1987, his successor, Eugene Sawyer, brought in a private real estate manager, Vincent Lane, to oversee the CHA. From 1988 until his departure in 1995, Lane initiated various experiments at CHA developments, but possibly of greater importance, began to articulate a philosophy of public housing redevelopment—emphasizing mixed-income communities—that would become the cornerstone of subsequent CHA restructuring. During the last five years, the CHA has pressed ahead with major redevelopment plans at complexes such as the Cabrini-Green, ABLA, and Henry Horner Homes, while also pledging—via its Plan for Transformation, released in January, 2000—to completely rebuild or rehabilitate its portfolio of properties.

Two Lane-era initiatives illustrate the virtues and limits of his vision for public housing. In the South Side Oakland neighborhood, one of Chicago's poorest communities, Lane authorized the rehabilitation of two CHA high-rises, which were grandly renamed Lake Parc Place.[11] Recruited as residents, were 140 "very poor" public housing-eligible families and an equal number of "working poor" families. Lake Parc Place's new occupants were to test the proposition—dubbed the "Mixed-Income New Communities Strategy"—that the more affluent residents, by keeping alert to and regulating the behavior of other tenants, would serve as the bulwark of a sustainable residential community. Another innovation at Lake Parc Place was the CHA's contracting out of maintenance work to private vendors.

Given the novelty of its tenant selection strategy, coupled with Vincent Lane's insistent advocacy, various social scientists examined Lake Parc Place and produced fascinatingly ambiguous findings. One team of researchers concluded that "Lake Parc Place was successful in persuading non-project people (that is, the 140 working poor families) to move into public housing in a high-poverty neighborhood and in getting both project and non-project residents to feel safe and satisfied, to interact with neighbors, to form friendships with neighbors, to support the building's rules and norms, and to volunteer in activities that maintain order and help the community and children."[12] But a second study "found that the majority of residents—project and non-project residents alike—feel a sense of ownership in the success of the complex and feel that their involvement—not management initiatives or role modeling—has been key to Lake Parc Place's success."[13]

Due to the expense involved in rehabilitating just these two high-rises, the variety of mixed-income redevelopment pioneered at Lake Parc Place was not repeated. In 1993, the CHA won a $50 million HUD/HOPE VI grant to demolish three high-rise buildings and rebuild, mainly on Cabrini-Green property, an equivalent number of low-rise residential units. Lane, however, encountered opposition from Cabrini-Green residents, who complained that the CHA was not consulting them, as well as other local government officials, who were unwilling to cooperate with Lane as his dream for Cabrini-Green expanded. By 1994, Vincent Lane spoke in these terms of Cabrini-Green: "We need socioeconomic diversity or we will never solve the problems of the inner city…if we can do this at Cabrini and by McCormick Place and at Henry Horner, I predict you will see people moving from the suburbs back downtown, more commercial space being used and our schools upgraded."[14] Mixed-income development was coming to encompass a much broader slice of the employment and income spectrum than at Lake Parc Place, and Lane was reimagining Cabrini-Green's makeover as a full-scale neighborhood redevelopment campaign.

In 1995, the CHA's Lane era abruptly halted. Due to a variety of internal management problems, HUD took over the operations of the Chicago Housing Authority.[15] Until 1999, and the agency's return to local control, the CHA was directed by a former HUD official, Joseph Shuldiner, a tough-talking administrator who energetically reorganized the agency's internal operations. During his tenure, the CHA won several additional HOPE VI grants and pushed ahead with a Cabrini-Green neighborhood redevelopment plan consistent with Vincent Lane's latter, expansive ambitions for that project. The Shuldiner CHA also initiated a viability assessment process, as required by the Congressional Omnibus Consolidated Rescissions and Appropriations Act (OCRA) of 1996. The CHA examined the physical condition of developments holding 10,000 apartments to determine if rehabilitation represented a more cost-effective strategy than demolition coupled with the issuance of Section 8 vouchers to displaced tenants. The result of this exercise was the agency's determination that a majority of the assessed developments could not be economically rehabilitated.[16]

In mid 1999, federal officials returned control of the CHA to local administrators and, within a few months, the CHA won HUD approval of its Plan for Transformation, a series of documents defining the agency's course of action for the current decade. The Plan for Transformation envisions a very different CHA. Ongoing demolitions—which ultimately will eliminate all of the agency's "family" high-rise structures (51 as of early 2000)—will reduce the CHA's housing stock to 25,000 units, an 18,000 unit reduction from the agency's maximum portfolio in the 1980s. All these 25,000 CHA apartments will be newly constructed or rehabilitated. Most of the newly constructed units will be located in mixed-income redevelopments at major existing complexes, such as the ABLA, Cabrini-Green, and Robert Taylor Homes. Senior-citizen apartments will number 10,000. The CHA will also contract out social services and building maintenance. As of January 2000, the CHA estimated that 6,000 families (in addition to the several thousand who had left its developments during the 1990s) would be relocated from public housing. The estimated cost of the Plan for Transformation is $1.5 million. The proposed completion date for this massive endeavor is 2010.[17]

The Plan for Transformation proposes to completely reshape Chicago public Housing. Nevertheless, its main provisions were perfectly foreseeable. The OCRA-mandated viability assessment found that the cost of rehabilitating most of the CHA's larger developments would exceed the expense of demolition and the issuance of Section 8 vouchers. Since the mid 1990s, at complexes such as ABLA and Cabrini-Green, the CHA had already begun planning processes intended to produce mixed-income redevelopment blueprints.

In mid 1996, resident leaders at several CHA developments formed the Coalition to Protect Public Housing (CPPH). Their impetus was the series of Congressional actions that ultimately eliminated the "one-for-one" rule requiring the demolition of public housing units be accompanied by the provision of an equivalent number of new public housing or Section 8 units.[18] Across the country, the elimination of the one-for-one rule has yielded plans to redevelop public housing in which one-third or fewer of new residential units will be reserved for public-housing occupancy.[19]

The CPPH, in alliance with advocacy groups such as the Chicago Coalition for the Homeless and the Jewish Council of Urban Affairs, has sought to influence both federal policy-makers and local officials. The coalition, however, has not managed to draw much public attention to the ongoing reshaping of the CHA, nor has it seemed to have much effect on CHA plans for particular developments. Probably the CPPH's greatest success was achieved in 1999, when its public demonstrations and threats to sue induced the CHA to add a relocation contract to CHA leases (Wright 2006). The relocation contract spells out a legal "right to return" for public-housing resident who have fulfilled the terms of their leases but are required to vacate their apartments during project redevelopment.

Even before the approval of the Plan for Transformation, the vacating of CHA buildings produced a stream of relocating former public-housing residents. Many of these individuals and families sought to use Section 8 (in 1999 renamed "Housing Choice") vouchers to find private-sector housing. Others simply moved from their CHA dwellings. For many of these families, the experience of relocation seems not to have been especially successful. Journalists have reported on the unwillingness of neighborhood residents in various parts of the metropolitan area to welcome former public-housing residents.[20] Several researchers have found that most former CHA residents relocate to heavily African American, economically marginal neighborhoods, areas that, in effect, represent but a small step up from public housing.[21] In January 2003, the independent monitor retained by the CHA to review its relocation services wrote:

In July, August, and September 2002, the large number of HCV (Housing Choice Voucher)—eligible families still in CHA buildings, coupled with imminent building-empty dates, and the relatively small number of relocation counselors, caused a rush to place families in rental units. This in turn led inevitably to placing families hurriedly, and to relocating families into racially segregated areas already overwhelmingly populated by low income families. We were told.... residents were moved to HCV units without having had any real opportunities to make thorough and thoughtful surveys of available private rental units.[22]

The ongoing transformation of public housing in Chicago has, thus far, produced an extremely mixed record. Across the city, thousands of public-housing units have been demolished, whereas new construction and rehabilitation (other than at senior-citizen developments) has proceeded very slowly. Agency-resident relations—long a sore point—have been redefined, but not clearly improved by the CHA's efforts to downsize and contract out supportive services. The deconcentration of Chicago's public-housing population, a policy goal initially advanced by Vincent Lane, has been compromised by the CHA's haphazard relocation services. Even at showpiece developments, such as ABLA and Cabrini-Green, where plans to produce attractive new mixed-income communities have been promoted by the CHA and blessed with the active support of Mayor Richard M. Daley, resident discontent and erratic consultative practices are much in evidence.

## Public Housing Transformation and the New Chicago

The transformation of public housing in Chicago is part of a national trend in domestic policy emphasizing a devolution to the states of formerly federal government-led initiatives in social welfare and housing, as well as the scaling back of public bureaucratic program implementation in favor of market-based solutions.[23] Nevertheless, the current close partnership between the CHA and Mayor Richard M. Daley's city government reflects another set of emerging circumstances. In the last decade or so, a very evident local policy consensus has emerged that seeks to reposition Chicago as an up-to-the-moment postindustrial metropolis. This new consensus reflects how the city's business, civic, and political leadership has come to view the shifting contours of Chicago's economy, and it is very much reflected in the "global city" agenda of the Daley administration.

For the rank-and-file Chicagoan—or the foot-loose conventioneer—this policy consensus has been writ large on the cityscape of central Chicago. Not only has the Daley administration pushed the major infrastructure developments, in many smaller ways, central Chicago-based arts organizations, universities, and other units of cultural capital have received governmental support. The ultimate aim of these initiatives is to enhance Chicago's status as an inviting, varied, and exciting world metropolis.

A secondary effect of this program of core-area physical and cultural enhancement has been the explosion of upscale residential development in neighborhoods adjoining the Loop. In the case of both new residential construction and loft conversions, much of this development has occurred in areas once dominated by manufacturing, warehousing, or transportation infrastructure. In effect—and to borrow metaphors from no less than Richard M. Daley—an emergent Martha Stewart's Chicago is rising directly atop the sands of an ebbing Nelson Algren's Chicago.[24] One of the ironies of the recent boom in residential construction in areas such as the Near South and West Sides, or in the public housing enclave of Cabrini-Green in the otherwise up-scale Near North Side, is that much of the city's public-housing construction during the 1950s and 1960s had been placed in these very neighborhoods. Usually their demographic composition had been African American, or on the verge of becoming so, and just as often in that era, the proximity of these neighborhoods to railroads, factories, and highways was viewed as an environmental liability. In effect, housing for low-income African Americans was wedged into what were perceived to be among the least desirable sections of the city.

What a difference two generations make! As the middle class and wealthy return to central Chicago, neighborhoods formerly dominated by public housing are being domesticated as safe residential havens. Although a low-income, largely racial minority population will remain in areas such as Cabrini-Green, or on the Near West Side margins of the rebuilt ABLA and Henry Horner Homes, these remnant public-housing residents will no longer be the dominant population bloc as subsequent residential development fills in the empty parcels left by public-housing demolition (or before that, by industrial migration and residential abandonment). As Chicago makes the turn into the new millennium, the sharp racial conflicts over neighborhood succession that marked the 1960s, or for that matter, the racialized political conflicts of the Harold Washington mayoralty of the 1980s, seem to have vanished. Nevertheless, in accompaniment to the emergence of a central Chicago that is the workplace, home, and playground of the affluent, great care is being taken to create residential environments and commercial areas that will conform to the up-market expectations of the downtown area's newcomers.

## NOTES

1. Fuchs, Esther R. Mayors and Money: Fiscal Policy in New York and Chicago. Chicago: University of Chicago Press, 1992.

2. Hirsch, Arnold R. Making the Second Ghetto: Race and Housing in Chicago, 1940-1960. New York: Cambridge University Press, 1983.

3. Bowly, Devereux Jr. The Poorhouse: Subsidized Housing in Chicago, 1895-1976. Carbondale: Southern Illinois University Press, 1978.

4. Hirsch, Arnold R. Making the Second Ghetto: Race and Housing in Chicago, 1940-1960. New York: Cambridge University Press, 1983.

5. Biles, Roger. Richard J. Daley: Politics, Race and the Governing of Chicago. DeKalb: Northern Illinois University Press, 1995. Pages 171-173.

6. Rubinowitz, Leonard S. and James E. Rosenbaum. Crossing the Class and Color Lines: From Public Housing to White Suburbia. Chicago: University of Chicago Press, 2000.

7. Henderson, Harold. "Scattered Successes." The Chicago Reader. October 14, 1994.

8. Venkatesh, Sudhir Alladi. American Project: The Rise and Fall of a Modern Ghetto. Cambridge, MA: Harvard University Press, 2002. Pages 33-34.

9. Bogira, Steve. 1986. "Prisoners of the War Zone." The Reader (Chicago) (3 October).

10. Venkatesh, Sudhir Alladi. American Project: The Rise and Fall of a Modern Ghetto. Cambridge, MA: Harvard University Press, 2002. Page 118.

11. Schill, Michael H. "Chicago's Mixed-Income New Communities Strategy: The Future Face of Public Housing?" In Affordable Housing and Urban Redevelopment in the United States, W. Van Vilet, ed. Thousand Oaks, CA: Sage Publications, 1997.

12. Rosenbaum, James E., Linda K. Stroh, and Cathy A. Flynn. "Lake Parc Place: A Study of Mixed-Income Housing." Housing Policy Debate 9(4):703-40, 1998.

13. Nyden, Phillip. "Comment on James E. Rosenbaum, Linda K. Stroh, and Cathy A. Flynn's 'Lake Parc Place: A Study in Mixed-Income Housing.'" Housing Policy Debate 9(4):741-748, 1998.

14. Bennett, Larry. "Postwar Redevelopment in Chicago: The Decline of Politics of Party and the Rise of Neighborhood Politics." In Unequal Partnerships: The Political Economy of Redevelopment in Postwar America, G. Squires, ed. New Brunswick, NJ: Rutgers University Press, 1998.

15. Banisky, Sandy. "Chicago Housing Authority Watches Its Best Efforts Fail." Baltimore Sun. June 18, 1995.

16. Henderson, Harold. "There Goes Their Neighborhood." The Chicago Reader. May 29, 1998.

17. Chicago Housing Authority. "Plan for Transformation." January 6, 2000.

18. Wright, Patricia A. "Community Resistance to CHA Transformation: The Coalition to Protect Public Housing's History, Evolution, Struggles and Accomplishments." In Where Are Poor People to Live? L. Bennett, J. Smith, and P.A. Wright, eds. Armonk, NY: M.E. Sharpe, 2006.

19. Salama, Jerry J. "The Redevelopment of Distressed Public Housing: Early Results from HOPE VI Projects in Atlanta, Chicago, and San Antonio." Housing Policy Debate 10(1):95-142. And Goetz, Edward G. Clearing the Way: Deconcentrating the Poor in Urban America. Washington, D.C.: Urban Institute Press, 1999. Pages 59-61.

20. McRoberts, Flynn and Abdon M. Pallasch. "Neighbors Wary of New Arrivals." Chicago Tribune. December 28, 1998.

21. Popkin, Susan J. and Mary K. Cunningham. "CHA Relocation Counseling Assessment." Washington, DC: The Urban Institute, 2002; Fischer, Paul. "Where are the Public Housing Families Going? An Update." Report Prepared for the Sargent Shriver National Center on Poverty Law, Chicago. January 2004.

22. Independent Monitor's Report No. 5 to the Chicago Housing Authority and the Central Advisory Council. Chicago. January 8, 2003.

23. O'Connor, Alice. Poverty Knowledge: Social Science, Social Policy and the Poor in Twentieth Century U.S. History. Princeton, NJ: Princeton University Press, 2001; Goetz, Edward G. Clearing the Way: Deconcentrating the Poor in Urban America. Washington, D.C.: Urban Institute Press, 2002. Pages 59-61.

24. Daley, Richard M. Speech to Chicago Greening Symposium. March 8, 2002. www.ci.chi.il.us (accessed 27 August 2002).

# Latino Immigrant Civic Engagement in the Chicago Region

By Magda Banda and Martha Zurita

*As discussed in the following article, politics occur not only at the level of voting but also by participation in neighborhood and civic organizations. This participation has led to significant victories by Latinos in the Chicago region. Chicago is no longer just a black–white city but has become a multi-racial city. Thus, the incorporation of Latinos into the political fabric of the city is important.*

At the very core of our society is the active participation of its members. It is a concept as old as our country. However, not all members of our society, particularly immigrants, have access to our more official form of participation, namely voting. As such, it is important that everyone have access to various forms of participation so that their voices can be heard and needs be met. This paper examines the civic participation of Latino immigrants in the metropolitan Chicago region, as well as the role of community-based organizations as facilitators for many Latino immigrants' civic engagement.

## Introduction

In the metropolitan Chicago region, as with other parts of the country, the growth of the Latino population is significant and truly noteworthy. From 1990 through 2004 the population of Latinos in the region grew by 95 percent, to comprise 20 percent of the region's total population. During the same time period, the region's non-Latino growth rate was only four percent.[1] In 2004 one in five Chicagoland residents was Latino and Chicago had the third largest Latino population in the nation, after Los Angeles and New York. Most of the growth of the Latino population in the state was experienced in the six-county Chicago region. Ninety-two percent of the state's Latinos were concentrated in metropolitan Chicago, compared to 62 percent of non-Latino Illinoisans who resided there, according to the 2000 Census.

Today, we know that the large majority (79 percent) of the region's Latinos are of Mexican descent.[2] Latinos of Puerto Rican origin comprise eight percent and South Americans four percent. Central Americans make up three percent of the region's Latinos. Cubans account for one percent of the region's Latinos and Latinos of other origins make up five percent.[3]

The growth of the Latino population cannot be discussed without examining the impact of immigration; a significant portion of the Latino growth from 1990 to 2004 was due to immigration, primarily Mexican immigration. In 2000, almost half (47 percent) of the Latino population in the six counties was foreign born.[4] In DuPage, Lake, and Kane Counties, the majority of their Latino populations were born outside of the United States (51 percent, 53 percent, and 52 percent, respectively). The city of Chicago has rates similar to the region; 47 percent of the Latinos residing in Chicago were born outside of the United States.

## Latino Voting Rates in Illinois

Although the Latino population is booming in terms of growth rates, they have low number of voters, which translates into limited impact on policy. Using voter registration and voting as one important measure of civic participation, we see that in Illinois, Latinos show significantly lower participation than Whites and African Americans. In the November 2004 election, less than 60 percent of Latinos in Illinois were citizens, which clearly lowered the number of Latinos who could vote.[5] (See Figure 1.)

This was quite the opposite for Whites and Blacks whose majorities were citizens (98 percent and 99 percent, respectively). With less than 60 percent of the Latino population being citizens, it was not a surprise that only one-third (33 percent) of all Latinos in Illinois were registered to vote, whereas 75 percent of Whites and 72 percent of Blacks were registered. In terms of those that actually went to the polls, less than 30 percent of Latinos in Illinois voted, compared with 66 percent of Whites and 67 percent of Blacks. It is important to note that Latinos have voting rates similar to other groups; 86 percent of all Latino registered voters voted during the November 2004 election, compared to 88 percent of Whites and 93 percent of Blacks. Due to their citizenship status, however, many Latinos do not qualify to vote; less than one-third of Latinos in Illinois have their voices heard through voting. As such, it is imperative that Latinos, particularly immigrants, have their voices heard through other forms of civic participation.

**Figure 1. Reported Voting and Registration for Voting-Age Population for Metropolitan Chicago, 2004.**

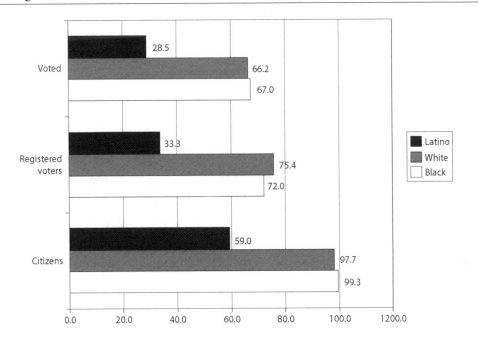

## Latino Immigrant Participation in Chicago Region

In the summer of 2003, the Institute for Latino Studies conducted an unprecedented survey of 1,500 Latino households in the Chicago region. This rich dataset examined many facets of their lives and will create a richer understanding of this population, which will then enable policymakers and social service agencies to serve them better. One area examined in the household survey was householders' level of civic participation. The sample in the study was representative of the Latino population. More than half (53%) of the survey respondents were foreign-born, who were the focus of this analysis. There were many types of civic involvement that the survey measures, such as membership in block clubs, Parent Teacher Associations, hometown associations, and religious organizations. Overall, the involvement in these types of activities was relatively low. The participants' involvement was lower than Latinos nationally.[6] However, similar to national trends, Chicagoland Latino immigrants participate at higher rates in religious (12 percent) and school-related organizations (7 percent).

The percentage of foreign-born participants who were registered to vote was also low. Less than 30% of participants were registered to vote where they lived. When examining the levels of immigrants registered to vote by age group, we see that the older age cohorts, 50-64 and 65+ had higher rates of voter registration, 61% and 66%, respectively. However, the voter registration levels of the younger cohorts were significantly less. This is particularly true for those 18-24 and 26-35 years of age whose levels were 8% and 11%, respectively.

**Figure 2. Foreign-born Latino Participation in Groups by Type.**

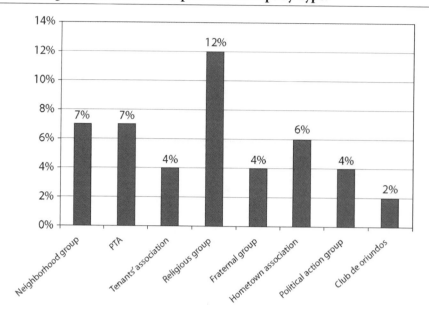

**Figure 3. Foreign-Born Latino Registered Voters and Citizens by Age Group.**

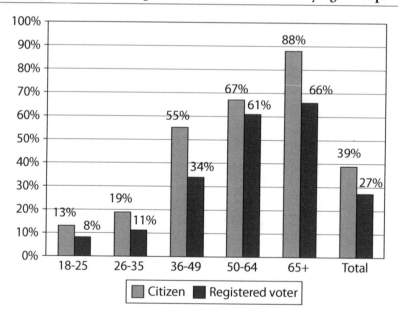

In Figure 3, we see that the younger age cohorts have the lowest rates of citizenship, which is to be expected. As such, it is understandable that they have the lowest rates of voter registration. However, the largest disparities between citizenship and voter registration are in the 36-49 and 65+ age cohorts.

A significant relationship was found amongst the views of immigrant respondents and their levels of participation in activities. There was a significant relationship, for example, amongst those who have worked with neighbors on neighborhood issues and those who felt that people like them could make their community a better place to live (r = .16). [7]

There was also a relationship between people's interest in politics and their memberships in specific types of groups, such as clubs de oriundos or clubs de paisanos (r = .12). Similarly, a relationship existed between people's interest in politics and their working with their neighbors on neighborhood issues (r = .12). Furthermore, the more people believed that public officials cared about people like them thought, the more likely they were to work with their neighbors on neighborhood issues (r = .12).

## Reasons for Low Civic Participation

As with any population, there are various reasons for low levels of civic participation. Through a study conducted by the Institute for Latino Studies in the summer of 2004 on the development of Latino leadership, researchers identified specific challenges to Latino immigrant civic participation. These reasons were the following: Latinos' lack of trust and fear of being exposed; political indifference; lack of resources and time; limited English proficiency; and lower levels of formal educational attainment.

Since many of the communities in which these groups work include recent newcomers who are not familiar with U.S. systems, there is a need to gain their trust, in order for them to work with the organizations and take on issues of importance to them. This lack of trust is even more present for those who immigrated without proper documentation. Undocumented immigrants are more fearful of being exposed, due to the threat of being deported. As such, they are less likely to challenge the status quo or injustices, because they do not want attention brought to themselves or their status.

Some immigrants from Latin American countries, particularly Mexico, bring with them a viewpoint of political indifference deriving from experiences with local and federal governments in their home countries. During the Latino leadership study in the summer of 2004, many interviewees mentioned "political apathy" as a challenge to Latino immigrant participation.

Due to limited finances, immigrants may have to work more than one job in order to make ends meet. In the metro region, for example, the median income for foreign-born Mexican householders in 1999 was $40,700.[8] This was much less than the median income of non-Latino Whites in the region, which was $60,128.[9] As a result, many people face time constraints to participate in outside activities, particularly if these activities do not provide financial resources to the family or immediate returns or wins. Limited financial resources then act as a hurdle to civic engagement for some.

Another major reason some Latino immigrants do not participate civically is limited proficiency in English. People's comfort level with English, particularly conversational

English, can affect their participation levels. From the interviewee's perspective, if one cannot speak English fluently, one might not feel comfortable or confident expressing oneself in front of an audience or policymaker.

Civic participation rates are higher among individuals with higher educational attainment levels.[10] However, 66% of Mexican immigrants in the metro region have less than 12 years of schooling.[11] The low level of formal education among Latino immigrants has been identified as a challenge by many interviewees from the ILS leadership study.

> I only had a high school education, but felt that I had more sense than [policymakers]. I was still intimidated to face better educated people.
>
> —Magdalena, 50-year-old leader, Mother of 6

## Immigrant Stories

*Mrs. Sandra Martinez. Mother of 2, Mexican, 31 years old*

Sandra moved into a new neighborhood on Chicago's south side five years ago. Although she has lived in the U.S. for ten years, she only recently became engaged in community organizing trainings and movements approximately three years ago, when organizers invited her. She had many doubts as to what services were available and how to participate in community activities. Through the organization's trainings, Sandra became involved in the New Americans Initiative and the efforts for driver's licenses for undocumented immigrants. Prior to her involvement in the organization, Sandra was unhappy in her neighborhood and planned to move out…

*Ms. Alejandra Gomez, Single, Mexican, 19 years old*

Alejandra has lived in the U.S. for five years. She has been involved with a community-based organization for approximately one year. A speaker came to her high school and talked about a leadership program targeting undocumented student issues. There were a few reasons that moved Alejandra to become involved. First of all, the issues facing undocumented students directly affected Alejandra. Secondly, her major was justice studies because she likes to "fight for people's rights."

Before becoming involved with the organization, Alejandra was not aware of the issues affecting her. "I knew I was undocumented but I didn't know what it was … the Dream Act, the Student Adjustment Act. [Then] I found out." Being part of the leadership trainings allowed Alejandra to see not only that she was not alone as an undocumented student, but that she could push for legislation. "I got to see I wasn't the only one affected. I got to see others like myself and it inspired me. I felt that I was not alone as an undocumented student….I also developed leadership skills because I was shy before. Also, my English skills improved. I learned about U.S. government systems. I met people working in politics. I got to be on TV and was even interviewed....Most importantly, I'm informed now and know what's going on with the Dream Act and similar policies."

Alejandra feels more ready to help others. The program has had an exponential result in terms of how it touches people indirectly. She was able to reach out to people in two ways: she shared her enthusiasm for organization with people close to her and was also able to put what she learned into practice through her participation in public events and speaking with politicians about issues. "Of course, I always recommended it because of things I learned—to be activist, develop as leader, reach out to other people, and network. It's great... for students who are interested in fields dealing with government....I recommend it to friends and family." Alejandra believes that she helps improve her community, particularly by educating policymakers on issues affecting her community. "I'm helping my community behind the scenes... I've spoken with Alderman Manny Lopez and told him about my situation as an undocumented student. I've talked with [then State Senator] Miguel del Valle. I went to Springfield. I've spoken with Congressman] Luis Gutierrez."

## Significant Victories

Through their civic engagement, Latino immigrants, as well as others, have had significant impact on their communities and the state of Illinois, which will benefit families today and in the years to come. One such example was the 2004 passing of *Illinois House Bill 60*, which extends in-state college tuition for undocumented students who have attended Illinois high schools for a minimum of three years. Also, in 2004, was the passing of the *Illinois New Americans Initiative*. It is a $9 million, three-year citizenship acquisition program aimed at immigrants in the state. Additionally, the *Illinois Family Care program* was passed in 2004. This program is another major accomplishment that benefits 80,000 uninsured families.

It is through the work of non-profit agencies, some local and others not, that Latino immigrants' participation in civic life is facilitated. There were various ways in which organizations engaged community members. One way was by working on specific campaigns or issues impacting the community, such as driver's licenses for undocumented drivers or in-state college tuition for undocumented students. Another way was involving community members in specific local projects, such as increasing Local School Council nominations for local schools. Other organizations sponsored residents to attend traditional community organizing workshops, such as with the Industrial Areas Foundation (IAF).

## Parting Thoughts: Need for Facilitating Organizations

Clearly, in order for Latino immigrants' voices to be heard, there is a need for alternative forms of civic participation. As stated earlier, less than 60 percent in Illinois are citizens and only one-third of all Latinos over age 18 are registered to vote. Yet, the data from the

Institute for Latino Studies' household survey in the summer of 2003 show that Latino immigrant householders are not involved at high rates. The Institute study on Latino leadership during the summer of 2004 found that there is a need for organizations to facilitate the civic engagement process. This need exists for various reasons: Latino immigrants' lack of trust and fear of being exposed; political indifference; lack of resources and time; limited English proficiency; and lower levels of formal educational attainment. In the end, the Latino leadership study found that engaged community residents, along with facilitating organizations, have significant impacts on their communities and society, just as our nation's forefathers had envisioned.

## Notes

1. U.S. Census Bureau, American Community Survey, 2005 and http://www.nd.edu/~chifacts/.
2. U.S. Census Bureau, American Community Survey, 2005.
3. "Other" category includes people identified only as "Hispanic" or "Latino."
4. Paral, T. Ready, S. Chun, and W. Sun. 2004. *Latino Demographic Growth in Metropolitan Chicago*. Research Reports v 2004.2. Institute for Latino Studies, University of Notre Dame.
5. U.S. Census Bureau, Current Population Survey, November 2004.
6. Boraas. 2003. *Volunteerism in the United States*. Monthly Labor Review (August 2003).
7. The Pearson's Correlation Coefficient (r=.16) was calculated using respondents' feeling that people like them could have an impact in making their community a better place to live and if they and their neighbors worked on neighborhood issues together in the last two years. This relationship was significant at the 0.01 level. A perfect positive linear correlation would be 1.00, whereas a perfect negative linear correlation would be –1.00.4
8. Paral, R. & T. Ready. (2005). *The Economic Progress of US- and Foreign-Born Mexicans in Metro Chicago: Indications from the United States Census*. University of Notre Dame, Institute for Latino Studies.
9. Paral, R., Ready, T., Chun, S., & W. Sun. (2004). *Latino Demographic Growth in Metropolitan Chicago*. University of Notre Dame, Institute for Latino Studies.
10. Boraas, S. (2003). *Volunteerism in the United States*. Monthly Labor Review.
11. Paral, R. & T. Ready. (2005). *The Economic Progress of US- and Foreign-Born Mexicans in Metro Chicago: Indications from the United States Census*. University of Notre Dame, Institute for Latino Studies.

# Part III

## Chicago Politics

# Chicago Politics

Throughout the history of Chicago politics, there have been seven eras, each with different characteristics. We are now entering a new eighth political era:

1. 1833–1860: Booster Regime of businessmen as mayor and aldermen in which there weren't many partisan divisions until the end of the period.
2. 1860–1871: The Civic Wars of the Partisan Regime during the Civil War when the tensions and political divisions were so great that the City Council couldn't meet for four months during 1862–1863.
3. 1871–1931: The period of the first political machines and the Council of the Grey Wolves in the city council.
4. 1931–1983: Urban Growth Machine and Rubber Stamp City Council were begun under Mayor Cermak and were perfected under Mayor Richard J. Daley and perpetuated under Mayors Bilandic and Byrne.
5. 1983–1987: Council Wars and Progressive Regime under Mayor Harold Washington.
6. 1987–1989: Chaos, Fragmented Council, Weak Mayor period under Mayor Sawyer.
7. 1989–2011: The New Machine and Return of the Rubber Stamp City Council under Mayor Richard M. Daley.
8. 2011–Present: The post-Daley era of Chicago politics with a new mayor and a new city council.

The political machine grew up with the city after the Great Chicago Fire. The first political boss was Michael McDonald, a gambler-saloonkeeper who noticed the common bonds between the criminals and politicians and introduced them to each other. But more than spawning corruption, the machine served the rapidly growing ethnic communities in Chicago during the last part of the nineteenth and the first part of the twentieth century.

Originally there were multiple political machines, both Democratic and Republican in Chicago, governed by patronage and corruption. The City Council of Grey Wolves was run by cliques of machine aldermen in a constant struggle with reformers. Then in 1931, Anton Cermak created a single Democratic machine, which was continued after his death by Mayor Ed Kelly and party boss Pat Nash. After a brief interlude under Mayor Martin Kennelly, Richard J. Daley came to power and perfected the Democratic Party machine.

The Richard J. Daley machine had a distinctive set of features, which refined the machine politics that had governed most of the larger East Coast and Midwest cities. It was an economic exchange within the framework of the political party and an economic growth machine that married that political party to big businesses in a public–private partnership.

Patronage jobs at City Hall begat patronage precinct captains who contacted voters and persuaded them to trade their votes for machine candidates for favors and city services. Government contracts from City Hall convinced otherwise Republican businessmen to give the campaign contributions necessary to fund campaign literature, walk-around money, and bribes. These contributions of precinct work, money, and votes won elections for the Richard J. Daley machine, which then controlled the government so that the mayor could distribute the spoils that kept the machine running. Mayor Richard M. Daley continued some of the practices of his father, but he once again modernized Chicago politics and government.

As shown in Figures 1 and 2, old-style patronage and corruption of the Richard J. Daley machine now coexists with multi-million-dollar campaign contributions from global corporations, high-tech public opinion polling, and media manipulation in the Richard M. Daley machine. The ward organizations, and especially Richard M. Daley organizations like the Hispanic Democratic Organization (HDO), worked the precincts while city contractors and construction labor unions still contributed money to the mayor's campaigns and to the aldermanic campaigns he supported.

In a major change from past regimes, rich individuals, global businesses, law firms, and financial institutions contributed the millions of dollars necessary to hire national political consultants to do public opinion polling, direct mail, and slick TV ads. The payoffs in the new Daley machine were also different. There were still patronage jobs given to precinct workers and contracts to contributing businessmen, just like under the Richard J. Daley machine. But at the end of the twentieth century and the beginning of the twenty-first, amenities like flowers in the parkway, wrought iron fences, Millennium Park, and, most importantly, a tax structure favorable to the new global economy were added. The election campaign of Mayor Rahm Emanuel raised even more money from the global economy. It remains to be seen if he will continue the other aspects of the Richard M. Daley machine.

## The New Machine vs. the Old Machine

Despite superficial similarities, such as having a Mayor Daley in charge of the city of Chicago, several aspects of the new machine differed greatly from the early political machines. Patronage/precinct organizations were supplemented with media-based, synthetic campaigns. Campaigns were centered on the candidate more than on the party and ward organizations were supplemented by special Daley political organizations. The new Daley

## Figure 1: Richard J. Daley Machine

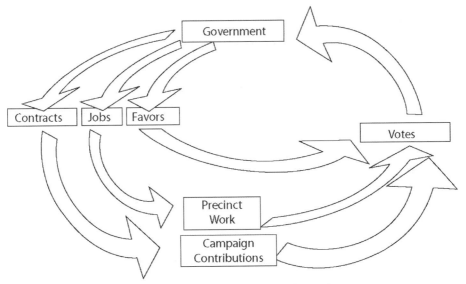

Source: Created by Dick Simpson, based on course lectures by Milton Rakove.

## Figure 2: Richard M. Daley Machine

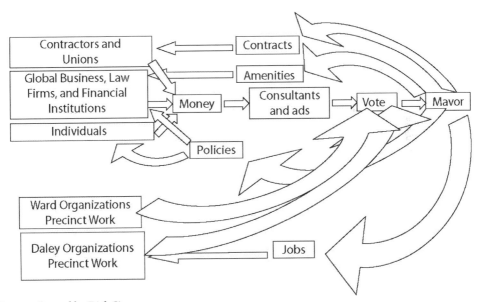

Source: Created by Dick Simpson.

rubber-stamp city council no longer had a significant opposition faction to oppose the mayor. Instead of being segregated into submachines or excluded entirely, minorities and other potential opposition groups were co-opted and rewarded with jobs and contracts for working within the system. Public policies were reoriented toward the global economy and no longer solely focused on local development interests.

In political campaigns, money is equivalent to power, influence, and access. Therefore, power players in the new Daley Machine can be partially tracked by examining the major sources of campaign revenue. In 2003, Richard M. Daley raised 27 percent of his campaign funds from financial services and law firms. He raised another 11 percent from wealthy individuals. Most of these were in the global economy sector. He raised only 10 percent from labor unions and 25 percent from developers and real estate. So,more than one-third of his money came from the global economy, one-third from the old economy, and one-third from smaller sections. Only three percent came from political party organizations.

There was an important change in the 2007 elections when labor unions contributed over a million dollars to the mayor's aldermanic opponents and refused to endorse Daley's reelection. On the other side, global firms like Wal-Mart and Target, fighting against Chicago's Big Box ordinances that would have mandated higher wages and health benefits, supported the mayor's aldermanic allies and the mayor with several hundred thousand dollars in contributions. All of these patterns of contributions continued in the 2011 city elections.

A critical cog of the old and the new Daley machines in government was the Chicago City Council. The Chicago City Council since Richard M. Daley became mayor in 1989, was once again a rubber stamp. For instance, from 2003 to 2006, in three and a half years, there were only forty-nine divided roll-call votes in the council instead of the hundred per year that were more the norm historically. The council became less controlled by the mayor after 2006 as he lost four key council votes in 2006–2007 and had to use the mayoral veto for the first time in his or his father's mayoralty. The new city council that took office in May 2007 was a weaker rubber stamp than past councils because nine new aldermen were elected, most with the backing of unions and neighborhood organizations over pro-Daley incumbents. But the pattern of autocratic mayoral control and a weak council has characterized twenty-first century Chicago under Richard M. Daley.

The machines of Chicago have been both Republican and Democratic, suburban and inner city. Even today, the Republican Machine of DuPage County is the mirror image of the Democratic Machine of Chicago. These political machines have been defined as permanent political organizations or political parties, which are characterized by patronage, favoritism, loyalty, and precinct work. An inevitable side effect of machine politics is corruption, scandals, and inefficient government service delivery.

With the 2011 election we begin a new era in Chicago Politics. Mayor Rahm Emanuel was elected in a campaign in which he raised more than $12 million dollars and in which, like Mayor Daley's campaigns, the money was raised from the global economy. In fact, nearly half of his campaign contributions came from out of state. In the city council that was elected at the same time, nearly one-third of the members are newcomers. Many incumbents retired and other long-time aldermen were defeated. With a new mayor and a new city council and changed political conditions, some Daley machine traditions will be continued, but Chicago may also evolve to a new form of politics.

# Chicago Politics and Community Development

## By Douglas Gills

*Independent, community based, "outsider" organizations crystallized their efforts to bring Harold Washington to the mayor's office in 1983 and reelected him in 1987. After his election, he kept his commitment to these organizations by allocating more city resources to community organizations to deliver human services, aid local economic development, and build affordable housing. In return, these organizations supported him during the battles of "Council Wars."*

*The "rainbow coalition" of neighborhood organizations is now gone. In the 2011 Chicago mayoral election, white, Latino, and African American constituencies each put forward their own candidates. Nonetheless, the Harold Washington-Neighborhood Movement model of politics still remains a compelling template for the future.*

Harold Washington's election as Chicago's first black mayor in April, 1983, was the product of unprecedented participation in the local electoral process by large segments of Chicago's racially, ethnically and socio-economically diverse population, segments which had been previously alienated from the political mainstream. This participation was facilitated by the formation of a loosely unified coalition of reform-minded institutional elites (insiders) and progressive community activists and political insurgents (outsiders).

But what was most striking was the extent of organization and the painstakingly developed programmatic focus of the "outsider" part of the coalition. In Chicago during 1982-87, movement politics was as important as "insider" maneuvering. It had its own logic and rules

Douglas Gills; Pierre Clavel & Wim Wiewel, eds., "Chicago Politics and Community Development," *Harold Washington and the Neighborhoods: Progressive City Government in Chicago, 1983-1987*, pp. 242-247. Copyright © 1991 by Douglas Gills. Reprinted with permission.

of organization. One can identify three main groups, loosely organized around three main ideas. First, his electoral base was overwhelmingly black in composition, with the critical support of poor Latinos and poor whites. There was tremendous electoral mobilization of the black community under united black leadership.

Blacks, in the main, had endured decades of political exclusion and public neglect. Even while their numbers had increased significantly, they had received little more than symbolic participation in the economic and political life of the city. The black community organized politically, in both formal and informal ways, with a near single-minded purposefulness.

Second, the coalition received the support of reform-minded liberal whites, Jewish and black business elites who joined the Harold Washington electoral coalition. For these, and to some extent the other elements of the coalition, there was a consensus that the conventional practice of machine politics had to be rejected. Were Chicago to go forward into the 21st Century, it had to shed its image of racist politics, corruption, graft, patronage and unmerited privilege. There was a pervasive assault upon the patronage-based political machine of the regular Democratic Party inherited from the era of mayor Richard J. Daley.

Third, the movement underpinning Harold Washington's campaign and his early administration was marked by aggressive, vocal and independent action on the part of people associated with neighborhood organizations and community action groups. These community activists had been isolated from meaningful political participation in prior regimes. Now, they pressed their demands for a neighborhood agenda that included greater effective input in decision-making about the city's future and a greater share of city funds to be expended in the neighborhoods relative to the central business district, O'Hare, and the Near Loop lake front areas.

The other part of the story is that, among movement elements, while the most obvious thing is the mobilization of the black and other "national" groups—e.g. Latinos, poor whites, ethnics—a critical part of movement organization and the dominant substantive program came from the economic development initiatives that had emerged over a period of years from the community-based organizations and networks. The community-based network was critical to the larger outsider social movement and coalition, providing a large part of its organizational basis and the substance of much of its policy direction. As a result, the community-based movement was prominent in Washington administration initiatives after the 1983 election.

## Economic and Political Background

The old political arrangement of the "machine" associated with Richard Daley, mayor during 1956-76 and his successors (Michael Bilandic and Jane Byrne) through the 1983 election had been based upon doling out patronage in the form of jobs, contracts and personal loyalties between machine elites and their ethnic-based constituencies. It had become increasingly inappropriate to address the needs of large numbers of Afro-Americans, Latino and Asians which had begun to occupy Chicago's neighborhoods in the periods following World War I and World War II. In fact, the twenty years of Chicago's race relations leading into the 1983 mayoral election was marked by a series of recurrent political confrontations, protests and disruptions of normal patterns of urban behavior. This was due to the ever present effects of an increasingly intense urban crisis.

It was an economic crisis, but it manifested itself in the political arena as the heightening contradiction between declining sources of public revenues and growing level of legitimate demands for public services and assistance.[1] In short, the ruling elites could not rule through the traditional arrangements, and vast sectors of the population grew increasingly intolerant of "business (or politics) as usual." The government thus became a contested arena of political battle.

Thus the urban crisis had several interrelated dimensions: economic, fiscal, and political. In past studies of Chicago politics many have argued the inter-connectedness of these elements.[2] But what the Washington election made clear was the underlying importance of a fourth dimension—the direct mobilization of a new social base. Much of this new politics is non-institutionalized (i.e. movement politics or social protest politics), social movements and factions that came from fundamental shifts in the city's political economy—a social crisis marked by the inability of large segments of the population to gain income adequate to support viable households. The consequences were increased crime, deterioration of major social institutions and the breakdown in the quality of community life.

## Development of Community Organizations Through the 1983 Election

The economic changes in Chicago increased the differences between the older white ethnic neighborhoods and the newer neighborhoods occupied by peoples of color. The first were ethnic based, the latter were communities based upon socio-economic and political conditions of exclusion from the mainstream. There is the tradition of Chicago as a city of diverse neighborhoods organized around institutions of cohesion such as church, school or union meeting hall. These traditional neighborhoods were thought to possess a positive sense of cultural (ethnic) identity. On the other hand, the new "neighborhoods" were a post-industrial, post 1960s phenomenon. These new neighborhoods were demarcated by the common condition of their residents—homogeneously black or brown, homogeneously poor and depressed, homogeneously identified by the prevalence of deteriorated housing and commercial districts, and by public sector neglect.

The traditional type of neighborhood organization was improvement oriented, exclusivist and conservationist. The more recent form of organization typically emerged around the need for defense from racist attacks, resistance to withdrawal of public services, and mobilized around demands for improvement in the standard of living and quality of life. Rather than resulting from concerns about preservation of status, the new neighborhood organizations were instruments to fight back and for community reform.

They often produced leadership with more radical or progressive orientations than their predecessors.

By the end of the 1970s, a shift occurred towards "developmentalism" and policy "advocacy." This shift toward power politics and away from protest was based on the reality that blacks, Latinos and poor whites constituted the new majority in Chicago.

## Politicization

The CBO (community based organization) social policy movement was converted into a political movement and steered into the electoral process through (1) broadening the base of the coalition by identifying the new allies on a mass scale, and (2) a process of agenda-building and popularization of a new emerging consensus that Byrne and the Machine could not/would not deliver on this agenda.[3]

Political organizing through the electoral process broadened the base of the movement. It provided the opportunity to dismantle the political machine and set the stage for social and public policy reform under the leadership of Harold Washington.

## Coalition Agenda-Setting

The Chicago Rehab Network and the Community Workshop on Economic Development both drew upon the common experiences of their diverse member groups in order to shape a neighborhood agenda, particularly around housing, land use, economic development and resource allocation for depressed neighborhoods. The 1981-1982 period in Chicago was replete with numerous protest struggles within public institutions as the crisis deepened. Perhaps the most significant development for our current discussion was the struggle to prevent Chicago from sponsoring a World's Fair in 1992. The World's Fair was not merely an opportunity for Chicago to have a good time or to host a big party. At the core of the issues surrounding it was a plan for the economic redevelopment of the near south side.

There was an operative consensus that the Fair was ill-designed, if it should be held at all. Similarly, other developers who used the city capital development dollars should provide revenues to support housing, economic development and job generation in the neighborhoods, it was argued. Individuals and groups networking around CWED, the Chicago Jobs Council, Chicago 1992 Committee, the Rehab Network and Center for Neighborhood Technology began to advocate a comprehensive urban development policy with the following key components:

a. Housing and commercial development without the displacement of indigenous residents and businesses.
b. Community-directed economic and housing development that secured the interests of local groups and included the input of community based groups in the planning, implementation and benefits of private-public development ventures.

c. The city should encourage "balanced-growth" between the business district and depressed neighborhoods and linkage between large developments using public resources and the need for reinvestment in the neighborhoods.

d. When developers wanted to do business with the city, they should expect to hire Chicagoans first, respect affirmative action and minority set-aside agreements and support community-based initiatives in economic development by providing technical and financial assistance.

e. Banks and other lending institutions holding city funds or city employee pension funds should be pressured to support community-based redevelopment projects by reinvesting in depressed neighborhoods and by lending to public-private partnership ventures.

f. The city should view community-based non-profit development organizations as legitimate partners in community redevelopment projects.

g. The city should shift a larger share of its CDBG dollars into direct support of housing, commercial and community redevelopment initiatives and into direct staff development and capacity-building among neighborhood development organizations and agencies.

## The Community-Based Network in the 1983 Election

The same forces which came together to support Jane Byrne and to defeat Michael Bilandic in 1979 were at the front lines of the movement to defeat Byrne and elect Harold Washington in 1983 and again in 1987. The associational networks with linkages into the black, brown, poor white and liberal lakefront communities made possible the transformation of mass social protest into a massive political mobilization inside the electoral arena.

There was a coincidence between this reform neighborhood development agenda and the core demands of the black empowerment movement for fairness, open government and ethical practices. When stripped of its ideological and rhetorical symbolism the neighborhood development agenda was compatible with the short term aims of the black empowerment and Latino empowerment movements. The neighborhood movement demanded equitable resource allocation to black and Latino communities, enforcement of affirmative action and minority set-aside mandates, access to government policy making, to information and to public office holders, along with the elimination of patronage with respect to public employment, contracts and public service provision. One reason for this compatibility of interest was due to the origins and development of the community development movement out of, and alongside of, these nationality movements among black and Latino community activists.

This movement, then, fed into the three main social bases within Harold Washington's coalition. There was the nationality vote: most blacks, a majority of Latinos and a significant number of reform-minded whites. The Latino and progressive white vote was very critical to his election. In the primary election of 1983, the critical ingredient was progressive whites. Although Washington received 80 percent of the black vote, 17 percent of his coalition was white and that provided him with the margin of victory. In the general election, Latinos provided the critical margin of victory. He was able to improve from 25 percent of the Latino vote in the primary to about 65 percent of the Latino vote in the general election.

Washington garnered 75 percent of the Puerto Rican vote, 62 percent of the Mexican vote, and 52 percent of the Cuban vote.

## Harold Washington in Office 1983–87: Limitations on Reform Gains

I think that the Washington victory and the consolidation of his administration resulted in the institutionalization of a new base of power in the opposition to the machine. It is not clear if it functioned any differently, but it was not the machine as we knew it. In fact, I remember Washington speaking at a rally in front of the Daley Plaza during the 1983 campaign, when he said that "The machine, as we now know it, is dead." At subsequent times he would speak of the machine and patronage in the same terms. Most people only focused on the fact that the machine was dead, as opposed to the notion that the machine as we know it is dead.

The community-based organization provided an excellent alternative. It did not provide direct patronage, but it was possible to build up a patronage type army, a machine army, without the individual (privilege) payoff. It was possible to use the new neighborhood agenda as a frame within which access was given to neighborhood based actors, without the corruption that is associated with the under-the-table deals of the previous ward bosses.

There were a number of more immediate results for the neighborhood organizations as well. *We got greater access to decision making,* implementations and evaluation, and just plain old information. There was *more equitable resource distribution* across Chicago. There was *more budgetary scrutiny.* Another strength of the administration was the establishment of *more representative government.*

### Limitations of the Washington Program

There was also a down side for the community organizations: to some extent and for some time there was a *loss of independence and initiative among CBOs.* Second *the movement was coopted* to the extent that such thoughts prevailed as 'We can't do anything to embarrass the mayor" or "we put him there so we have to support him." The missing factor, which had been present in 1983, was the mobilizing base that had been provided by the CBOs. How did we lose this? This question hangs over us now.

It is clear that by 1987 Harold Washington was funding a number of organizations that differed markedly from the original CBO constituency: neighborhood retail and industrial retention organizations are examples. Many of these did not meet CDBG guidelines for low income eligibility. The coalition was weaker as a result in 1987. Thus, community-based participation was perhaps the most problematic aspect of the Washington administration.

# Conclusion: Toward a New Agenda

I think that there are important implications of the Washington Administration at both the local and the national level. The Washington victory and subsequent governance period represented a magic moment of international importance. To say that is to say there was one thing beautiful about it, and something that brought the dead to life. People who had been emotionally, spiritually dead, came alive! I saw and worked with winos, who put on ties and picked up their pens and clip boards and walked precincts during the Harold Washington campaign. Harold was correct to say "You go out of the city, you go out of the country, you go out of the continent and people will say 'How's Harold, what's happening in Chicago. '"

Now, what's the road forward? *We need a mass organization that can take-up substantive issues on the basis of a mass common program.* Existing community groups have by necessity had to form coalitions. What we need is a monolithic organization, a unifying homogeneous mass organization that can raise up a standard of struggle around class based issues facing the vast numbers of citizens.

Second, *we need independence and initiative in the movement.* We've lost some of that and until we regain it, regardless of who is elected Mayor, we are at a loss for it. Until we do this we will compromise the progressive character of our politics, whoever gets to be mayor. Harold was less effective because he didn't have a strong independent movement. He *was* the movement!

If that initiative had been there we could have clarified the lines between who runs and who really rules Chicago. If this had been happening, then LaSalle Street would not have been able to bulldog Harold into making compromises that were not in the best interests of the City. Washington would have been able to say: "My hands are tied, my constituents are saying this is what I should do."

# Notes

1. See James O'Connor, *The Meaning of Crisis: A Theoretical Introduction* (Cambridge, Mass.: Basil Blackwell, 1987); T .Robert Gurr and Desmond King, *The State and the City* (Chicago: Univerity of Chicago Press, 1987); Roger Friedland, *Power and Crisis in the City* (New York: Schocken Books, 1983); and Terry N. Clark and Lorna C. Ferguson, *City Money* (New York: Columbia University Press, 1983).

2. Clark and Ferguson, *City Money;* Larry Bennett, Gregory Squires, Kathleen McCourt, and Phillip Nyden, *Chicago: Race, Class, and the Response to Urban Decline* (Philadelphia: Temple University Press, 1987); and Abdul Alkalimat and Douglas Gills, *Harold Washington and the Crisis in Black Power* (Chicago: Twenty-First Century Books, 1988).

3. See Alkalimat and Gills, *Harold Washington;* also Melvin Holli and Paul Green, *The Making of a Black Mrryor* (DeKalb: Northern Illinois University Press, 1984).

# Reform by Lawsuit

## By Don Rose

*In this article, Don Rose an independent political consultant and journalist, argues that real political reform in Chicago has come through the Courts.*

Richard M. Daley will leave a schizophrenic legacy: developing and beautifying his city, boosting its economy and its arts, bringing it together socially and politically, while a cesspool of corruption, segregation and repression lingers just below the surface.

Richard M. Daley's Chicago, despite its enduring problems, is but a faint shadow of its even more corrupt and racist self. A sedulous, decades-long reform effort cleaned up the worst abuses of Richard J. Daley's Chicago, though the son at times struggled to turn back the clock. But what if I told you that the key reformers were not legislators, civic leaders or community organizers, but were in fact an unlikely combination of a moderate Republican senator and a handful of crusading lawyers?

Yes, we've elected dozens of reform-minded politicians in the past half century—including a mayor who died too soon—but the genuine, longest-lasting reforms, including some that made possible the election of other reformers, were handed down from the bench, thanks to those creative, often brilliant attorneys. This is their story.

\* \* \*

On that fateful April night in 1955, when Richard J. Daley was elected mayor, a red-faced, beer-bellied, saloonkeeper and alderman named Mathias "Paddy" Bauler, danced a little jig and immortally proclaimed, "Chicago ain't ready for reform yet!"

Not only was it not ready for reform, but Daley would soon retool its fearsome Democratic machine into the nation's most powerful political organization—based on a new model—while the old urban machines were gasping and wheezing their last. He did it by incorporating the business and financial communities—State Street and LaSalle Street—two traditional elements of WASP-ish reform, which initially opposed his election fearing Chicago would become a "wide open town."

Their unwritten pact was first, give free reign to business and real estate development in Downtown Chicago; second, control the spread of the burgeoning black population whose second "great migration" was under way, threatening the central business district's white sanctity.

Patronage was the fuel that kept Daley's vast machine humming, along with authoritarian control of the election process, gerrymandering of the city's 50 wards, power over the courts and use of the police as a personal army.

Politics being intrinsically tied to race, Daley used every possible instrument of government, from schools, housing and employment to protective and recreational services, to suppress the African American population, creating the nation's most segregated city with the largest contiguous area of black residence outside of Africa.

It would be more than a decade before the first freshets of reform would begin the circuitous process of eroding machine politics. It took federal legislation, a potent local civil rights movement, a handful of reform politicians and most of all, that cadre of inspired young lawyers, who filed the suits that crippled the machine and began the process of bringing equal rights and equal justice to this most unequal of big towns.

Ironically, it took a Republican senator to help reform litigation succeed. Federal judges of both parties in the Northern District of Illinois were every bit the political hacks as Chicago municipal judges who typically emerged from the ranks of precinct captains and owed first loyalty to the bosses. The federal bench included Daley law partners and cronies who reliably ruled against anything resembling reform.

Elected in 1966, Charles Percy, changed the game at the urging of the Chicago Council of Lawyers, a new reform-minded bar association fed up with the Chicago Bar Association's then-obeisance to the Machine. The Council asked Percy to let it vet his nominees and recommend qualified, nonpolitical candidates for federal courts.

He did and they did. By the mid-1970s half the hacks were gone—replaced by independent-minded judges of both parties who ruled on most of the lawsuits that reined in the excesses of the political machine and called a halt to institutional racism in most operations of local government.

## Patronage

In 1969, a 25-year-old candidate for delegate to the Illinois Constitutional Convention filed a federal suit charging that political patronage and the use of public employees in campaigns was an unconstitutional intrusion into the election process—essentially, requiring political work by public employees was illegal.

Judge Abraham Lincoln Marovitz—a "beloved" character around town and one of Daley's closest cronies—threw the case out. Michael Shakman lost the election by some 600 votes, fewer than the number of patronage workers in his district. An appeals panel including two non-Daley Democrats reversed Marovitz and the case wound up back in District Court where rulings eventually tipped to the plaintiff.

Daley was hammered by the facts and finally agreed to a consent decree that would limit patronage abuses of employees. The decree took on the name of the plaintiff.

As the case wended its way through the courts in the 1970s, more units of government were put under its rulings. In 1979, two years after Daley's death, patronage hiring was ruled illegal.

Units of county and state government came under the hiring decree in the 1980s. A city scheme to circumvent hiring laws by using employment agencies was uncovered in 1994. Angered, Judge Wayne Andersen appointed a monitor to oversee the city's hiring practices—while a new Daley, Richard M., elected in 1989, tried to vacate the decree.

The notorious "hired truck" scandal, which exposed massive political hirings, found 40 workers guilty of rigging tests and interviews to get political workers hired. Patronage-based groups such as the Hispanic Democratic Organization were disbanded. Top aides of the younger Daley, including patronage chieftain Robert Sorich, went to jail.

"Shakman" remains the longest running reform saga in Chicago history, still making headlines. Election after election demonstrates a decrease in the Machine's strength as the grip and power of patronage continue to weaken—but does not disappear.

## Rigged Elections

Another case filed during the Illinois Constitutional Convention elections has also had a lasting impact. ACLU lawyer Bernard Weisberg, who became a federal magistrate, questioned why Illinois Secretary of State, Paul Powell, assumed the power to place candidates of his own choosing in top positions on the ballot, even though several candidates may have been in line at the same time when the filing office opened.

An unabashed Powell blustered of course he "breaks ties" himself. Otherwise, who knows, "a commonist" might get the number one spot—deemed a substantial advantage. Weisberg filed a federal suit and got a quick win. A lottery system was ordered in case of "ties" at time of filing. Every jurisdiction in Illinois now uses the ballot-placement lottery to assure fairness.

Weisberg won his election and helped draft a powerful civil liberties article for the new Illinois Constitution. When Powell died, shoeboxes stuffed with $800,000 in cash were found in his office. Not because he won the lottery.

Massive vote fraud was endemic in hundreds of Chicago's 3000 precincts, largely because the election judges, appointed by party committeemen, were machine partisans—including so-called Republican judges who theoretically kept the proceedings bipartisan. Poll watchers were often ejected and results juggled while police averted their eyes.

In 1972, a reform Democratic candidate distributed poll watcher credentials to the Chicago Tribune, which exposed major vote fraud in a Pulitzer Prize-winning series. The Independent Voters of Illinois sued the election board.

Thanks to the appointment of a top Secret Service man as Election Board chairman, a consent decree permitted the watchdog group Project LEAP (Legal Elections in All Precincts) to edit and rewrite the confusing judges manual. Further, LEAP was authorized to credential and assign election judges if Republican or Democratic committeemen failed to do so by a date certain.

Honest election judges equal honest elections. Scrub, rinse, repeat.

\* \* \*

Gerrymandery preserves incumbency. It excludes political undesirables.

Chicago's 50 wards varied widely in population well into the 1960s—the largest was five times the size of the smallest. The gadfly Sherman Skolnick sued under the 1962 one-person, one-vote Supreme Court ruling and a remapping following the 1970 census was ordered to equalize ward populations.

When the new map was drafted it became clear that equality of size did not assure fairness in racial and ethnic representation. Indeed, council cartographers cleverly used creative techniques, including dilution and concentration, to short-change African American communities of three potential black aldermen and avoid creating a Latino ward.

The concept of racial equity in political representation did not quite penetrate enough judicial minds in a 1971 suit challenging the remap, but a decade later things changed. A judge ruled for the excluded minorities but not broadly enough. The case was appealed and won. In 1986, during Mayor Harold Washington's first term, a new judge ordered seven wards redrawn with black or Latino majorities and special elections held. Victories by two black and two Latino Washington supporters finally gave the mayor a majority in the City Council.

A suit following the 1990 census eventually created the first Latino congressional district in Illinois. That and the successful earlier suits were filed by Washington's former corporation counsel Judson Miner, a founder of the Chicago Council of Lawyers, who later hired and mentored a young lawyer named Barack Obama.

## Police Spying

If a police state is one where the military is used for domestic political control, Daley's Police Red Squad brought us close. It began early in the century as intelligence-gathering on anarchists and other "subversives." Under Richard J. Daley, spying expanded to a vast range of community groups, civil rights and civil liberties organizations—including the ACLU and NAACP—any that ever criticized his regime. It planted undercover agents and provocateurs in neighborhood associations as well as independent political gatherings. Victims ranged from liberal aldermen to missionary nuns to actual radicals—none of whom had done anything remotely unlawful.

The Red Squad spied on meetings and marches, photographing participants and sharing files with the FBI, military intelligence agencies and the CIA. Hundreds of thousands of persons were illegally surveilled, phony charges made, negative information passed on to right-wing reporters and, in some instances, organizations were taken over by the plants and led into disruptive actions. Some of the violence at the 1968 Democratic convention was perpetrated by the squad's provocateurs.

Two similar suits were filed, one on behalf of the Alliance to End Repression network by Richard Gutman, the other by Doug Cassel and Robert Howard on behalf of several individuals and organizations with extensive Red Squad files. (Disclosure: I was a plaintiff.) Howard was affiliated with several public-interest law groups.

The cases were merged for trial and, after 11 years, won smashing victories against all spy agencies except the CIA. In 1985 the city was fined and subjected to a strong court order prohibiting investigations of lawful conduct.

## Segregation

Following passage of the 1949 National Housing Act, the City Council passed an ordinance permitting aldermen to reject public housing in their wards. Most white aldermen did, allowing only a few white projects to be built, while venal black council members wanted as many dependent African American citizens as possible in theirs. Miles of Chicago Housing Authority high-rises built during the 1950s and '60s warehoused vast numbers of blacks, setting in stone the city's pattern of racial segregation—blacks south and west, whites up north.

In 1966, the ACLU, with lead lawyer Alexander Polikoff plus now-Federal Judge Milton Shadur and Bernard Weisberg sued the CHA challenging segregation in site selection and tenant assignment under the constitution and civil rights laws. Lead plaintiff was activist Dorothy Gautreaux of the Altgeld Gardens project, where Barack Obama would years later become a community organizer.

The goal was scattered-site, integrated public housing—long a dream of early CHA idealists who were forced out for their views.

Gautreaux won in 1969. Judge Richard Austin ordered multiple scattered site developments. But the city stonewalled, resisting every inch of the way. In 1987 Judge Marvin Aspen wrested control from the recalcitrant CHA and broke the logjam. He put a savvy, progressive developer in charge and soon small, subsidized CHA developments that blended into their communities appeared throughout the city, albeit to a limited extent.

In settling a related suit, the U.S. Dept. of Housing and Urban Development created the Gautreaux program that enabled 7,500 families to move into better neighborhoods in both city and suburbs from 1977 to 1998. They lived in private dwellings, rent partially subsidized through vouchers.

Though the larger pattern of city segregation could not be broken, thousands of housing options were opened to minorities through housing mobility. By a fraction, we are no longer the nation's most segregated city.

July 4, 1965, civil rights leader Al Raby filed a well-documented complaint with the U.S. Department of Health, Education and Welfare charging Chicago schools were intentionally segregated through a multiplicity of methods including discrimination in construction of new schools, overcrowding black schools and juggling school boundary lines. It further charged discrimination in teacher assignment and unequal availability of ancillary services. Citing the 1964 Civil Rights Act, the complaint followed years of protests and boycotts, mostly aimed at the obdurate Chicago School Superintendent Benjamin Willis.

Commissioner of Education Francis Keppel cut off federal funds for Chicago schools, but Daley instantly called President Lyndon Johnson, who instantly ordered Keppel to reverse his decision.

The issue did not die. Lawsuits filed over the next 15 years, including some by the U.S. Departments of Justice and Education, were based on the same essential issues raised by Raby. Those agencies found the school system violated the U.S. Constitution and the Civil Rights Act. In 1980, the Chicago school board agreed to a detailed order to desegregate as best it could and correct the inequities.

Magnet schools and other nostrums were expanded, but the system was 85 percent minority, limiting the amount of genuine integration possible. What they proved is that separate is not equal, as the Supreme Court ruled before the first Daley was elected.

The proportion of blacks on the Chicago Police Department actually dropped between 1958 and 1968. First they were a quarter of the population and a quarter of the force; a decade later, 35 percent of the population but only 15 percent of the force. Further, the newly formed Afro-American Patrolmen's (now "Police") League documented numerous complaints about blacks being disproportionately rejected in hiring, while those on the force were discriminated against in assignments and discipline.

The Chicago Lawyers Committee for Civil Rights Under Law, working with AAPL leaders Renault Robinson and Howard Saffold, recruited several of Chicago's bluest-ribbon law firms to launch a series of suits against the police department charging discrimination in hiring, job assignment and promotions. The Department of Justice again got into the act, based on the massive amount of U.S. funds going to the police, charging the city and CPD with both race and gender discrimination.

The cases were consolidated at trial. In 1976, Judge Prentice Marshall, one of Senator Percy's appointments, ruled Chicago "knowingly discriminated against women, blacks and Hispanics in the employment of police officers and that the most effective remedy to cure that constitutional malaise is the economic sanction of withholding revenue sharing funds until [they] meet the affirmative requirements of the decree entered pursuant to this decision."

The police department had to change its ways. Minority participation is up, discrimination down—but not out. Discrimination in testing and promotions continue to generate lawsuits.

A parallel story can be told about the Chicago Fire Department. In 1973, the Department of Justice brought suit for discrimination in hiring: only about 5 percent of the department was black. A 1980 consent decree required it to be brought up to 45 percent. The city hired no firefighters for years before giving in. Minority employment, now in the thirties, rises slowly.

Even the Chicago Park District discriminated. Journalists' investigations exposed dramatic differences in the funding, maintenance, recreational services and facilities offered in black and Latino parks compared to those in white areas. Photos of disrepair in black parks were shocking. Citizen groups sued and again, the Department of Justice stepped in. The result was a consent decree against the Chicago Park District putting it under federal oversight for six years. The head of the parks at that time was Ed Kelly, a northside ward boss—later a key organizer of an unsuccessful white racist rebellion of Democrats against Washington, who had upset Jane Byrne in the 1983 mayoral primary election.

## The Future

The combined force of the lawsuits that crippled patronage, made elections fairer, aided independent candidates and empowered minority populations made it possible for Harold Washington to beat the machine. But he died too soon. The 2010 Democratic primary elections saw major offices, including president of the Cook County Board, fall to black and Latino reformers. Machine bosses openly blamed their losses on the decline of patronage. Thanks again, Shakman.

Things have improved in the years from Daley to Daley, but not all things. Old problems were solved, some remained, others morphed into different shapes like the "Terminator" villain. Tax increment financing, created to save blighted areas, too often rewards the rich and robs the poor. Privatization results in corporate welfare that imposes debt on generations to come. Whole neighborhoods are left to rot while millions romp joyfully in Millenium Park.

It's time for a new cadre of inspired young lawyers who will file the suits that will bring a new wave of reform to the ills of the new century, regardless of who succeeds Richard M. Daley. Chicago may yet, be ready for reform.

# Patronage: Shakman to Sorich

*In 1969, Michael L. Shakman filed suit against the Democratic Organization of Cook County, in an attempt to adjudicate the then standard practice of hiring and firing based on politics and not necessarily aptitude. In 1972, the parties reached an agreement prohibiting politically motivated firings, demotions, transfers, or other punishment of government employees. A 1979 court ruling led to a 1983 court order that made it unlawful to take any political factor into account in hiring public employees. Those decisions along with companion consent judgments—collectively called the Shakman Decrees—are binding on most city, county and statewide offices. The following excerpts are from the 1979 Shakman ruling and the later case of Robert Sorich and his co-defendents.*

## Judgment in Shakman v. Democratic Organization of Cook County

Now, therefore, upon the consent of the parties aforesaid, it is hereby Ordered, Adjudged and Decreed as follows:...

C. The provisions of this Judgement apply to each and all of the following:

1. defendant The Democratic Organization of Cook County, a corporation;
2. defendant Democratic County Central Committee of Cook County and all members thereof;
3. defendant City of Chicago, a municipal corporation;
4. defendant Richard J. Daley, individually and as President of The Democratic Organization of Cook County, Chairman of the Democratic County Central Committee

of Cook County, Mayor of the City of Chicago and Democratic Party Ward Committeeman for the Eleventh Ward of the City of Chicago; ...

11. defendant Richard B. Ogilvie, individually and as Governor of the State of Illinois;

12. defendant Edmund J. Kucharski, individually and as Chairman of the Republican County Central Committee of Cook County; ...

14. the successors of each of the foregoing defendants in each of their aforesaid capacities; and to

15. the present and future officers, members, agents, servants, employees and attorneys of each of the defendants and others named or referred to hereinabove, and all others in active concert or participation with any of the defendants or others named or referred to in (1) through(15) above who receive actual notice of this Judgment by personal service or otherwise.

D. It is declared that compulsory or coerced political financial contributions by any governmental employee, contractor or supplier, to any individual or organization and all compulsory or coerced political activity by any governmental employee are prohibited, and, once hired, a governmental employee is free from all compulsory political requirements in connection with his employment. However, governmental employees may engage on a voluntary basis, on their own time, in any lawful political activity (including the making of political financial contributions).

E. Each and all of the defendants and others named or referred to in paragraph C above are permanently enjoined from directly or indirectly, in whole or in part:

1. conditioning, basing or knowingly prejudicing or affecting any term or aspect of governmental employment, with respect to one who is at the time already a governmental employee, upon or because of any political reason or factor.

2. knowingly causing or permitting any employee to do any partisan political work during the regular working hours of his or her governmental employment, or during time paid for by public funds; provided that nothing contained in this subparagraph (2) shall prohibit governmental employees from voluntarily using vacation time, personal leave time or from taking non-paid leaves of absence to do political work, but permission to do so must be granted non-discriminatorily.

3. knowingly inducing, aiding, abetting, participating in, cooperating with or encouraging the commission of any act which is proscribed by this paragraph E, or threatening to commit any such act.

**By Judge Nicholas Bua**
**September 24, 1979**

### Patronage Hiring by the City of Chicago

...17. The City of Chicago (the "City") presently employs approximately 40,000 to 45,000 persons, Of these employees approximately 18,000 are police or fire officers.

18. The City hires many of its employees on the basis of regular Democratic political sponsorship, as described below...

19. The City gives preference in hiring for many City jobs to persons who are politically sponsored by Democratic Party ward committeemen or other Democratic regular organization officials. About one-half of the people hired by the City in recent years other than as police or fire officers were for jobs for which preference was given to persons with Democratic Party sponsorship.

20. For a number of City jobs persons normally can be hired only with regular Democratic *political sponsorship.*

21. Most of the City jobs for which such political preference is given are not policy making or confidential in nature. These jobs include, without limitation, jobs as garbage collectors, building inspectors, street cleaners, clerks, technicians and supervisors.

22. The City often informs Democratic Party officials of City job openings of which public notice is not otherwise given.

23. Persons applying for some City patronage jobs have been told by City officials that to get a job or learn about job openings the applicant must see the Democratic Party Ward Committeeman.

24. Persons hired for City jobs with Democratic political sponsorship as described above do not have civil service, contractual or statutory protection against arbitrary discharge.

25. By the conditioning and basing of terms and aspects of hiring for many positions with the City of Chicago on political factors, those employees of the City are coerced into political work and support for the regular Democratic organization.

26. This support helps the regular Democrats win elections in the City of Chicago and Cook County. It provides them with a significant advantage in those elections ....

### Political Sponsorship

...120. Usually, persons get sponsorship for a City, County, County officer, Park District, or Forest Preserve District job from a regular Democratic organization official either after having done or upon the expectation that they will do political precinct work (such as door to door canvassing, putting up posters, etc.) on behalf of candidates endorsed by the sponsor.

121. Democratic political sponsorship for government jobs is usually communicated by a sponsorship letter to the employing office.

122. Members of the regular Democratic organization generally sponsor persons for governmental employment on the basis, among other considerations, of their support or promise of support of the regular Cook County Democratic organization, the sponsor's ward or township organization or other party units and of their endorsed candidates. Many such job applicants are required as a condition of obtaining such sponsorship to do or to promise to do precinct or other political work for such endorsed candidates or to make or to promise to make financial contributions to party organizations.

123. Usually, no person is sponsored by regular Democratic organization officials for public jobs if he or she has in any open way been a worker or partisan of any political group opposed to or by the regular Democratic organization of the sponsor. On some occasions such persons are so sponsored if they agree to switch political affiliation and agree to support the regular Democratic organization and its candidates ....

### *Political Impact of Democratic Patronage Practices*

129. The patronage employment system described above helps regular Democrats win elections. It provides a significant advantage in Chicago and in Cook County, Illinois, to candidates supported by the regular Democratic organization and a corresponding disadvantage to opposing candidates, including independent candidates and Republicans. Independent candidates have essentially no patronage precinct workers and Republicans in Chicago have few patronage precinct workers.

130. Democratic party officials believe that patronage hiring is very important for them to maintain their election advantage.

## Opinion: Shakman v. Democratic Organization of Cook County

**By Judge Nicholas Bua**
**September 24, 1979**

There are, on the average, over 250 governmental employees per ward in the City who were sponsored by the regular Democratic organization for their job. Since the City wards average about sixty precincts per ward, there are, on the average about four patronage government employees in each precinct in the City. A significant number of these persons do political work on behalf of persons supported by sponsoring regular Democratic organization officials.

Most importantly, the defendants admit that the political precinct work done by these patronage workers "helps elect candidates supported by the various members of the Democratic County Central Committee," They also admit that "[t]his is one of the purposes of giving the preference in hiring."

The court holds that the plaintiffs have a right to an electoral process free from deliberate governmental discrimination against their views. The factual record before the court conclusively demonstrates, beyond any existence of a genuine issue of material fact, that the defendants deliberately use the challenged patronage practices to help elect regular Democrats and help defeat their opponents. This purposeful, deliberate discrimination gives the defendants an actual, significant advantage in elections. This is not to say, of course, that patronage workers are the dominant force in every election. The plaintiffs do not claim that they are. The parties agree that many factors, including campaign money, television exposure, racial or ethnic background, etc. may influence the outcome of the election. The point is that patronage workers give an important advantage to regular Democrats. The regular Democratic defendants are using the government to further their own political interests by giving preferences for many government jobs only to those who have worked and/or will promise to work for regular Democratic candidates.

The court concludes that the patronage practices challenged by the plaintiffs infringe their rights as candidates and voters under the first and fourteenth amendments to the Constitution of the United States and 42 U.S.C. SS 1983. 1985. The challenged practices are not necessary to the furthering of any compelling government interest. Accordingly, the court holds that the challenged practices violate the Constitution of the United States…

# U.S. v. ROBERT SORICH, TIMOTHY MCCARTHY, JOHN SULLIVAN, and PATRICK SLATTERY

*Robert Sorich was Assistant Director of the Mayor's Office of Intergovernmental Affairs (IGA) from 1993 to 2005. As such, Sorich was often referred to as the "patronage chief." Federal prosecutors claimed that Robert Sorich and his co-defendants, Timothy McCarthy, John Sullivan, and Patrick Slattery, used their official city positions to hand out patronage jobs to those with political sponsorship and connections. Thus, violating the Shakman Decrees. The following includes excerpts from the 2006 U.S. Government findings of evidence (proffer) in the Sorich case; and the United States Court of Appeals (7th District) ruling upholding the conviction.*

# The Government's Proffer Regarding the Existence of a Scheme and Basis of Agency Admissions in the Sorich Case

As alleged principally in Count One, Sorich and McCarthy worked with and directed other City officials to corrupt the City's personnel process by directing the awarding of certain jobs and promotions in non-policymaking positions to candidates pre-selected by IGA [Mayor's Office of Intergovernmental Affairs] through sham and rigged interviews coordinated by personnel directors and conducted by interviewers. In addition, defendants and co-schemers concealed and otherwise protected the joint criminal activity from public exposure and possible criminal prosecution. The government submits the following summary of evidence:

## A Background Concerning the Typical Hiring and Promotion Process for City Operating Departments.

### *Summary of the scheme to rig the hiring and promotion process*

In fact, however, as set forth herein, the City's hiring process for certain jobs in certain departments covered by the Shakman decree was controlled by IGA, including defendants Sorich and McCarthy, during the relevant time periods. The government has not alleged that IGA controlled the award of all Shakman-covered positions, but rather that IGA's control focused on certain Operating Departments and certain positions. Campaign coordinators, union leaders, and other politically connected people nominated job candidates to Sorich and McCarthy. After participating in the decision to predetermine the winners for these particular jobs, Sorich and/or McCarthy communicated with personnel directors and other employees of the Operating Departments and then provided the personnel directors with lists of preselected candidates that IGA wanted the Operating Departments to place in those positions.

After receiving names from Sorich or McCarthy, the personnel directors screened for those candidates, causing them to be chosen from among other eligible candidates so that IGA's candidates would be certain to be included on referral lists for interviews.

Interviewers from the Operating Departments then conducted sham interviews. As described in detail below, in some hiring sequences, personnel directors identified IGA's preselected winners to the interview panelists, so that interview panelists would give the IGA picks the highest numerical ratings on interview rating forms, without regard to the candidates' relative qualifications. In other hiring sequences, interviewers just left the numerical ratings blank on the interview rating forms, and the personnel director filled in the scores later, after getting the winners' names from IGA. In yet other hiring sequences, the interviewers or their managers obtained the names directly from IGA. However the names were delivered to the Operating Departments, the highest scores were assigned to favored candidates on the basis of their IGA designations, without regard to the Operating Department's evaluation of the candidates' relative qualifications.

* * *

### Sorich's Maintenance of a Secret Jobs List in the 1990's

Beginning in 1989 and continuing to the present, there was an administrative assistant at IGA who worked first as an assistant for Sorich's predecessor at IGA, and after that person left in or about 1993, she became Sorich's assistant ("Sorich's secretary"). She worked for Sorich and, beginning in or about 2001, McCarthy as well.

The Chicago Department of Transportation (CDOT) manager's organization was not the only political organization at CDOT [which was awarded Shakman-covered jobs]. Another top CDOT official had a political group comprised primarily of African-Americans. Although that group originally was a part of the organization that the CDOT manager inherited, it operated separately during the time the CDOT manager ran the organization. Sorich's secretary confirmed that Sorich was in contact with both the CDOT manager and the head of the African-American organization.

In addition to her typical secretarial responsibilities for Sorich (and later McCarthy), Sorich's secretary had what she described as a "secret" job responsibility related to hiring and promotions in City employment. She was responsible for maintaining lists and files related to requests for jobs or promotions that campaign coordinators (such as Harjung, Katalinic, Tomczak, and HDO officials), aldermen, union officials, and others brought to IGA.

During the 1990's, Sorich's secretary kept a software program tracking employment-related requests on a City-owned laptop in her office, but did not tell others why she had the laptop there. Sorich's secretary also kept paper files tracking jobs and sponsors. There were also boxes of index cards kept in Sorich's office and/or Sorich's secretary's office. The index cards included employee names, job titles, and requests, and political sponsorship.

Sorich provided his secretary with the information to put in the database. Before meetings with campaign coordinators, aldermen, and others, Sorich sometimes asked his secretary to print out the jobs list by sponsor, so that he could talk to the sponsor about what requests had been granted and what requests had not. The jobs on the list were covered by the Shakman decree, including Motor Truck Drivers, Laborers, and Tree Trimmers. At one point, Sorich told his secretary to use the laptop at home and not at work. She then printed Sorich's lists at home, and brought them to him at the office.

Sorich's predecessor at IGA told Sorich's secretary to maintain the database and files, but not to tell other people that she was maintaining such lists and files.

As of December 1997, the jobs list contained over 5,700 entries relating to political employment requests.

# Federal Appeals Court Decision

Despite the existence of a federal consent decree and other measures that for decades have sought to bring more transparency and legitimacy to the City of Chicago's civil service hiring, patronage appointments have continued to flourish. These defendants were key players in a corrupt and far-reaching scheme, based out of the mayor's Office of Intergovernmental Affairs that doled out thousands of city civil service jobs based on political patronage and nepotism. The government alleged that the defendants concealed what they were doing by falsely assuring city lawyers that their hires were legitimate, and then shredding evidence and hiding their involvement once a criminal investigation began. After an eight-week jury trial, three of the defendants were convicted of mail fraud and the fourth of making materially false statements to federal investigators. The centerpiece of their appeal is a challenge to the government's theory of prosecution: they contend that their behavior, while dubious, is not criminal, and that the honest services mail fraud statute, 18 U.S.C. § 1346, is unconstitutionally vague. We conclude that the defendants' actions do constitute mail fraud, and that the statute is not unconstitutionally vague as applied to the facts of this case. The defendants also argue that they did not deprive the city or the people of Chicago of any money or property, but the jobs that they wrongfully gave away were indeed a kind of property, so we reject this argument. Individual defendants also challenge the sufficiency of the indictment, the connection to the mails, and the sufficiency of the evidence against them, while one defendant argues that he was entitled to a sentencing adjustment for playing a minor role. Finding none of these arguments persuasive, we affirm on all counts.

# Background

The beating heart of this fraudulent scheme was the mayor's Office of Intergovernmental Affairs (IGA). Formally, the office serves as a liaison between the City of Chicago and state and federal governments and has no role in hiring for the city's 37,000 or so civil service jobs. Informally, the office coordinated a sizeable portion of the city's civil service hiring, ferreting out jobs to footsoldiers in the mayor's campaign organization and to other cronies.

The government introduced a substantial amount of evidence describing both the contours and the details of this long-running operation (it has likely been in place since before any of these defendants came to work for the city). We view the evidence in the light most favorable to the government since the jury found the defendants guilty. It includes testimony from former department heads, political campaign coordinators, personnel managers, and workers both hired and rejected; wiretaps of conversations; and documentary evidence, including hiring records, sham interview forms, and lists tracking job applicants and their sponsors. The most dramatic document is a spreadsheet showing all 5,700 patronage applicants and their sponsors between 1990 and 1997. The spreadsheet was kept on defendant Robert Sorich's laptop computer, and he attempted to destroy both the list and the computer, but both were turned over to the FBI in 1997 pursuant to a grand jury subpoena. FBI analysts were able to recover the spreadsheet.

Rather than describe this evidence in detail, we will provide an overview here, and will supply any relevant specifics in the analysis section below. Sorich was the mayor's so-called "patronage chief," and held the title Assistant to the Director of IGA. Defendant Timothy McCarthy was Sorich's deputy from 2001 to 2005 and often stepped into his shoes. Campaign coordinators would pass Sorich lists of campaign workers and volunteers whose names he would then send to the heads of various city departments—Aviation, Streets and Sanitation, Sewers, Water, etc.—for jobs. Defendants Patrick Slattery and John Sullivan held high positions in the Department of Streets and Sanitation.

During both individual and mass-hiring sequences, departmental managers like Slattery and Sullivan would hold sham interviews and then falsify interview forms in favor of the pre-selected "winners." The interview forms were often filled out weeks after the interviews, with one pile for blessed applicants (to be given high scores), and another for everybody else (to be given low scores). Some positions, such as tree trimmer, required merit tests but the results were frequently ignored. Evidence showed that Sorich even pressured departmental managers to hire applicants with drinking problems for positions that involved overseeing workplace safety.

This all went on despite the existence of multiple laws and personnel regulations forbidding the use of political considerations in hiring for civil service jobs, and mandating the awarding of those jobs on merit. These laws largely stem from the "Shakman Decrees," which are two federal consent decrees banning the use of politics in City of Chicago hiring that came into being as a result of litigation in the 1970s and '80s. Members of the scheme falsely signed "Shakman certifications," attesting that particular hiring sequences had not been influenced by political patronage.

# Daley vs. Daley

By David Bernstein

*For much of the past half century, a mayor named Daley has towered over Chicago. In this article, David Bernstein compares the reigns of father and son, assessing their triumphs and failures, their impact on the city—and what their enduring dominance at the polls says about us.*

On a blustery morning early in March, Mayor Richard M. Daley was running late for a constituent's birthday party. A very important constituent, practically family: the City of Chicago. One hundred seventy-one years old this year, Chicago was being feted at the History Museum in Lincoln Park, and the second-floor banquet hall was decked out for the occasion—there were hot dogs, balloons, and a cake decorated with the stars and stripes of the city flag. By the time the mayor walked in, 20 minutes behind schedule, the Marist High School Jazz Band was playing an impromptu recital of the school fight song to fill the dead air for the few hundred guests.

Waiting to be introduced, the mayor fixed his windswept comb-over and straightened his blue pinstripes. When it came his turn to speak, he read his prepared remarks in a robotic monotone. Rattling on about the founding father Jean Baptiste Pointe du Sable, the city charter, and world's fairs past, the mayor seemed bored—like a man who has spent six long terms schlepping to untold thousands of such ceremonial events.

About halfway through, the mayor paused. Perhaps he sensed his lackluster performance, because he looked up at the audience and started speaking off the cuff. He riffed about the visit he'd made earlier that morning to an eighth-grade class in the tough Back of the Yards neighborhood on the city's South Side—at a school named for his late father, Mayor Richard J. Daley. With passion in his voice, he mused about how many of these young, mainly Hispanic and black students were succeeding in the classroom despite the daily scourge of gangs, guns, and drugs they faced. Then, in one of his characteristic non sequiturs, he segued into a story about the meeting he'd had the day before with the former British prime minister Tony Blair and how the city must meet the vast and varied challenges of the global economy. His face flushed as he stressed the need for safer neighborhoods, better schools, new libraries, and vibrant cultural attractions. His boyish enthusiasm spoke better than words of his love for the city and for a job he [gave] no indication of ever leaving.

## Like Father, Like Son

Richard Michael Daley, who turned 66 in April 2008, is the country's longest-serving big-city mayor—at press time, 7,059 days as "The Man on Five" in City Hall. When he serves out the rest of this term ending in 2011, he will have surpassed by four months the 21 years and 8 months his father, Richard Joseph Daley, spent in office before suffering a fatal heart attack. Together, the Boss and Son of Boss have ruled the city for 40 out of the last 53 years and nearly a quarter of Chicago's history. The marks of their tenures are everywhere—from the big stuff like the mass of highways and towering skyscrapers, O'Hare International Airport and Millennium Park, to the smaller things, such as bicycle lanes, wrought-iron fences, and well-illuminated streets.

Over the years, they have inspired many Chicagoans with a feeling that the city works, even when it sometimes doesn't. In the process, their overwhelming popularity with voters has brought stability to a city government that, by tradition, has been politically unruly. (Consider: Chicago went through five mayors in the 13 years between the reigns of Daley I and Daley II.)

\* \* \*

## Politics: The Machine Gets Retooled

"Organization, not Machine," Daley I would sternly correct people who criticized his vast political operation. "Get that. Organization, not Machine." Whatever you call it, Daley I and his political army counted as many as 35,000 to 40,000 patronage workers who could be relied on to deliver a 400,000-vote margin in each election.

Daley I, of course, did not create Chicago's political machine; Mayor Anton Cermak did it a quarter century before Daley—forging a loose coalition of ethnic duchies ruled by politicians and hoodlums who divided up the spoils with little thought for the public interest. But it was Daley I who turned Cermak's Model T organization into a political muscle car. He changed the existing feudal system, allotting authority to the ward bosses but holding them responsible for taking care of city services and turning out the vote. In return, the ward chieftains surrendered control of the city government to him. Daley I also modernized the machine by cozying up to big business. "He's often thought of as the last of the old-time bosses," says the veteran political consultant Don Rose. "But he was the first of the new-time bosses by bringing LaSalle Street into the Machine."

* * *

To Daley I, however, the Machine was a necessary appendage to municipal governing. "Good politics is good government," he used to say. In addition to delivering votes, ward bosses were also expected to deliver city services 365 days a year. By the end of Daley I's first term, there were 475 new garbage trucks, 174 miles of new sewers, 69,600 new street and alley lights, 72 downtown parking facilities, 2,000 more police officers, and 400 additional firefighters.

As chairman of the Democratic Party of Cook County and the head of the patronage system, he larded city departments with political workers. "No job was too small to get their attention," says the former Illinois governor Dan Walker, who often clashed with Daley I. "They would fight over a janitor job as strongly as they would fight over a cabinet job." A *Chicago Tribune* investigation in 1974 found that the city had squandered $91 million in its annual budget because of padded payrolls. In Daley I's administration, changing a light bulb was no joke; it required five city workers, according to the paper.

At the same time, Daley I employed some of the city's best and brightest policymakers and technocrats, and if a politically connected city commissioner was a loafer or a drunk, Daley I would make sure he had a competent deputy to run the department. "One of the myths about Richard J. Daley is that he was just a politician," says Paul Green, a political scientist at Roosevelt University. "He loved to govern. He loved to run things."

Bill Daley says his father doled out patronage jobs, not just as rewards for his political supporters, but also to lend a hand to the needy: "My dad would go to wakes, and the widow would be there with a couple of kids, and she'd say, 'I don't know what I'm going to do, Mr. Mayor.' He'd say, 'Call my office tomorrow—we'll see what we can do.'" Today, adds Bill Daley, "you can't do that. You'd go to jail."

By the time Richard M. Daley became mayor in 1989, the Machine of the old days was "dead, dead, dead," as Harold Washington had famously declared. Television advertising had all but replaced precinct captains for attracting votes. As Daley I's longtime press secretary, Earl Bush, noted in the early 1980s, "A bucket of coal won't buy anybody today." Election laws had also changed in the face of the 1979 *Shakman* decrees, which barred politically motivated hirings and firings.

Daley II did not seek the Machine's Lazarus-like return, and he didn't aspire to be party chairman—leery of the "Boss" stigma that would have come with the title. Asked once by a *Tribune* reporter why he had not followed his father's blueprint, Daley II was quoted as saying: "Parties aren't what they used to be. People don't vote for parties. They vote for the person. It's all television money and polling now. It's not parades. It's not torchlights and songs." His observation might be even more true today. Does anybody anymore even know who is chairman of the Cook County Democratic Party? (It's Joseph Berrios. Next question: Who the hell is that?)

But Daley II had other reasons for bucking the Machine establishment. It didn't want him. The old guard's loyalty toward Daley I did not extend to the son, especially after the 1983 mayoral race, when the young Daley finished an embarrassing third, and many of his father's old allies blamed the son for splitting the white vote with the incumbent mayor, Jane Byrne, and allowing the relatively unknown legislator Harold Washington to become Chicago's first black mayor. Furthermore, the ward pros saw young Daley as a threat to their power. For his part, Daley felt no loyalty to the Machine. "I don't owe the Democratic Party anything," he was quoted as saying. In 1991, he made the break official when he pushed to change the Democratic mayoral primary to a nonpartisan election.

The split from the old Machine made Daley II more palatable to lakefront liberals and other good-government types, or "goo-goos," who had viewed his father as anathema. "There were a few of us at first," recalls John Schmidt, who had fought Daley I and later became Daley II's chief of staff. "We gave credibility to one another."

But in place of the old Machine, Daley II set up his own independent political organization. He formed groups, such as the now-defunct Hispanic Democratic Organization (HDO) and the Coalition for Better Government, and installed get-out-the-vote workers in every ward who were loyal to him and to candidates who supported him, not necessarily to the full Democratic ticket. Roughly half of the 1,000 or so HDO members were on the public payroll, according to the *Tribune*.

Beyond running city hall, the mayor has extended his power across the city. He controls at least a half dozen other agencies with taxing powers, including the Chicago Public Schools, the Chicago Transit Authority, the Chicago Housing Authority, the Chicago Park District, and the Metropolitan Water Reclamation District.

His influence stretches further with his family ties. Through his brother John, who chairs the Cook County Board of Commissioners' powerful finance committee, the mayor wields clout in county matters. (The [then] board president, Todd Stroger, was a Daley-appointed alderman before being elected in 2006 to fill his father's shoes.) Another brother of the mayor, Michael, practices law at Daley & George, a clout-heavy law firm. His brother Bill, of course, was commerce secretary under Bill Clinton and is well connected inside the Beltway and in the business world. [Now, of course, he is President Obama's chief of staff.]

Daley II cements his power through his vast influence—or perceived influence—over government levers and funds. Dick Simpson, a political science professor who served two terms as an independent alderman in the 1970s, says Daley II depends on the practice of pay-to-play "pinstripe patronage"—that is, handing out lucrative government contracts and other economic favors to clout-heavy political supporters and campaign contributors.

\* \* \*

Daley II denies that he has created a new Daley machine. "My political organization is myself," he once said. Again, whatever you call it, his mighty political operation would probably put a proud smile on his father's face. "I think Rich didn't say, 'I have to copy what my dad did,'" says Bill Daley. "But he was smart enough to say, 'If it worked for him...'"

Northerly Island, the 91-acre peninsula just east of Soldier Field, was eerily quiet one day last winter, the only sounds the crying of gulls and the tranquil Lake Michigan surf. From the narrow strip of lakefront park, the downtown skyline seems a world away. "You can sometimes see coyotes out here," a park district worker told me as I wandered the island.

What's unseen, hidden under eight inches of grassy turf, is the former Meigs Field runway, bulldozed with six gigantic X marks on March 30, 2003, by Daley II's order. For years the mayor had wanted to close the tiny private airport and turn it into a park, but was thwarted by the governor at the time, Jim Edgar. When Daley II finally acted, he did so stealthily at night, and without prior approval from the city council, the state legislature, or even the Federal Aviation Administration. The destruction of Meigs was denounced as an illegal land grab, but the mayor said he acted to protect downtown Chicago from a possible terrorist attack.

The move was vintage Daley II: one-man rule, a governing style taken right out of the Daley family catechism.

Although you'd hardly know it from most of the last half century, Chicago's charter—in effect, the municipal government's constitution—actually gives the city council vast power over vital city functions. Daley I altered the balance, and his son has followed suit.

Shortly after his election, Daley I wielded the clout behind his double role as mayor and party chairman to undo the civil-service reforms enacted by his predecessor, Martin Kennelly. He wrested control of the budget from the city council, stripping aldermen of their most important function. He also limited the ability of council members to grant routine favors—often in exchange for bribes—such as doling out driveway permits and zoning variances. Bob Crawford, the retired political editor at the news radio station WBBM-AM, says Daley I was simply doing what any good in-charge leader does. He recalls the mayor as once proclaiming, "Show me a mayor who has no power and I'll show you a mayor who doesn't get anything done."

Wearing his two crowns, Daley I had near absolute rule over the city and county governments, the Chicago-area state legislators, and even the judiciary. Inside the Washington Beltway, he was considered a political kingmaker. "Dick Daley is the ballgame," as Robert F. Kennedy famously put it.

Daley I wielded his power untouched by guilt. He thought of himself as a different breed of "Boss": personally honest and civic-minded, unlike the crooked pols of Chicago's past. "My decisions are not what is good for Daley, but what is good for the city," he once told a reporter, and he probably believed it.

In 21-plus years in office, Daley I never lost a vote in the city council. He and his floor leader, the wily 31st Ward alderman Tom Keane, would cut backroom deals and then present them to the full council to rubber-stamp. As the old warhorse Edward Burke, who has served in the council since 1969, once described the role of aldermen in those days: "We were useful to fill chairs and vote the way we were told to vote. That was the extent of it."

Early on, the mayor faced occasional opposition—11 Republicans served on the council in 1955. By the mayor's final term, there was one. (Today, there's still just one: Brian Doherty, of the 41st Ward, on the far Northwest Side.) By the 1970s, 37 of the 50 aldermen had been handpicked by Daley I and afforded him unquestioning obedience. Leon Despres, from Hyde Park, who served 20 years in the council from 1955 to 1975, remained the mayor's most persistent critic. Sometimes Daley I would grow irritated and cut off Despres's microphone in mid-speech. In 1965, the mayor even ordered the council's sergeant-at-arms to force Despres to stop arguing and sit down. As Mike Royko observed: "Until that time the mayor never had an alderman defy him when he said, 'Sit.' In fact most of them not only sit, they bark and roll over." Dick Simpson, a thoughtful critic of both Daleys, says of the father: "The longer he stayed in, the more iron-fisted he became and the more rubber-stamp the council became. That's somewhat true, but not quite the same, with Richard M. Daley."

On taking office, Daley II quickly tamed the council that had paralyzed Harold Washington. By his second term, the mayor had near lockstep loyalty. A 1978 state law allows the mayor to fill aldermanic vacancies in the council, and since 1989, Daley II has appointed 31 aldermen, including 16 of the current 50. Even with such a solid base of seat-fillers, Daley II, like his father, leaves little to chance. Ed Burke (20th), the council's finance chair, and Patrick O'Connor (40th), Daley II's unofficial floor leader, carry the mayor's water in the council. The former 23rd Ward alderman and city clerk James Laski says Daley II also has city hall enforcers to twist the arms of aldermen to ensure loyalty. "You need a job, you need extra trees cut down in your ward, you need some more money for streets and alleys, or getting funding for a library or a senior center, all those things," says Laski, who recently finished an 11-month prison stint for accepting $48,000 in bribes. "They hold those little carrots in front of you, saying, 'You want dis, you want dat, you want dis—we need dis, dis, and dis.'"

Though Daley II denied it, such horse-trading reportedly took place before the council's recent 33-to-16 vote approving the mayor's controversial plan to build a new children's museum in Grant Park. Afterwards, several aldermen privately told reporters that top city officials had promised them perks and favors in exchange for supporting the mayor.

In the last few years, as corruption scandals have weakened Daley II politically, more aldermen have shown a willingness to confront him, and he has even lost a few votes. The experience seems to have pushed him to wield as heavy a gavel as his father once did. At a council meeting last February, for example, Daley II unleashed a tirade against 2nd Ward Alderman Robert Fioretti, who had voted against the mayor's plan to raise the real-estate transfer tax to aid the CTA. (The tax increase passed 41 to 6.) With his fists clenched, Daley II laid into Fioretti: "If Alderman Fioretti believes they don't need the CTA in his ward, then stand and say, 'CTA, bypass my people.'... You'll last about half a day.... They'll have to send 911—police and fire—to protect you and your families."

## Race: Searching for Harmony

Through the Machine—relying mainly on Dawson and the "Silent Six," the group of black aldermen loyal to Daley I—the mayor managed for years to keep the racial cauldron from boiling over, as it did in other cities. His solution for keeping the city together was to keep it apart via segregation. "Integration didn't help [Daley] politically," says Adam Cohen, an editorial writer for *The New York Times* who co-wrote (with a *Tribune* editor, Elizabeth Taylor) the 2000 biography of Daley I, *American Pharaoh*. As long as the black vote bloc was concentrated and segregated in ghettos, says Cohen, the mayor could more easily control it without scaring off white voters.

But the relative calm didn't hold. After Martin Luther King Jr.'s assassination on April 4, 1968, rioting broke out in more than 150 U.S. cities, but the unrest was perhaps worst in Chicago. By the end of three days of chaos, 11 people were dead, 300 had been arrested, and thousands more were homeless. Seeing his city up in flames, Daley I issued orders that have lived in infamy: "Shoot to kill any arsonist" and "Shoot to maim or cripple any looters." (The orders were never actually issued to police commissioner James Conlisk during the riots; rather, the mayor announced them at a press conference on April 15th, a full week after calm had been restored.) Bill Daley defends his father's saber rattling: "He honestly believed that [someone who throws a Molotov cocktail] was putting someone's life at risk that was innocent, and that would justify a shoot-to-maim or shoot-to-kill order. Tell me why this is so illogical."

Logical or not, many people viewed the order as racist. Family, friends, and former staffers insist that Daley I wasn't racist. He was simply a pragmatist who believed at his core that in Chicago, everybody, no matter what race, has an equal opportunity to succeed through hard work, just as he had. "I'm a kid from the stockyards," he used to remind people. If anything, his supporters concede he was a product of his segregated upbringing in Bridgeport.

Others disagree. "Oh, sure he was racist," says his old council foe Leon Despres. "Daley Sr. really was a partisan for segregation." Bob Crawford, the radio newsman who covered Daley I for eight years, is more circumspect: "Some people say 'racist'; I would say, 'somewhat bigoted.' But it all came back to politics with Daley; if anything was too risky, why do it?"

By the late 1960s, Daley I's tight political grip on the black wards had begun to loosen. (By his last election, in 1975, he would receive only half the black vote.) Anger toward Daley I and the Machine swelled up after the deadly predawn police raid in 1969 on the Black Panthers' headquarters that ended in the suspicious deaths of two Panther leaders, Fred Hampton and Mark Clark. The tipping point came in 1972, when Congressman Ralph Metcalfe Sr., the former Olympic sprinter and longtime protégé of Dawson, split with Daley

I's Machine and joined the chorus of protest after two prominent black doctors were alleg-edly beaten and harassed by police. "It's never too late to become black," Metcalfe said.

Daley I couldn't adjust. He continued to surround himself with a monolithic group, and he kept blacks at arm's length. "He didn't really have black people in his inner circle," says Cohen. "He had blacks in the submachine, but their responsibility mainly was to turn out votes." Under Daley I, only two blacks headed city departments (health and human services). And it wasn't until 1971 that Daley I slated a black candidate, Joseph Bertrand, to run for a citywide office (treasurer).

Times were different for Daley II. By 1983, blacks had taken to the streets once again, this time celebrating Harold Washington's mayoral victory. The euphoria was tempered by the "Council Wars," which earned Chicago an embarrassing reputation as "Beirut on the Lake." Mayor Washington died in November 1987, and in 1989 Daley II won the office in the most racially polarized vote in the city's history. "I had whites, blacks both yelling at me," the mayor recalls today. "I'd go to one parade, they'd yell; I'd go to the other parade, they'd yell." He received just 7 percent of the black vote that year.

Much of the black community's hostility stemmed from lingering resentment toward his father. But to the surprise of many, Daley II has calmed the city's political and racial upheavals. "He knew he wouldn't be around long as mayor if he had a racially divided city," says Bill Daley. "And the big concern in 1989 when he won was, 'Will he be fair to the black community?' A lot of people in the black community thought they were never going to get streets cleaned, no snow pickup, no nothing—that Rich Daley would just ignore them."

Within days of being elected, Daley II introduced his new cabinet, and half of the 24 ap-pointees were minorities. By his third term, the African American newspaper *The Chicago Defender* endorsed Daley II over a black challenger, U.S. Rep. Bobby Rush. "The evidence is clear that the young Daley is much more accepting of blacks than his father was," says Timuel Black. "Maybe it's the times."

Maybe, but it's definitely smart politics. African Americans account for about two-fifths of Chicago's population. This mayor "recognizes something that his old man would've found very, very hard," says the retired federal judge and former U.S. congressman Abner Mikva, who used to clash with Daley I, "and that is that the African American population is not just a piece of a jigsaw puzzle that you fool around with when you're drawing maps and assigning places at the table."

Daley II has set up additional chairs for other minorities, too, particularly Latinos, Chicago's fastest-growing ethnic group. (Latinos make up a quarter of the city's population.) UIC's Dick Simpson argues that the increased role of Latinos in Chicago politics has caused blacks to lose ground. In recent years, for example, the share of city contracts awarded to African American businesses has dropped to 8 percent, the lowest level since Daley II took office.

Still, Jesse Jackson acknowledges that race relations in Chicago are markedly better under Daley II—though much remains to be done. "The city is still the Loop and the Northwest Side," says Jackson. "The South Side, West Side still don't exist."

* * *

## Business and Public Finance: Precarious Prosperity

Daley I's fiscal management has been widely hailed as a textbook example of how to run a big metropolitan economy. He was a micromanager who forged strong ties with the city's blue-blooded, typically Republican businessmen while keeping labor unions happy by making sure there were always construction projects with high prevailing wages. The strategy helped him save the city. "The Chicago he inherited in 1955 really was a sleepy town with a downtown that was on the skids," says Adam Cohen. "The Chicago he left behind at the end of his life was much, much grander."

But it wasn't easy. In the two decades he held office, Daley I faced a steadily declining tax base and an economy in transformation. The city's well-to-do and middle class were fleeing to the suburbs, followed by many businesses—manufacturing industries as well as office jobs and retail shops. Faced with a teetering business district, the mayor determined that the city's well-being depended on reinvigorating the Loop. Thus, says the former *Tribune* urban affairs reporter John McCarron, Daley I "circled the wagons around downtown and helped keep it strong." He pumped fat public works projects into the Loop and spurred private development with flexible tax policies and permissive zoning. Essentially, his goal was to bolster commercial property so the city could boost the tax base and his patronage workers and union supporters could keep their good-paying jobs.

Critics griped that he ignored the neighborhoods—particularly ones in the Black Belt. Consider: by 1965, black unemployment in Chicago had reached 17 percent, well above the rate for whites. "What's good for State Street is good for Chicago, and what's good for Chicago is good for State Street," the mayor insisted.

A crafty administrator, Daley I knew budgets as well as politics. He relied on revenue bonds on top of gradual tax increases to pay for his numerous projects. In his first year in office, he got lawmakers in Springfield to support him in a city sales tax and a utility tax, which became a windfall for the mayor to make city improvements. (In 1970, Chicago got "home rule" status, which allowed the city to impose any kind of tax, except for income taxes, without the approval of the state legislature.)

For the first two-thirds of Daley I's reign, the city budget swelled with additional spending—expenditures increased 46 percent during his first term alone—and year after year property and other taxes climbed. Most of the increased spending was for major capital projects and expanded city services, not to mention for the bloated payroll of patronage workers. In 1971, for example, Daley I hiked property taxes by nearly 18 percent. But even as taxes reached levels never seen before, there were few complaints. The mayor's spending binge, says Despres, "created an atmosphere of bustling activity and prosperity," so taxpayers felt that they were seeing their tax dollars at work. "He showed results," says Despres. And when voters started voting down bond issues in the early 1960s—after all, they'd have to pay the interest on the bonds—Daley turned to an agency he had created, the Public Building Commission of Chicago, to borrow money without public approval. The commission became Daley I's "private bank account," says Ross Miller, an English professor at the University of Connecticut and author of the 1996 book *Here's the Deal*, about the infamous Block 37.

To sustain the boom, the mayor also tapped Springfield and Washington for funds. He got the state to pay the welfare costs of Chicagoans, and Cook County to pick up the tab for the city jails. And when the Chicago Transit Authority was flat broke, Daley I struck a deal with the state legislature to create the Regional Transit Authority, which infused suburban tax dollars into the city's transit system. By 1974, only 15 percent of Chicago's budget financed functions such as mass transit and welfare, compared with 73 percent in New York City, which, by then, was effectively bankrupt. At the height of the Great Society spending—from 1966 to 1970—Daley I helped obtain a 169-percent increase in federal aid for Chicago, according to political science professor Ester Fuchs's 1992 book *Mayors and Money*. And during his fourth term, Daley I boosted spending by 40 percent without even raising taxes.

If it all sounds too good to be true, it was—as subsequent mayors found out. In the 1970s the city's economy went into reverse. Between 1972 and 1984, the city lost 198,000 jobs, mostly in manufacturing. (By contrast, DuPage and northwest Cook County gained 156,000 jobs.) In addition, local tax revenue stagnated because Chicago was rapidly losing residents. Property taxes, for instance, funded 39 percent of the city's budget in 1970. By 1979, it had dropped to 27 percent. By 1980, the city was in serious financial trouble, and the credit rating agency Moody's downgraded Chicago's bonds.

What happened? When tax revenue slowed and federal and state funds leveled off in the mid-1970s, Daley I and his bean counters began secretly using "revolving funds," a budgetary gimmick of sorts that delayed paying bills, effectively hiding mounting deficits off budget. Meanwhile, the city resorted to borrowing to pay off past debts, but then used the new funds for operating expenses, not for debt repayment—in other words, robbing Peter to pay Paul, all the while maintaining an illusion of solvency. "All of this was swept under the rug under Richard J.," says Lois Wille. "And yet, he always had the reputation of being a good budget man."

When Daley II took the reins of Chicago in 1989, the city was bleeding a $105-million deficit. He turned it into a surplus by the end of his first term by slashing the city bureaucracy, reorganizing city hall, raising the water and sewer rates, and supporting a 20-percent state income tax hike that boosted school funding. "He's been a relatively good fiscal steward," says Ralph Martire of the taxpayer watchdog Center for Tax and Budget Accountability. Daley II has more or less held the line on property taxes—since taking office, they have increased an average of only 1.5 percent a year, according to the mayor's office. Daley II also cut taxes on businesses, and, like his father, focused much of his attention on keeping downtown Chicago prosperous by aligning with big business. But unlike Daley I, the current mayor has had a lot less state and federal aid (not to mention patronage) to dole out.

Under the mayor [Richard M. Daley], the Loop has flourished, and so have the nearby neighborhoods. New buildings have sprouted up, as have new businesses, including Boeing and MillerCoors, both lured here by the mayor. Between 2003 and 2006, Chicago's diverse economy grew by more than $27 billion. Tourism is thriving. Daley II has helped reinvent Chicago as a destination city, attracting a record 45 million visitors last year, according to Crain's, tying Chicago with Washington, D.C., as the country's eighth most heavily visited city. "Without the mayor, absolutely we would not have this renaissance in arts and culture in Chicago, never," says the city's culture czar, Lois Weisberg. "His father didn't have it, period."

In May, the magazine *Fast Company* selected Chicago as its "U.S. City of the Year." And in June, *Trader Monthly* ranked the city as "the world's top trading town," citing Chicago's thriving commodities and derivatives exchanges.

But the contrasts between the haves and have-nots remain. A 2006 study found that Chicago had lost nearly 600 businesses and more than 14,000 jobs within the city's poorest neighborhoods between 1995 and 2004. Critics say that Daley II, like his father, has focused too much attention on downtown development and not enough on historically underserved neighborhoods. If the city seems more prosperous, they say, that's only because gentrification has expanded to the near South and West sides. "Right now, you go northwest, there's, like, three jobs for every one person," says Jesse Jackson. "If you go south, there're six people for every one job. Here, taxes are up. Services are down. He has not addressed structural inequalities."

Some critics argue that the mayor's controversial use of tax increment financing districts, or TIFs, is a version of the budgetary sleight-of-hand practiced by his father. On paper, TIFs are supposed to freeze property taxes and earmark new revenues for economic development projects in blighted neighborhoods. The TIF, or something like it, is a common economic development tool in cities around the country. But as Ross Miller points out, "Chicago always does it bigger and better." According to the Cook County clerk's office, TIF revenues have grown from $10.6 million in 1989, when Daley II took office, to more than $500 million in 2006.

Urban affairs reporter Ben Joravsky, of the *Reader*, argues that Chicago's 160 TIF districts—particularly the nine or so TIFs in and around the Loop area—have become a "secret slush fund" for the mayor and aldermen to subsidize private developers (many of them friends or campaign donors to the politicians) in lucrative projects downtown. By Joravsky's count, TIFs suck away more than $500 million a year in property tax dollars that could be spent instead on parks, schools, libraries, and the city's ailing mass transit system.

* * *

Over the years, Daley II has shrunk the size of city government by privatizing some of its functions—an approach his father, the patronage king, would probably find unimaginable. Daley II started small, first with basic city services, such as towing, building management, and janitorial work. But by 2005 he had leased the Chicago Skyway to an Australian-Spanish consortium for $1.8 billion. Next, he leased four downtown parking garages to Morgan Stanley for $563 million. And he has proposed privatizing the city's parking meter collection and its waste sorting and recycling centers. The big enchilada, though, is Daley II's plan to privatize Midway Airport, potentially a $3-billion-plus windfall. If it happens—the city is currently evaluating bids—it would make Midway the country's first privately operated commercial airport.

\* \* \*

And while his father was strictly Chicago-centric, Daley II thinks globally. Last February, for example, he opened a new city office in Shanghai to woo Chinese industries here and assist local companies doing business in China. Listen to Daley II talk these days and you'll hear a lot of 'China this,' or 'China that'—the mayor knows China's economy is exploding and he wants to make sure Chicago doesn't miss out on the action.

But just as his father faced a drastic economic downturn after 15 or so years in office, Daley II is facing an economy that's sinking with no bottom yet in sight. In Chicago and nationally, home values are dropping, unemployment is rising, and commercial real-estate deals here have dried up. Daley II's legacy may depend in part on whether he can find his way through a tough economy.

\* \* \*

So far, Daley II has successfully quelled any career-threatening tax revolts. In 2003, when property assessments skyrocketed to 31 percent citywide, the mayor pushed state lawmakers to pass the 7-percent cap on assessment increases. Three years later, he encouraged extending the cap. But in late July of this year, the mayor said Chicago is facing the worst economy of his tenure. "This is a real crisis," he told reporters, adding that the city's budget shortfall was roughly "a couple hundred million."

## Public Works and Big Projects: From Concrete to Wrought Iron

Few mayors in America have physically changed the face of a city as much as the Daleys have done. Daley I kept Chicago broad-shouldered and brawny with new steel and concrete buildings. Daley II's legacy is the equivalent of a face-lift—beautification projects that have improved the quality of life in the city. As the *Tribune's* architecture critic Blair Kamin puts it: "Richard J. Daley is the classic modernizer. He's the guy who builds the bones of the city—expressways, bridges, O'Hare. Richie is essentially adding a new layer, Martha Stewartizing the city. His Chicago is a 'City That Plays' rather than just a 'City That Works.'"

And while the Daleys are most closely associated with big projects with high wow factor, they also made sure to focus on the practical nuts-and-bolts of the city—its infrastructure. They knew that if streets weren't cleaned, if potholes weren't filled, if the sewers flooded over, if the water wasn't drinkable, voters would hold them responsible on election day. Their attention to nitty-gritty municipal housekeeping has perpetuated the belief among many Chicagoans that, under the Daleys, the city runs smoothly.

\* \* \*

Daley I realized that the city had to change to keep up with the jarring shift from a manufacturing to a service economy. He knew that airports were replacing railroads. That office buildings were replacing factories. That commuters were replacing residents. And he built accordingly. McCormick Place secured Chicago's status as the nation's convention capital. The University of Illinois Chicago Circle Campus, which Daley I called his "greatest accomplishment," gave working-class Chicagoans a low-tuition state school near downtown, and in the process, though displacing a large number of residents, revitalized a decaying neighborhood. The opening of the Hancock in 1970 and Water Tower Place in 1975 pumped new retail-shopping life into the stagnant "Magnificent Mile." And O'Hare (1962) brought Chicago a modern airport, ensuring the city would stay the transportation hub of the nation's midsection.

His interest in building large and small—he also built the city's first bicycle paths and neighborhood health clinics—turned out to be good politics. More civic projects meant more patronage and jobs for his labor union supporters. Most of all, says Bob Crawford, when the city looks good—at least, its prominent public places—so does the mayor. "There's a saying that Chicago has a clean face and a dirty neck," says Crawford. "There's a lot of truth to that."

\* \* \*

Big projects continue to be Daley II's Achilles' heel. The O'Hare modernization project has been mired in corruption, cost overruns, and delays, caused in part by litigation by expansion opponents. For years, Block 37 in the Loop has been a civic joke. "That block was supposed to be paying off now between $30 million and $40 million in taxes a year," says Ross Miller. It's finally turning into a business, shopping, and entertainment center, but a plan to add a "superstation" express-train system to O'Hare and Midway has hit a snag.

Even Daley II's greatest triumph so far, Millennium Park, opened four years late and $325 million over budget. Only by going hat in hand to wealthy civic leaders, foundations, and corporations was he able to recoup about half the costs of the project. But the investment appears to be paying off. The park is now the city's second largest tourist attraction, drawing 3.5 million visitors last year. It has spurred significant residential and commercial development in the East Loop, plus billions more in sales and tax revenues from tourist spending....

## Scandal and Corruption: See No Evil

As mayors, both Daleys have maintained a pristine record of personal honesty. At the same time, ample instances of skullduggery, graft, and scandal have marred their administrations without sinking them. It's as if there were a long-standing—if tacit—pact between Chicago's voters and its pols: As long as officeholders deliver dependable city services, it seems, citizens will return the favor at the ballot box while tolerating the greasy wheels of politics. "There's corruption under every mayor," says Roosevelt's Paul Green. "Chicago is a tough city. It isn't Madison, Wisconsin." Many of the streets you drive on, Green says, are named for people "you wouldn't want to be in a lifeboat with, if they were alive."

By several accounts, Daley I candidly tolerated a certain level of graft as part of his management style. Leon Despres says that the mayor once told a group of University of Chicago professors, "I let them go so far and no further," referring to his Machine allies. "Daley wasn't given to preaching," Royko once wrote. "His advice amounted to: Don't get caught." Much to the mayor's chagrin, many people did—from average-Joe precinct workers to close friends and members of his inner circle, including alderman Tom Keane and the mayor's patronage chief, Matt Danaher.

Publicly, anyway, Daley II denounces corruption. When graft charges touch the current administration, he typically decries the problem, though he defiantly insists he knew nothing and blames the trouble on a few bad apples. Often, he rolls a few heads and then announces reforms that never seem to go far enough to cure the problems.

Though the scandals tarnishing the two administrations echo each other in many ways, they are also quite different. Many of Daley I's problems, for example, sprang from election-related corruption—cries of vote fraud rang out after every election, not a major issue today. And though patronage excesses were rampant under Daley I—"As corrupt as the city's hiring practices may be today, they're clean and pure compared to the old days," says Lois Wille—they weren't necessarily illegal at the time.

In 1969, Michael Shakman, a Hyde Park lawyer, sued the Democratic organization, claiming he had lost his bid to become a delegate to the state's constitutional convention in large part because of political patronage. Three years later Daley I and the *Shakman* plaintiffs reached an agreement that set strict limits on politically motivated hiring and firing. But the mayor largely ignored the federal court decree. He could get away with it because he was above the law, in many respects.

* * *

Another potential source of scandal, giving public jobs to friends and family, was done almost openly in Daley I's time. Mike Royko called the administration a family employment agency. For instance, when Richard M. Daley was fresh out of law school (and having taken three tries to pass the bar exam), his father gave him the job as an assistant corporation counsel. Another son, Michael, became the attorney for the Democratic Party of Cook County, which Daley I controlled. Those who questioned the jobs he got for his sons—they could kiss his mistletoe, as the mayor famously put it in 1973, after news broke that he had secretly switched millions of dollars in city insurance business to a little-known Evanston firm that included his son John.

It seems almost laughable now, but when Daley II rode into office in 1989, he vowed to end corruption in city hall. Just weeks into his new administration, he told reporters that his office had found loads of dubious contracts by his predecessors that qualified as boondoggles. "There's enough of them to hold your nose," he said.

Yet contract cronyism has thrived under Daley II. Over the years, the city has routinely doled out millions in contracts to clout-heavy friends and associates of the mayor who are usually generous campaign contributors—the so-called pinstripe patronage. Nepotism, too, remains alive and well under the current administration. A 1999 *Tribune* investigation found that 68 relatives of the Daley clan had been on the public payroll at one time or another since Daley II took office.

With teeth now behind the *Shakman* decree, this administration has been tangled in charges of illegal patronage. Most notably, a federal investigation in 2005 uncovered "pervasive fraud" in city hall's hiring and promotions. Daley II's former patronage chief, Robert Sorich, a Bridgeporter whose father was the official photographer for Daley I, was convicted in 2006 of rigging city hiring tests and faking interviews to benefit Daley II loyalists. Three other city hall insiders were also convicted in the scheme.

Last year, Daley II finally settled the city's decades-long legal battle with the *Shakman* complainants. His administration agreed to end all political hiring (which officials repeatedly insisted never happens anyway) and create a $12-million fund to compensate victims of illegal political discrimination. More than 1,400 people have received payouts from the fund, according to city records.

Outright graft has also remained an issue for this administration. In one of the most notorious instances, the *Sun-Times* revealed in 2004 that Daley II's administration had given out lucrative trucking contracts to politically connected companies in exchange for bribes. In many cases the companies did no work—they just paid and got paid. The mayor's Bridgeport friend Michael Tadin led the pack of hired-truck contractors. After the story broke, Daley II announced that he wouldn't take campaign contributions from city contractors anymore (although he hasn't sworn off donations from contractors with the city's pension funds).

The latest black eye for Daley II came this past May, when seven building department employees and eight private developers were nabbed in a bribery scam in which the builders allegedly paid off city inspectors to falsify or expedite inspections. "We're talking systemic corruption," said David Hoffman, the city's inspector general.

Saying the charges were "appalling and regrettable," the mayor denied the notion that corruption was widespread in his administration. "You cannot condemn everybody for a few," he told reporters. "I don't know if it's systemic, but you can't indict everybody on that." Still, when U.S. attorney Patrick Fitzgerald announced the indictments, he noted, "There's every reason to think there will be more charges to come in the future."

Mike Royko titled his 1971 biography of Richard J. Daley *Boss,* and the term perfectly fit the man and the times. When Chicago was still a lunchpail town, Daley I epitomized the hard-nosed, hard-driving chief of a gritty, rusting enterprise. Four decades later, in an era dominated by Wall Street, real estate, and the service economy, his son likes to describe himself as the CEO of the city, and that term also makes a nice fit, with its white-collar, corner-office connotations, its suggestion of efficiencies and eager MBAs.

Both terms come from the world of business, and at their best they express worthy styles of leadership. But the words also suggest a troubling contradiction when applied to a mayor: As any business executive would readily admit, a company is not run as a democracy. The unchecked power of both father and son has led to the most unfortunate aspects of their mayoralties—the autocratic tone, the lack of accountability on ethics, the fear of retaliation for opposing the Daley way.

Still, for many Chicagoans, it doesn't seem to matter. Democracy isn't part of the electorate's Faustian bargain with the Daleys. The father steered Chicago through hard and dislocating times while most other Rust Belt cities were sinking into misery. The son surfed the national urban boom to boost Chicago to new heights of attractiveness and world prominence. In both cases, the city got order, stability, and results in exchange for a benevolent dictator. Roosevelt's Paul Green suggests that voters are aware of the deal they've made and are happy with it, believing that "every time the city has gone down the drain is when the city council is in charge." The ballot-box results speak for themselves. Daley I never won less than 55 percent of the vote (his lowest, in 1955), and on four occasions, he exceeded 70 percent. Daley II racked up 72 percent of the vote in winning his last election in 2007.

\* \* \*

Just as the city craves the Daleys, the Daleys need Chicago. Daley I called being mayor of Chicago the "greatest honor that I could have." It's not surprising that he died in office. In the same way, Daley II often wears his love for the city on his sleeve. "I've said many times before that I believe I have the best job in the world," the mayor says. The lawyer Newton Minow, who has known a huge array of politicians in his long career, says of the father and son: "They have a mad love affair with this city."

This co-dependent relationship has its quirks and its costs. It excludes some people and overrewards others. It mixes pleasure with pain and makes both parties vulnerable. In the end, though—well, somehow it works.

# Part IV

## Chicago Government

# Chicago Government

Local governments in the Chicago region are fragmented and frequently dysfunctional, having been created in earlier times. The plethora of governments that have resulted inhibit accountability, efficiency, effectiveness, and coordination. At the same time, in the city of Chicago there is no participatory level of neighborhood government where citizens can have an active voice in affecting local decisions that most affect their lives.

As those who have studied Chicago city government have learned, it is inefficient because of the remains of patronage and the historical evolution of governmental services. Frequently in the past, the cost of city services has been 100% more than in other comparable cities. Continual budget cuts and the privatization of some city services have made government somewhat more efficient over the years, but waste still remains. Some governmental services are also not equitably delivered. It is not uncommon for black and minority communities to receive fewer city services than white communities within the city and in the suburbs.

The City Club of Chicago had proposed ten reforms that are needed for the Chicago City Council. These proposed reforms include:

1.  Public disclosure of information on legislation;
2.  Improving the City Council committee system;
3.  Better and more democratic City Council procedures; and
4.  Greater citizen participation.

Of the ten proposals, five have been partially adopted over the last fifteen years, but the council remains mostly unreformed. Since 1989 it has been a Rubber Stamp Council, simply endorsing the proposals put forth by the mayor's administration, rather than providing a legislative democracy. For instance, the city council often unanimously approves the mayor's more than six billion dollar city budget.

However, with the mayor and aldermanic elections of 2011, we are entering a new post-Daley era. At the same time political reformers have been elected President of the Cook

County Board of Commissioners and Governor of Illinois. By necessity the new mayor, County Board President, and Governor will have to cut expenditures to close permanent structural deficits.

Beyond the city of Chicago, there is a crazy quilt of 540 governments with taxing authority in Cook County. There is considerable waste, duplication, and inefficiency in these fractured, many-layered governments that have grown up haphazardly over the last 150 years. The multiplicity of local governments is the result of state constitutional limits on taxing and borrowing. New, special units of government, with their own taxing authority, were formed when a larger unit could not finance and administer a particular government service due to constitutional limits. Special districts were also created when a natural service area did not correspond to existing political boundaries (mosquito abatement districts) or to achieve economies of scale (Metropolitan Water Reclamation District). There are now more than 1,200 of these separate governments in the Chicago metropolitan region.

Perhaps the biggest problem in local government, however, is the political corruption that machine politics has brought. Public corruption in Illinois has a long history dating from the first scandal involving Chicago aldermen and Cook County commissioners in the 1860s. At that time they participated in a crooked contract to paint City Hall. Today, crooked contracts still cost the taxpayers millions of dollars a year and crooked politicians still go to jail.

More than 1,500 individuals have been convicted of myriad forms of public corruption since 1970. Among them thirty-one Chicago aldermen (current and former) have been convicted. Based upon the testimony before the Illinois Reform Commission, the cost of corruption, or "corruption tax," for the Chicago and Illinois taxpayers is at least $500 million a year.

Only comprehensive reforms can lessen the level of corruption. Chicago is currently the capital of corruption in the United States. Given the high cost of corruption, we cannot hope to adopt a prudent city, county, or state budget without such reforms. Without reform we will continue to pay too much for government services, we will keep honest businesses from locating here, and we will slow economic recovery from the current recession. While citizens will continue to distrust government at all levels and consider tax increases unfair, curbing public corruption is the first step in reestablishing trust and pride in our government.

# Blueprint of Chicago Government: 1989

By Dick Simpson, et al.

*Written in 1989, this report provided a detailed analysis of the agencies, budgets, programs, and staffing of executive departments and related agencies whose boards or commissions are appointed by the mayor. As Richard M. Daley was taking office, this report showed that progress had been made under Mayors Washington and Byrne, but there was much more to be done. Now that Mayor Daley's twenty-two year term of office has ended, this report can be used as a benchmark to gauge the progress that has been made. Only the Executive Summary is presented here.*

O ur report provides a picture of the agencies, budgets, programs, and staffing of executive departments and related agencies whose boards or commissions are appointed by the mayor as of 1989. We also outline some of the issues that the Richard M. Daley administration and Chicago now confront.

Our study concludes that the city has made progress in dealing with some of the issues cited in the 1979 and 1983 transition team reports. Our 1983 study, at the end of the Byrne and the beginning of the Washington administrations, highlighted four principal steps that needed to be taken at that time:

1.  Systematize the management of the executive branch of city government through better coordination and supervision of the principal government functions.
2.  Develop better management information systems and master service plans for long-term, effective service delivery by all municipal agencies.
3.  Specify functional responsibilities of each municipal agency and restructure some agencies to better meet their assigned responsibilities.

4. Create a more open and democratic governmental process.

The Washington administration made specific strides in each of these areas. It corrected some of the worst problems, and for the most part, these gains were maintained during the interim Sawyer administration. The gains included:

1. The establishment of a "deputy mayor" system of administrative assistants to serve as liaisons and to supervise the multitude of departments and agencies that report to the mayor. In addition to establishing a more coherent administrative structure, the city government was streamlined with more than 5,000 jobs cut from the city payroll. Thus, the same services have been delivered with fewer employees and only a modest budget expansion since 1983....

2. Management information was improved and new "master service plans" for service delivery were developed between some departments. However, in general, this is still the weakest aspect of the city government bureaucracy. While departments are now required to designate an information officer for public relations and freedom of information purposes, critical information for decision making or evaluation of a department's performance often does not exist or is not made available to those outside of the department.

3. New organizational charts for the city government as a whole and for individual departments now exist. Functions have been moved from one department to another to make the delivery of city services more rational and efficient. However, the Chicago Municipal Code, including the sections specifying the official duties of many departments, is hopelessly out of date. The Washington administration created commissions, eliminated nonessential departments, and switched functions among departments, but many departments such as the Department of Revenue still fail to adequately perform their assigned tasks....

4. The Washington administration made several important strides in creating a more open and democratic governmental process. Mayor Washington signed the Freedom of Information Executive Order that opened city documents to the public for the first time. His Affirmative Action Executive Order guaranteed women and minorities the right to powerful government jobs and contracts—and thereby made them a part of the government. The Latino, Asian American, and Women's Commissions articulate the needs of the disenfranchised and monitor governmental progress especially in affirmative action and minority participation. A new budget-making process makes public the proposed city budget earlier, provides information to communities, and invites more citizen input than ever before in Chicago's history. Community groups were also given Community Development Block Grant funds to deliver human services at the neighborhood level, with much more participation by citizens. However, the Byrne, Washington, and Sawyer administrations failed to create "Little City Halls" to provide citizen participation in planning and evaluating city services in their community. They failed to create neighborhood planning committees or community zoning boards to allow citizens a voice in planning the physical future of

their communities. And the city council remains unresponsive to all forms of meaningful citizen participation.

In the last decade, the city has moved forward. Therefore, we turn our attention in this report to six critical problems that must now be dealt with by the new Daley administration. Some are left from previous administrations, some have a new aspect. Some problems can now be resolved only because of the progress that has been made. For whatever reason, these six problems are evident throughout city government.

## Productivity

The current city deficit of $50-100 million [in 1989] requires the city to provide more services with fewer funds. New water and sewer rates have helped to close the gap and cutbacks of seven percent in the departments and 20 percent in city council committees help considerably. The state income tax increase will solve the deficit or shortfall. But as costs go up, Chicago residents will not be satisfied with fewer services. Therefore, even with state tax relief, the city government must insure that every program and department increases the productivity of its present resources.

City departments have grown up organically over the last century. Each was originally created with a clear purpose and, often, with a small staff. Each used the technology available at the time of its creation to deliver city services. Over time, however, conditions change, departments add more and more functions and personnel, and they continue to do things as they have in the past. There is no genuine zero-sum budgeting process, no rethinking of the entire operation of city agencies. When new tasks arise, a new commission or office has to be set up because the existing agencies are not flexible enough to change their focus and functions. This makes productivity, economy, and efficiency in government particularly hard to achieve. Nothing short of a review of every single activity of city government to determine anew whether the service should be delivered by the government, which agencies should do it, what is the appropriate technique or method to best perform the function, and restructuring city agencies to better perform these services, will suffice.

## Management Information

A major obstacle to improving productivity is that neither city officials nor the public can tell whether city departments are using their resources well. Unlike other cities, Chicago departments do not compile audited performance data on the goods and services that they deliver. Therefore, for most services it is impossible to calculate a reliable cost per unit and, thus, to set realistic goals of measurable increases in productivity. In general, no one knows whether Chicago services are produced as efficiently as services in other cities, whether some departments are becoming more productive, or whether other departments are lagging behind. The studies by the Better Government Association of a decade ago and the information gathered in 1988 by the city council Budget Committee under the chairmanship of Alderman Bloom (5th Ward) indicate that services cost from 50 percent to several hundred percent more to deliver in Chicago than in other cities. While advances have been made during the Washington and Sawyer administrations in providing the same city services with several thousand fewer employees, the lack of audited performance data and other reliable management information from the departments makes accountability and improved productivity very hard to achieve....

## Public Participation in Governance

In our reports in 1979 and 1983, it was clear that the excessive secrecy and closed decision making in Chicago government made it impossible for citizens to know what policies were being considered and what activities departments were undertaking. Mayor Washington's Freedom of Information Executive Order has made it possible for citizens to obtain some official information and former mayor Sawyer's continuation of the process of extensive public hearings on the 1989 city budget provided opportunities to express views on financial issues. Several agencies are also soliciting more active public participation in policy making. The Park District has established advisory committees to identify local residents' perspectives on park and recreation priorities. The Chicago School Reform Act will give local school councils important powers over personnel, resources, and educational policies.

It is essential, as a first step, that mechanisms be developed to increase public access to information and opportunities to comment on city problems. Departments must be required to issue reliable annual reports documenting policies and performance. The Municipal Reference Library must be expanded to provide sufficient staff to respond to public inquiries. The decision processes of both legislative and executive branches must become both more open and more predictable, so the public will know when and how to participate....

## Official Integrity

Major advances have been made since 1983. The signing of the Freedom of Information Executive Order by Mayor Washington and its re-adoption by Mayors Sawyer and Daley have guaranteed that basic information about public programs is available, although the formal freedom of information process is a long and complicated one.

The passage in 1987 of the first Ethics Ordinance in the history of the city was a significant advance. So was the establishment of a Board of Ethics to monitor city employees, to set standards, to provide decisions on critical cases, to collect information on campaign financing, and to provide reports to the government and the public. The passage of additional ethics legislation in the city council as part of the city council reform campaign has closed loopholes in some of the legislation and made aldermen accountable for at least some of their activities.

However, the failure of the Office of Municipal Investigation to curb wrongdoing by city employees and to develop prevention mechanisms to make corruption and favoritism by government employees more difficult has meant that the public still distrusts city government. There is the widespread belief that "clout" is required to get city service—that they are really political favors. Worst of all—witness the many convictions of city employees, including aldermen, judges, and inspectors—there is evidence that the government is still riddled with outright corruption and that justice has to be bought. Government services should become a citizen's right, not political favors up for sale to the highest bidder.

## Archaic Laws

The Chicago Municipal Code is out of date. It has not been rewritten or revised in a systematic way since 1939. It now needs to be completely overhauled. Pierre de Vise's 1987 study of the Chicago Municipal Code cited these basic problems: "obsoleteness, fragmentation, duplication, and a lack of precision and clarity." These problems still exist today. De Vise recommended that 20 entire chapters of the code such as chapter 108 (Private Bathing Beaches) and chapter 194 (Air Raid and Blackouts) be deleted. Other chapters will need to be revised and brought up-to-date....

## Conclusion

Overall, the city has made considerable progress during the last ten years. It might be said that the executive branch of city government has been brought from the 19th century into the 20th. The Shakman decrees to eliminate patronage abuses, the beginning of genuine affirmative action programs in hiring and in contracting, the development of a system of "deputy mayors" charged with supervising and coordinating agencies with related functions, and the opening up of city hall to provide minimum levels of public information and accountability were major steps forward. However, city government still costs too much, is too secretive, blocks full citizen participation in decision making, and continues to allow corruption to flourish.

The agenda...must be ambitious. Pragmatically, there is no choice but to increase productivity across every unit of government. Taxpayers are unwilling or unable to bear higher taxes from local government. They may be willing to support a modest state income tax increase; however, there are very strict limits as to the local government taxes they are willing to pay.

The Park District's efforts and the School Reform Act indicate the necessary future direction for Chicago government. The private sector must be involved, and the public must help set the policies and priorities of every unit of local government. The ultimate test of government is citizen satisfaction and support. Only if they have the information to know what their local government is doing on their behalf and a voice in government decision making will citizens be willing to bear the costs, make the personal sacrifices, and provide the political support for Chicago government to promote a better future for the city.

# A Tradition of Corruption

By Elizabeth Brackett

*Chicago and Illinois politics have been fraught with corruption for decades. This tradition of corruption has led, in many cases, to arrests and the prosecution of those involved. This should have served as a lesson and warning to Rod Blagojevich, yet surprisingly it did not.*

*The following chapters from journalist Elizabeth Brackett's book* <u>Pay to Play: How Rod Blagojevich Turned Political Corruption into a National Sideshow</u> *provides a portrait of former Illinois Governor Rod Blagojevich and the tradition of corruption in Illinois.*

I f Illinois isn't the most corrupt state in the United States, it's certainly one hell of a competitor." The FBI's Robert Grant hurled those words into the atmosphere at the press conference following the arrest of Governor Blagojevich. While it may have made some Illinois politicos wince, the FBI chief didn't receive much argument from them. Illinoisans have a long love/hate relationship with their state's reputation for producing scoundrels and scallywags. The colorful characters who dot the state's political landscape are part and parcel of the state's raucous, brawling identity, particularly in the city of Chicago.

The antics of Mike "Hinky Dink" Kenna and "Bathhouse John" Coughlin, two bosses who ruled Chicago's First Ward from the late nineteenth century until World War II, are legendary. The ward, which later became much of what is now known as "The Loop" in downtown Chicago was one of the most infamous havens for vice in the entire United States, home to magnificent gambling palaces, ornate houses of prostitution, and saloons, bars, and dives of immense variety. "Hinky Dink" was the brains behind the operation while the gregarious

"Bathhouse John" was the front man. As Democrats, the two men controlled the party and its coffers, and both served as alderman of the First Ward. They immediately sold protection to the ward's pimps, prostitutes, and gamblers, which included lawyers who would be on the spot if arrests came. In exchange Kenna and Coughlin received a cut of the proceeds from the illegal activities.

* * *

Corruption got an early start too in the state capital in Springfield. Governor Joel Aldrich Matteson (1853-1857) tried to cash in $200,000 in government script, explaining that he had "found" it in a shoebox. A judge bought the governor's explanation that he had no idea how the script had made its way into the shoebox. The judge agreed not to accept an indictment if the governor turned the money over to the state.

Another Illinois governor escaped indictment in the 1920s despite substantial evidence that he had embezzled more than $1 million in state funds while in office. Governor Lennington Small went on to serve seven more years in office.

And though he was never governor, Illinois Secretary of State Paul Powell appears to have gotten away with fleecing the taxpayers out of more money than anyone before him. Powell, who was elected to the office in 1964 and again in 1968, had a simple definition of political success: "There's only one thing worse than a defeated politician, and that's a broke one." Powell was never defeated and, as it turned out at his death, he was not broke either. The highest office Powell ever held was secretary of state, and the highest salary he ever received was $30,000 a year. Yet after a lifetime of public service, when Paul Powell died in 1970 at the age of sixty-eight he left an estate that exceeded $3 million. Police officers gathering up his belongings from the Springfield hotel suite where he had been living did not believe anything suspicious had occurred until they came across $800,000, *in cash*, stuffed in shoeboxes, briefcases, and strongboxes in the closet. Upon investigation they realized that when Illinois residents came to the secretary of state's office to renew their driver's license and were told to write out their checks simply to "Paul Powell," at least part of the money really did go to Paul Powell. Taxpayers were both aghast and amused by the idea of Powell stuffing hundreds of thousands of dollars into shoeboxes, all the while continuing his modest way of life.

Powell was emblematic of the Illinois politicians who built their political organizations—and apparently their personal fortunes—on patronage. In his role as secretary of state, 'Powell had more than two thousand jobs to handout. He understood and wielded the power those jobs gave him. Whenever the subject of state jobs came up, he was known to say, "I can smell the meat a-cookin.'"

Those who were awarded jobs were expected to give back, perhaps by working for Powell's election and reelections, or contributing to his campaigns, or both. This was the "pay-to-play" politics of its day, which at the time no one saw as corrupt. It was simply the "way things worked" in Illinois.

Political corruption in the state had its roots in the momentous population movements of the nineteenth century. As Irish, Germans, Poles, and others came to Illinois, jobs were hard to come by. The new immigrants faced intense discrimination and grew to realize they would have to organize themselves politically in order to gain power. As their political organizations gained strength and began taking control of precincts, then wards, and finally city and state governments, immigrant politicians built these organizations by handing out jobs. Once a new immigrant had a job, walking a precinct for a candidate or a political party seemed like a small price to pay for holding on to that job. It wasn't long before working a precinct became a requirement for getting a job, enabling these political organizations to gain more and more control over who would work in state and local government.

Richard J. Daley, the legendary boss of Chicago, took over the Cook County Democratic party when he became mayor in 1955 and proceeded to build the nation's strongest political machine. Daley's predecessor, Martin J. Kennelly, had been seen as an ineffectual reformer. So it was, on the election night when Richard J. Daley took the throne, that Alderman Paddy Bauler danced a jig and belted out his now-famous words, "Chicago ain't ready for reform!" Over-the next twenty-one years, Daley's machine delivered again and again in providing city services and in getting out votes for the Democratic party. Handing out city jobs in exchange for precinct work or political contributions was never seen as corruption. Rather, it was seen as a means of providing "good government and good politics," as the mayor liked to say.

\* \* \*

Richard J. Daley never ran afoul of the law because of personal or political corruption. Most Chicagoans believed he was a personally honest man. But plenty of those around him got caught with their hands in the city's coffers. Thomas Keane, Daley's longtime floor leader in the City Council, was convicted and served prison time for federal wire fraud and for making millions of dollars on secret land deals. The day after Keane's conviction, his law partner, Alderman Paul Wigoda, was convicted for income tax evasion on a $50,000 bribe he'd taken from a real estate developer for pushing a zoning change through the City Council. And the day after that Daley's former press secretary, Earl Bush, went down on eleven counts of federal mail fraud. It marked the beginning of the end of America's last great political machine.

\* \* \*

With so many Chicago politicians before him taken down by federal prosecutors, Rod Blagojevich had to know the rules had changed. But somehow he seemed to think those changes did not apply to *him*. Federal prosecutors and the FBI were amazed—and angered—by Blagojevich's brazenness in the wake of the convictions of politicians who preceded him. On the day of the governor's arrest, the FBI's Robert Grant told reporters,

"Many, including myself, thought that the recent convictions of a former governor [George Ryan] would usher in a new era of honesty and reform in Illinois politics. Clearly the charges announced today reveal that the Office of Governor has become nothing more than a vehicle for self-enrichment, unrestricted by party affiliation, and taking Illinois politics to a new low."

The low road of Illinois politics had been well-traveled by previous governors. Three of the seven who served before Blagojevich were convicted and served serious jail time.

* * *

In 2001, when Patrick Fitzgerald arrived in Chicago, political corruption trials reached a new level. Fitzgerald went after city, county, and state politicians with an aggressiveness never before seen from the U.S. attorney's office. One of the sacred cows he took on was the political patronage system in the city of Chicago. Richard M. Daley had been mayor for twelve years and held firm control of the city's political operations when Fitzgerald took over as U.S. attorney. The city had flourished in many ways under Daley's leadership, and he credited the professional managers and staff he had placed in key departments for the city's success. Revamping the city's schools under the leadership of his appointee Paul Vallas was the mayor's toughest challenge, and he touted the important progress Vallas made. Neighborhoods were revitalized across the city, helped by good economic times and a well-run city Department of Planning—led at one point by Valerie Jarrett, currently one of President Barack Obama's chief advisers. Where his father had been the "Boss," Daley frequently referred to himself as the city's "CEO." He did not take the job as chairman of the Cook County Democratic party, as his father had, and he often said that the Democratic machine and the old patronage system were long gone. Nonetheless, through his corporation counsel young Daley challenged the Shakman Decrees, alleging that they "interfered with the smooth operation of city government and were no longer needed."

It was an imaginative effort, but the argument came to a screeching halt on July 18, 2005, when Patrick Fitzgerald brought federal charges against leading city officials in Daley's administration for "violating the Shakman Decrees' against the political hiring and firing of city employees." in a news conference announcing the charges, Fitzgerald reiterated that "Every resident of Chicago has the right to compete fairly for a job if he or she is qualified, without regard to political affiliation or whether they do campaign work. Every applicant who sits for an interview is entitled to an honest evaluation. And the residents of Chicago are entitled to the best-qualified laborers, plumbers, foremen, and inspectors. And when a federal court order requires that people be hired or promoted without regard to political affiliation, the court order must be followed. Yet, for a decade, certifications by city officials that the law has been complied with have often been fraudulent. Qualified persons sat for interviews for jobs that had already been doled out as a reward for political work. The defendants are charged with a pervasive fraud scheme that included fixing applicant interviews and ratings, guaranteeing that preferred job candidates would be chosen over other equally or better-suited individuals, and then falsifying personnel documents to conceal their wrongdoing." He added, "The diversion of public resources to benefit political organizations, by using fraudulently obtained jobs and promotions as currency to compensate political workers, cheats the city and its employees, and improperly advantages those political organizations with influential government sponsors."

\* \* \*

## Get Me a Candidate

At age seventy-seven, life was good for Rade Blagojevich. A vigorous and proud man, he still worked around the house and was finally able to enjoy life at his own pace. His sons had graduated from college, and at last he and Millie were able to kick back a bit. But that was before a massive stroke took him to his knees. Rade found himself unable to walk or speak. He had been visiting his son Robert in Nashville when the stroke felled him. He was rushed to the emergency room where doctors worked frantically to reverse the damage to his body. But it was not to be. He was flown back to Chicago but was never able to return to his home again. He died ten months later. Rod Blagojevich was devastated by the loss of his father. For the first time he began thinking seriously about his own life and his own mortality. Perhaps it was time for a thirty-one-year-old bachelor to settle down, to find someone to share his life and begin a family of his own.

In another North Side neighborhood an attractive, dark-haired young woman was having similar thoughts. Twenty-three-year-old Patti Mell, a recent graduate of the University of Illinois with a degree in economics, had just broken up with her boyfriend. Her father, Richard Mell, the powerful alderman of the Thirty-third Ward, was beginning to worry about his daughter as she moped around the house after the breakup. He suggested she come with him to a ward fund-raiser he was holding that night in a North Side German restaurant. It would be good for her just to get out of the house, he told her.

A friend had persuaded Rod Blagojevich to come to the same fundraiser. Patti knew who he was. She had met the judge who presided over the courtrooms at Fifty-first and Wentworth, where Rod had worked as an assistant state's attorney. That meeting occurred at a summer wedding, when Patti was seated next to him during the reception. The judge—maybe with a fix-up in mind—told her about a dynamic young state's attorney who worked in his courtroom. And so, at the fundraiser, with Patti on his arm, the judge wasted no time in introducing the two unattached and seemingly lonely young people. Certainly Rod Blagojevich wasted no time in capturing the attention of the alderman's attractive daughter. The judge chuckled to himself as he overheard Rod telling her, "If you go out with me, I'm going to show you the time of your life." Later that evening Patti repeated those same words to her father: "Dad, if I go out with him, I'll probably have the time of my life." She accepted Rod's offer.

* * *

Two years later Rod was ready to get married, and Patti accepted his proposal.

* * *

Dick Mell had secured his prospective son-in-law a job on the city payroll just six months after Blagojevich began dating Patti. That was what Mell did. He found jobs for people who supported him and his Thirty-third Ward organization. He was a successful businessman, founding an automobile parts manufacturing firm with his wife in the early 1970s. The business provided a good living for Mell and his three children and enabled him to indulge in his passion—politics.

* * *

Rod Blagojevich slid easily into Mell's organization. City payroll records show he was being paid by as many four different City Council committees in one year. But Blagojevich told the *Chicago Tribune* he never worked in City Hall; rather, he said, he worked in Mell's ward service office where he organized community events and held free legal clinics. The U.S. attorney's office launched an investigation into ghost payrolling at that time, concentrating on whether some of those listed on city payrolls, like Blagojevich, were being paid for doing no work. A handful of Mell' s office workers were questioned, but the investigation never resulted in indictments. Blagojevich was snagged by the city's ethics ordinance, however, when he represented legal clients from his private law practice in personal injury and workmen's compensation cases. The ethics ordinance bars city employees from representing personal clients in cases against the city. The ethics complaint against Blagojevich went to the City Council Rules Committee, chaired by—who else?—Alderman Dick Mell. The charges were dropped.

Rod and Patti Blagojevich had been married for two years when the phone rang one Sunday evening. Dick Mell, on the other end of the line, needed a candidate to run for state representative—and he needed one *now.* "Are you interested?" he asked Rod. It was the beginning of Rod Blagojevich's political career.

[That career came to an end when, as governor, he was indicted and convicted of political corruption.]

# The Culture of Chicago Corruption

## By James Laski

*Former Chicago City Clerk Jim Laski was convicted of federal bribery charges in 2007 and served over a year in prison. In this excerpt from his book, he discusses the culture of corruption he witnessed and experienced for over 20 years in various governmental positions and elected offices. The article provides an insider's view of how the political machine gives birth to corruption.*

As an appropriate coda to my story, let's take one final, hard look at the world of Chicago politics. When looking at the Chicago political arena, the question immediately arises: How much is real, and how much is power and ego under the guise of public service? The culture of Chicago politics over the years has not been about *what* you know or how *hard* you *work*, but *who* you *know* and how much *money* you can *make*. Now, don't get me wrong. I'm a product of Chicago politics, and had taken full advantage of its perks and benefits, but what I'd never done was insult the public's intelligence. There are political leaders in Chicago today who still believe, but deny their feelings, that elected offices are not *earned*, but *inherited* or as under the old English monarchy, by lineage.

There is no clearer example of that policy than that of Todd Stroger, who [was until 2010] president of the County Board of Cook County, the second-largest county in the nation. His father, John Stroger, had served as board president for a number of years with distinction, until health issues forced him to step aside. Now, before he would announce his decision not to seek re-election, he had one more important task, and that was to cut one more backroom deal, by which he would call in all his favors and line up all the support he could for his son to replace him as president. Suggesting that his son start small and run for a commissioner's seat on the board instead of immediately seeking the presidency would have been insulting. Even though there were several higher-ranking county officials, including elected members of the County Board, who were more than qualified to run for the seat, it was decided that blood was thicker than experience, and that Todd Stroger was entitled to the job. This was a young man whom his father had hand-picked to be the area's State Representative, and then alderman of the 8th Ward. The few years Todd did spend in those offices were relatively quiet, with no real effort on his part to pursue any type of meaningful legislative agenda for his community. The most disturbing aspect of Todd's ascension to the County Board presidency was his total lack of seasoning and experience, although one could argue those could have been gained by just being on the job. My concern was his total lack of motivation and work ethic. I can state unequivocally that he had never been a pillar of ambition. In fact, the standing joke was who would be the latest to arrive at a city council meeting, Todd Stroger or Dorothy Tillman? When Todd arrived, invariably he would be either sitting in the chambers with his eyes on the verge of closing, or just gazing out into space, with a look of sheer boredom. He was so totally oblivious to what was going on during a meeting that he would usually have to ask either me or one of his colleagues what issue we had just discussed before he could vote.

Historically, Mayor Daley would not endorse a candidate ahead of time in the Democratic Primary, and would wait until the outcome to support the winner in the General Election. However, in Todd's case, Daley came right out and endorsed the young Stroger, touting his skills as a public servant. Of course, an agreement had earlier been reached between the elder Stroger and Daley for the mayor's endorsement. If anyone could understand the Stroger situation, it would be Daley, because he wouldn't be mayor today if this hadn't moved him, too, up the political ladder. He was blessed with the Daley name, which carries both respect and a Kennedy-like image in Chicago.

The most blatant example of nepotism in Chicago politics, however, certainly was Bill Lipinski's anointing his son Dan as successor to his Congressional seat. At the time of the coronation, his son was a professor at the University of Tennessee, and had not spent much time of late in Illinois. In fact, during my thirteen-or-so years with Lipinski, I never saw the slightest interest on Dan's part to follow in his father's footsteps. Despite that fact, after winning the Democratic Primary and stepping aside, Lipinski, along with his fellow Democratic committeemen, then appointed Dan to replace him on the November General Election ballot. Since that Congressional seat was primarily Democratic, and there was no significant Republican opponent even on the ballot, it was a forgone conclusion that young Dan would succeed his father as the next Congressman of the Third District of Illinois.

This, unfortunately, is the mindset of many of Chicago's political leaders....It's all about entitlement, which generally carries a strong political name, powerful support, and tons of money. Just ask Congressman Jesse Jackson, Jr., whose wife just won a seat on the Chicago City Council. She defeated a candidate put up by former alderman and now County Commissioner Bill Beavers. By the way, that hand-picked candidate was Beavers' own daughter. So, in that particular election, Jackson carried more clout than the Beavers name.

When discussing Chicago politics, one must invariably return again to Mayor Richard M. Daley. About three years ago, Daley's friend and former alderman and floor leader, Pat Huels, and I spent the entire morning sharing stories while struggling through eighteen rounds of golf. One thing I learned that day was how involved in, and committed to, Daley is to his political/power agenda. When Lipinski first ran for congress back in 1982 against incumbent John Fary, Daley, according to Huels, gathered his inner circle together to discuss the race. That group included Huels' brothers Bill and John, Huels himself, and Tim Degnan. Surprisingly, Daley was concerned about Lipinski's chances, and supposedly told everyone at the meeting to make sure that Lipinski would win before advising him to stick his neck out for him. Daley did not want to burn bridges until he was reasonably assured of Lipinski's chances, and then, and only then, would he move forward to insure victory for Lipinski.

* * *

Again, I am not trying to minimize my own mistakes, or make excuses for my past misconduct. Nor, on the other hand, am I minimizing accomplishments of mine that I am proud of, such as introducing initiatives in Chicago that helped save lives and taxpayer dollars. I am particularly proud of my work on behalf of the senior citizens, children, and working men and women of this city. However, I would be less than honest if I did not concede that these were overshadowed by my own greed, and by my relationship with the Joneses. During my sentencing, Judge Norgle expressed his sympathy for my wife and children, but placed their pain and suffering at my doorstep, where it truly belongs.

The business of Chicago politics has always had a unique reputation for its own style of power and corruption, at times resembling a pool of sharks attacking its prey. It's a game that can leave its players morally, ethically, and even spiritually bankrupt. I have lived, accepted, and thrived off a system that tempted me, betrayed me, and ultimately cost me my freedom. In the final analysis, I have only myself to blame for this nightmare, but this brand of politics was in place long before I came on the scene, and will continue to thrive.

Over the years, increased FBI investigations and media scrutiny have forced the business of "old-time politics" to become much more sophisticated and covert. The Daleys and Lipinskis of the last couple of decades have orchestrated and manipulated this system for their own benefits, and to satisfy their own thirst for power and financial reward. In short, they have become the new architects of POLITICS, CHICAGO STYLE.

# Ethics Reform Agenda

## By Pat Collins

*Former U.S. attorney Patrick Collins prosecuted Chicago corruption before Governor Pat Quinn asked him to lead the Illinois Reform Commission. Here, he details his recommendations based upon his experience and findings. He lays out a four-fold program for curbing corruption in Illinois. His first three reform proposals were 1) campaign finance reform, 2) redistricting reforms, and 3) a greater use of wire-tap evidence. This article covers his fourth proposed reform, greater citizen participation.*

What we have experienced in Illinois over the last decade is unprecedented. In the last five years alone, successive governors—representing both major political parties—and those in their respective inner circles, have been charged with serious public corruption crimes. Outside the governor's mansion, at the city, county, and state level, investigative reporters and federal prosecutors have revealed all-too-frequent political scandals and breaches of the public trust. Even with the media casting an intense spotlight and prosecutors aggressively pursuing criminal cases, the steady drumbeat of corruption revelations seems to continue unabated.

Coupled with the widespread effects of this culture of corruption, we also have a dysfunctional democracy in which the decisions made and agendas set by our government often ignore or diverge from the most important issues that affect citizens across the state. The result is that our government leaders continue to delay and avoid important public policy decisions without consequence. While I don't know whether the culture of corruption has directly caused this dysfunctional democracy, I do believe the two are related. More importantly, this dual problem serves a one-two punch on Illinois citizens and defines our current political life.

Given this track record, what should be done to change our political culture in Illinois?

* * *

## Do We Want People to Participate ... or Not?

In order to complete a reform agenda discussion, we must take stock of the citizens' participation in the electoral process. At the core of a healthy and functioning democracy is a government that encourages civic participation in the political process and, after the elections are over, offers transparency in its government operations. In the spring of 2009, aided by the efforts of the Illinois Reform Commission (IRC) and our quarterback on this issue, Hanke Gratteau, the Illinois legislature took some important initial steps to improve transparency in government by amending the state's Freedom of Information Act (FOIA), the flagship transparency statue. A good start, but only a start.

In this chapter, I'd like to discuss four tangible reforms that would improve our political and governmental processes and result in a more healthy democracy. These ideas are not advanced as cure-alls, but rather illustrate the types of reforms that should be advanced by the reform movement and embraced by independent-minded lawmakers to improve the functioning of our democracy.

### The February Primary Date Should Be Moved Back to June

Right out of the gate, staring right at us as I write this book, is a major problem that should be addressed: the date of the Illinois primary.

"Did you ever try to pound a yard sign into the ground in Illinois in January?" Duane Noland, my fellow IRC commissioner, captured, in one sentence, what is fundamentally wrong with Illinois' decision to retain its February primary and reject a later primary date. Noland, who possesses the quick wit and homespun wisdom of the Illinois' heartland, was no stranger to Illinois government and politics. He served honorably in both the Illinois House and Illinois Senate and, in serving, developed appreciation for public officials and candidates for public office. He does not view members of the legislature as evil or crooked; to the contrary, he thought members of the legislature and statewide offices come to Springfield to do the right thing.

Conducting a primary in the dead of winter, however, makes no sense. It insults the democratic process by automatically lowering the level of citizen participation. There are a myriad of negatives to the primary date:

1. Given the cold and probable inclement weather, we all but guarantee a lower turnout;

2. We unfairly force candidates to compete with the holiday season for the public's attention;
3. We hold elections before the commencement of the legislative session and thereby deny voters the right to evaluate the candidates based on the success (or failure) of that legislative session;
4. We dramatically lengthen the general election campaign, which typically is more costly and thus requires greater fundraising. The longer campaign cycle also diverts government officials' focus away from their important job of governing.

In short, a February primary effectively provides a built-in benefit to the incumbent candidates and detriment to the challengers. It is these "Incumbent Protection Act" provisions that make a fraud-weary citizenry even more cynical and thereby less likely to engage in the political process.

Prior to 2008, Illinois had a mid-March primary. In 2007, in a public nod to Illinois' favorite son, Barack Obama, on his journey to the White House, Illinois moved up its primary in a purported attempt to become more relevant to the presidential election process, Ironically enough, due to the fact that the Obama–Clinton race went well into that summer; the movement of the primary from mid-March to early February provided no meaningful electoral boost to then-candidate Obama. Nevertheless, with the presidential campaign now over, there is simply no persuasive justification to keep the current date, particularly in non-presidential years. It should have been moved forward, but it wasn't. So, as a state that serves as an important barometer on electoral participation in our nation, we've made it harder for citizens to participate during a most critical period in our history. That's cynical and simply wrong.

The fact is that this primary date issue has taken on additional significance in the 2010 election cycle. A good recent sign for our democracy is that for some of the most important, high-profile races—such as governor—we have had hotly contested primaries on both sides of the aisle. No doubt some entrants into these important races were motivated by the desire to answer the call to serve Illinois in a time of need. Yet, by virtue of the legislature's decision to keep the February date, all the candidates who are attempting to distinguish themselves in this critical election cycle are facing obstacles that need not—and should not—ever have been there.

As part of our reform proposals, the IRC pushed for a June primary date, but we received very little support inside the walls of the state Capitol. We were told that there was simply no real support in the legislature for such a measure. Of course not, those inside state government only saw their own vulnerability if the primary date was moved to a time when more citizens would be more likely to participate in the electoral process. Chalk another one up for the "Incumbent Protection Act."

## Illinois Should Study and Pursue Mail-In Voting to Enhance Citizen Participation

Given the state of our democracy, I think we should take the electoral participation issue a step further and consider more dramatic proposals to engage our citizens. In that effort, our legislators should think "outside the box" to bring these electoral enhancement proposals to the table. One such proposal that merits study and analysis for potential adoption by Illinois is statewide mail-in voting. While a relatively recent phenomenon in the electoral process—it has only been around about 30 years—mail-in voting now decides everything from local elections to presidential elections in certain jurisdictions. The experience of the state of Oregon, which is the only state that has adopted statewide mail-in voting, deserves particular study. Why can't we allow everyone to have this same opportunity to vote without taking time off work or having to go out in bad weather and wait in line to do so? Again, those who want to control the end result will be against any movement in this direction, but what about the rest of us? The truth is that, with the recent adoption of "no-excuse absentee voting," where voters can now vote weeks before the election, we are moving in that direction already. Why not take the next step?

In fact, inspired by the Oregon experience, a pilot project to allow mail-in voting in Illinois was already proposed. In 2009, HB 1113 proposed that mail-in voting be attempted in the 2010 general election in a county selected by the State Board of Elections. HB 1113 was a modest but appropriate proposal that never got very far.

The potential benefits of mail-in voting to Illinois voters are substantial: higher turnout rates; more efficiently managed (and possibly cheaper) elections; and—given the "take home test" nature of mail-in voting—more informed decision-making by voters. For example, voters who want to vote intelligently in elections for judges would have the opportunity to research the judicial candidates' positions and endorsements before casting their ballots at home, without having to bring cumbersome lists into the voting booth, or worse, voting in an uninformed manner.

Of course, the key potential pitfall—the risk of compromising the integrity of the ballot process—is a serious one that cannot be ignored, especially in Illinois, with our history of voting fraud and ballot manipulation. The Oregon experience has not yielded significant concerns about enhanced ballot manipulation, but Illinois has a more troubled history regarding vote fraud. Accordingly, we need to explore technological protections. For example, a simple bar code on each ballot might allow the voter to trace his or her vote from beginning to end.

The results from Oregon and other jurisdictions that have adopted mail-in voting are hard to ignore. For the last three presidential races, Oregon has had some of the highest voter-participation rates of the 50 states. While Oregon has a history of citizen activism, are Oregonians a fundamentally more engaged group, even than, say, their Pacific Northwest brethren? Unlikely. The most likely distinguishing factor is the ease of ballot access.

As to the concerns of increased risk of ballot integrity issues, clearly much study would need to be done here. However, with the growing usage of the absentee ballot process in Illinois and across the country, the risk of ballot compromise is already upon us. Other issues, such as the potential "poll tax" nature of the mail-in voting process can be addressed in a number of ways, including by providing a number of free, secure drop-off sites.

To be clear, I do not suggest that mail-in voting is some form of panacea, or that it should be adopted immediately without substantial review and study. Further, some current ballot-access experts believe we should focus more on easing voting registration requirements (e.g., to make same-day registration a reality) in order to enhance voter turnout rates. However I raise mail-in voting and same-day registration as the types of targeted measures that might provide a positive boost to our disaffected electorate—an electorate who needs every reasonable opportunity to participate in the electoral process in easier and more accessible ways.

## The Legislature Should Permit Bills with Meaningful Support to Get to the Floor

While most of the discussion in this book has been devoted to the merits of reform proposals, based on my IRC experience, a spotlight needs to be shone on the Springfield legislative process—or lack thereof. Though some may think that the process is simply "inside baseball" stuff that is not important to the ultimate outcome, nothing could be further from the truth. During the 2009 legislative session, two significant pieces of legislation exposed fundamental flaws in this legislative process: the campaign finance reform bill and the Video Gaming Act related to the capital bill. By and large, the key provisions of these important bills were "negotiated" behind closed doors. When final bills were brought to the floor, votes were then taken promptly with little substantive public debate. What alarmed some of us rookie observers of the legislative process was that this appears to be standard operating procedure in Springfield. That is not healthy for democracy but, we were told, it wasn't about to change. Two procedural fixes should be considered, to increase the likelihood we don't replicate the results of the 2009 session:

1. Decreasing the influence of the too-powerful House Rules Committee;
2. Increasing the scrutiny major bills face by requiring substantive testimony and public release of the final bill before votes are taken.

As to the first, during our IRC hearings on government transparency, Illinois State Comptroller Dan Hynes testified about his frustration with the legislative process. In his brief tutorial on "How Laws Are Made 101," Hynes talked about the powerful function of the House Rules Committee, which serves as the gate-keeping mechanism for a bill on its way to a vote on the floor. He said, "The Rules Committee is where good bills go to die." That is precisely what happened to House Bill 24, a solid piece of campaign finance legislation that imposed meaningful contribution limits on all players. The key provisions of HB 24 were supported by reform groups and were, in fact, quite similar in many respects to the campaign finance bill advanced by the IRC.

By the end of the legislative session, HB 24 had garnered substantial bipartisan support to the point where over 50% of the *entire* House supported the measure. In a fairly dramatic development by Springfield standards, Democratic Representative Julie Hamos, in an end-of-session speech in support of HB 24, implored her Democratic colleagues not to "follow along like lemmings" to her party leadership's opposition to the bill. Her bold action did not carry the day. Even though HB 24 had enough support to pass the full House if called to a vote on the floor, the bill never got out of the Rules Committee and therefore could not be voted on by the full House or Senate. That's just wrong.

While HB 24 was bottled up in committee, the leadership-sponsored campaign finance bill, House Bill 7, sailed through the process. And what a "process" it was. The final version of HB 7 was negotiated behind closed doors and ultimately released at 2:30 in the morning. That same day, before any meaningful public discussion could take place, the bill was called to a vote in the Senate Executive Committee, and that same evening it was brought to the floor of the full Senate for a vote. Months later, after Governor Quinn reversed course and properly decided to veto HB 7 as inadequate reform, the successor campaign finance bill was again negotiated behind closed doors, albeit with the participation of some reform groups. Yet again, the final bill was released and votes were taken before the public was given any meaningful period to discuss, debate, and potentially refine the' provisions. What kind of a democratic "process" is that?

\* \* \*

The current use of the committee system and behind-dosed-doors dealmaking has had a significant effect on efforts to pass all kinds of important legislation. In a democracy, it should not be difficult to get bills with broad-based support to the floor of the legislature (like HB 24), nor should it be easy to pass bills from both chambers with little public vetting.

So what's to be done? As we proposed in the IRC process, the House and Senate should adopt rules requiring that each bill introduced to the House Rules Committee or its Senate equivalent, the Assignment Committee, be subject to a full committee vote if the bill has a threshold level of support. I would add a requirement that the lower threshold needs to include at least one member from the majority party to avoid minority party manipulation of the process.

The naysayers say that the internal rules of the House will never change because Speaker Madigan won't let them. Of course, they are right for now. The internal rules will not change without a transformation in the mindset of rank-and-file legislators, particularly those in the House of Representatives, where Speaker Madigan wields virtually exclusive control.

Yet we have seen some positive changes in the Senate recently on the gate-keeping committees, and it is up to House members to show their constituents they want to improve our democracy. They have another chance this spring to show us they want to do better.

As to the second issue, significant bills such as a multi-billion-dollar public works project with video poker expansion should have substantive public hearings and a period between public release of the bill and a vote. We need public testimony on major pieces of legislation, as well as a meaningful period for the public and legislators to read and comment on the language of significant bills, *before* the vote. How is this unreasonable when we are talking about fundamentally altering legalized gambling in our state? We must give more than lip service to democratic principles to avoid legislative train wrecks like we now have with the video poker debacle.

## Technology Should Be Utilized to Enhance FOIA and, Ultimately, Make It Obsolete

"Sunlight is said to be the best of disinfectants." Those oft-quoted words of a legendary Supreme Court justice almost 100 years ago have particular application in Illinois today. Indeed, there is a pretty good argument that more transparency throughout Illinois government is the best first step to exposing, and thereby improving, the political culture of our state. In fact, as noted earlier one of the tangible reforms emanating from the 2009 legislative session was the bolstering of key provisions of Illinois' Freedom of Information Act, the so-called FOIA. These measures, and the ultimate bill, were advanced by Attorney General Lisa Madigan, with an assist by the IRC and other reform groups. But that was just a start.

The truth of the matter is that government has done far too little to harness the tremendous benefits of technological advancement to shed light on the democratic process. Actually, the ultimate goal of the effort to make government more transparent should be, in effect, to make FOIA obsolete. That is, instead of citizens submitting a written request to a state agency like the Illinois Department of Transportation to obtain information on a construction contract, that information should be posted or otherwise available online so that the request never has to be made. After all, citizens shouldn't have to ask in order to find out what their government is doing. As we learned and heard during the IRC process, injecting government with a sense of institutional transparency will take time. Further, the transition to an on-line world may, in many cases, require substantial upfront costs. Such costs may be particularly steep in these tough budget times, but government leaders and respective agency heads should push to make incremental transitions to a more transparent democracy. For a democracy that is not transparent is no democracy at all.

# Justice: Chicago Style

By James Touhy and Rob Warden

*Operation Greylord, an undercover federal government investigation of the court system, ended with conviction of more than nine judges, thirty-seven lawyers, and nineteen assorted court personnel on charges of bribery, official misconduct, theft, tax evasion, conspiracy, and corruption. In short, Greylord proved that judges were being bribed to fix cases in Cook County. The county's court system has been as corrupt as other branches of government in Illinois.*

To understand the Chicago courts and the origins of Greylord, it is first necessary to understand how the court system works in the context of Chicago politics. The Cook County Circuit Court was dominated for many years by Richard J. Daley, the last of the big-city political bosses. Daley derived his power over the courts not from being mayor of Chicago but from being chairman of the Cook County Democratic Central Committee, which was to Cook County what the Politburo is to the Soviet Union.

As chairman of the central committee from 1953 until his death in 1976, Daley controlled tens of thousands of jobs ranging from garbage collector to assistant city attorney. The patronage system provided legions of election workers known collectively, together with the party bosses, as the Democratic Machine. Daley treated the judiciary as just another part of the county's overall patronage system. He parceled out jobs here and there as rewards for good performance by committeemen, Chicago aldermen, and other politicians. The more votes a politician could deliver, the more jobs Daley gave him. A judgeship was the grand patronage prize. About half of the county's judges were elected in general elections. To get elected, in most cases, one had to be slated by the central committee. To be slated, one had to be approved personally by the chairman. Thus, although judges were chosen in popular elections, in a very real sense only one vote counted—Daley's.

The elected judges, called full judges, in turn selected the rest of the judges, called associate judges. Daley exercised enormous influence over the full judges in their choice of associate judges. On both levels, selection was by connection. The full judges also elected a chief judge from their ranks—the ultimate in organizational perversity: a supervisor being chosen in a popularity contest by those he was supposed to supervise.

In addition to Circuit Court judges, the central committee also slated—and therefore assured the election of—eighteen judges of the First District Illinois Appellate Court, which hears appeals of Cook County cases, and three of the seven judges of the Illinois Supreme Court. The Supreme Court was empowered to fill any vacancies on the lower court that occurred between elections, but unofficially delegated the appointment authority in Cook County to its three Cook County members, who in turn, unofficially delegated it to Daley.

Republicans hadn't been much of a threat in the city since the Depression. Countywide, the Democrats could dominate because there were more Democrats in the city than there were Republicans in the suburbs. Occasionally, however, Republicans could grab a countywide office. Daley hated that. He particularly hated having Republican state's attorneys—which happened twice during his reign—because they invariably created headlines by indicting Democrats. However, by selecting the right candidate—one, say, who was not himself under indictment—the Democrats never stayed out of office long.

The Machine's power was curtailed in 1970 as a result of a federal lawsuit brought by a young lawyer named Michael Shakman, but, partly through inertia, it kept functioning into the early 1980s. After Daley died, however, the absolute power he enjoyed was never again vested in one person. The mayors who followed him did not chair the Democratic Central Committee. The Shakman litigation reduced the power of patronage by forbidding firing for political reasons, thus rendering the politicians powerless to compel public employees to perform election work. After Daley's death, further Shakman litigation was settled with a court-approved agreement forbidding hiring for political reasons—the death sentence for the Machine.

During the period pertinent to Greylord, however, the Machine was the mechanism for judicial election. Exceptional legal talents occasionally ascended to the bench under the system—but usually only by accident. In 1975, for instance, Daley had the central committee slate Joseph Gordon for the Circuit Court. Gordon, a bright and highly regarded former law professor, would have been an outstanding member of any judiciary, but that had little to do with why Daley selected him. When Daley's youngest son, William, was having trouble with his grades at John Marshall Law School, Gordon tutored him privately. For this, Daley was grateful. He expressed his gratitude by making Gordon a judge.

Before 1964, judicial terms were four years. To stay in office, judges had to be selected by the committee every four years, which meant that they had to stay in the committee's favor. This gave politicians tremendous potential to influence cases. Any judge who offended a Democratic politician ran the risk of being dumped at the next slating session.

For many years, pressure had been building to replace the political selection system with a merit selection system. A merit system had been operating effectively since 1940 in the two largest counties of neighboring Missouri. Under the Missouri system, a panel of judges, lawyers, and laymen screens judicial candidates and nominates three for each vacancy. From the three, the governor chooses one.

In 1960, the American Bar Association issued a report praising Missouri's system, saying that a judge there "no longer has to be fearful of any of his judicial pronouncements displeasing the political bosses." The report encouraged merit selection proponents in Illinois. The Chicago Democrats, of course, ardently opposed the idea. However, to head off merit selection, they agreed to a general restructuring of the judiciary.

Under the rubric of "reform," the Illinois General Assembly approved a constitutional amendment, which, after approval by voters, went into effect in 1964. The amendment created a commission of judges with power, in cases brought to its attention by the Illinois attorney general, to remove or suspend judges for misconduct. It also increased the terms of full judges from four to six years and made it possible for judges to stay in office without reslating. To become a full judge, a candidate still had to run in a partisan election, but thereafter only had to stand for retention. The names of judges seeking retention were on a nonpartisan ballot. Retention initially required a majority vote, but that was later changed to 60 percent. The change made sitting full judges somewhat less susceptible to political pressure, but they still owed the Machine. As Democratic Committeeman Vito Marzullo, one of the Daley allies, put it: "Don't think that these people are ingrates. They always cooperate with the party that put them on the bench whenever they can."

In 1980, fourteen years after the so-called reform, 45 men and women appeared before the committee seeking slating for nine full judgeships. Several spoke of their academic records and the scholarly articles they had written. Committeeman Nicholas B. Blase unimpressed. "The difference between them is whether they've done their homework for the Democratic Party," Blase said. "We must bring people up from ward organizations and ultimately reward them."

Better to be direct, if you were a candidate. "It is morally proper to reward people for past service to the party," Associate Judge Edward H. Marsalek told the slate-makers. "I never do anything as a judge to cast any ill feeling toward this organization," said Associate Judge A. Ellis.

The reformed system put the major figures of the scandal on the bench. Ray Sodini, the hung-over gambling court judge who sometimes delegated his responsibility to a police sergeant, was sponsored by Congressman Daniel Rostenkowski, who later became chairman of the House Ways and Means Committee and Democratic committeeman from the Thirty-second Ward. [And was later convicted of political corruption.] Dollars Devine was sponsored by Neil F. Hartigan, former lieutenant governor and committeeman of the Forty-ninth who later became attorney general. Frank Salerno, the judge who gave his girlfriend a hot mink, was sponsored by Edward R. Vrdolyak, alderman and Democratic committeeman of the Tenth Ward, who switched to the Republican Party after Harold Washington, the city's first black mayor, was reelected. [Vrdolyak was also convicted of political corruption.]

Other legislative "reforms" helped set the stage for the Greylord scandal. In 1963, the General Assembly amended the Illinois Code of Criminal Procedure to eliminate bail bondsmen. Rather than having bondsmen post the full amount of defendants' bonds, levying a ten percent fee, the new law allowed defendants to be released after posting ten percent of their bonds with the clerk of the court. After defendants appeared in court, their bonds were refunded by mail. In 1969, the General Assembly amended the Bail Reform Act to allow defendants to sign over bond refunds to attorneys of record.

The hustler was born.

* * *

Judge Brocton Lockwood, a judge from Marrion, Illinois who cooperated with the federal authorities in the Greylord investigation, concluded:

> Chicago has a one-party, that operates for the benefit of the government and not for the people. Lawyers compromise so that nobody's a clear loser, and everybody stays a little happy.

Dan Webb, who was the attorney who directed the operation, became a fervent campaigner for merit selection of judges:

> There is no question in my mind that you can make all the changes you want in the brick and mortar of the system, but it's the people you appoint to the bench who choose to become corrupt. There is only one way to prevent that from happening in the future, and that is to try to find a better way to select the men and women who serve as judges.

# Part V

## Global Chicago

# Global Chicago

As a global city, Chicago is a tourist and convention destination. It has more than 10 million visitors a year at cultural sites like Navy Pier, the Art Institute, and various museums. Thousands attend Chicago sporting events at Wrigley Field, Cellular Field, Soldier Field, and the United Center. People from the metropolitan region, the nation, and the world come to Chicago for knowledge, entertainment, shopping, and vacations. Mayor Richard M. Daley in a 2007 speech at the University of Illinois at Chicago said, "If you don't become a global city, you live in the past."

Although Chicago has achieved the status of a "global city," it is struggling to become a global city that is both livable and humane. One in which wealth and prosperity are shared. Foreign Policy magazine ranks Chicago as the eighth most important global city in the world. To reach this status of a global city, Chicago has become an influential hub of business, culture, sports, and international policy debate. We have drawn people from around the world, both to visit and to settle here. Nonetheless, we have uneven scores on the global city index. We rank twelfth in business activity, but only twentieth in political engagement—that is how a city influences global decisions. We also rank only twentieth in cultural experience.

Post-industrial Chicago's economic transformation began in the 1970s. Our switch to the post-industrial economy is as momentous as the Industrial Revolution in the nineteenth century and it is marked by Chicago's:

1. Becoming the immigration capital of the Midwest.
2. Continuing to have the most manufacturing jobs in the country.
3. Quietly gaining the most high-tech jobs in the country.

By 2001, there were two and a half times as many service as manufacturing jobs in the Chicago metropolitan region. According to Saskia Sassen in her book *The Global City*, the definition of a global city is a site for "the production of specialized services needed by complex organizations ... for running a spatially dispersed network of factories, offices, and

**Figure 1. Change in Share of Families by Income Class, 1970-2005.**

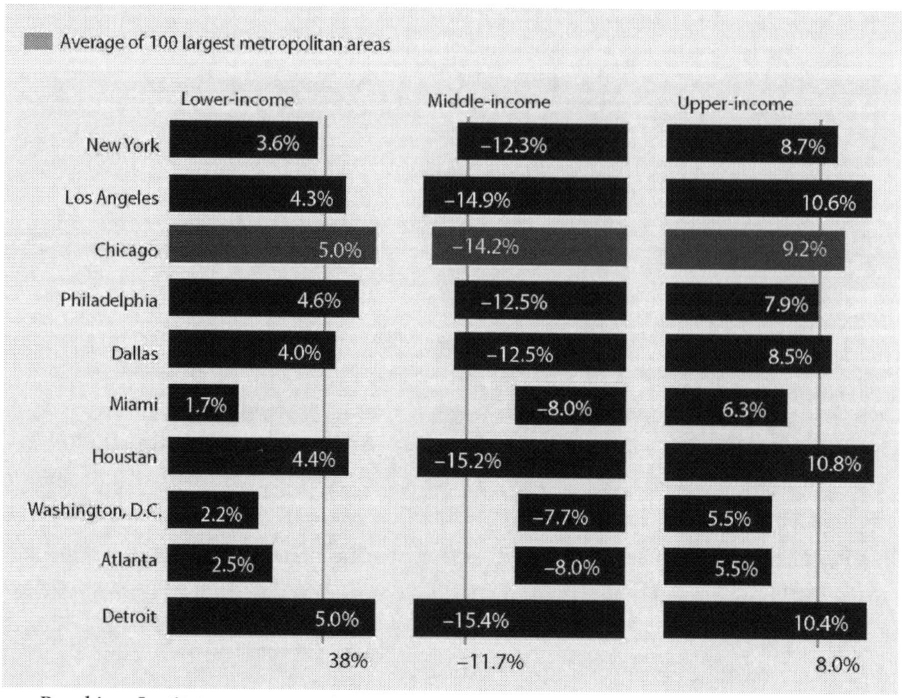

Source: Brookings Institute.

service outlets; … and the production of financial innovations and the making of markets, both central to the internationalization and expansion of the financial industry." These are services produced for firms rather than individuals. Chicago has excelled by attracting law firms, future markets, and consulting firms among other service firms.

The downside of the globalization of Chicago has been not only a "widening color gap," but also a shrinking middle class and a widening wealth gap between the rich and the poor in the region. The forces of globalization have produced fewer jobs that pay middle-class wages, but more jobs that pay higher- and lower-class wages. This increasing inequality has been called by some, an hourglass economy. As quantified in Figure 1, this shrinking of the middle class is a trend that is impacting metropolitan areas throughout the United States.

The articles in this section explore whether or not Chicago can make it in the long run as a global city, how that transformation is occurring, and how the forces of globalization are changing the "Hog Butcher of the World."

# A Global City

## By Adele Simmons

*Chicago's rich immigrant tradition since its inception has made it an international city long before "global city" became a buzzword. Through business, medicine and science, art, and music and dance, Chicago exhibits its global heritage.*

In Chicago, my hometown, the local florist's lilies may come from Holland, the grocer's grapes from Chile, the computer assembler's chips from Taiwan, the bicyclist's brakes from Japan. While those goods are flying in, Chicago academics are flying out—to advise the governments of Chile, Indonesia, and Nigeria, to name a few. Scientists from all over the world gather to conduct experiments at our laboratories—particularly Argonne National and Fermi Laboratory—and human rights activists from every continent doff their hats to their comrades here, without whom the new International Criminal Court might not exist. Chicagoans import and export goods, ideas, and people, hourly. To us, this is no big deal.

The fact that Chicago has become one of the world's great global cities has yet to impress most Chicagoans, in part because the global fabric is so thickly woven here. In a city with 130 non-English newspapers, where an emergency call to 911 can be responded to in 150 languages, a foreign tongue turns few heads. Similarly, no face seems out of place—each one seems legitimate for a Chicagoan. (We concede native status without much regard for nativity. If you're here, not living in a hotel, and not wearing any Green Bay Packers paraphernalia, we assume you're one of us.) Immigrants make up 22 percent of the city's population and they send an estimated $1.8 billion annually to the families they've left behind. Entire villages depend on that Chicago money. To us, this is old news. People have always come. Money has always gone back.

A Chicagoan who favors a local Korean dry cleaner, the Thai restaurant down at the corner, and an Eastern European tradesman recommended by a neighbor is unlikely to pay much notice to the Loop offices of foreign multinationals like Societe Generale, Sumitomo Bank, and ABN Amro. Similarly, the consular offices of seventy nations, clustered mostly around the Loop, make few Chicagoans ponder the city's place in the world. We expect those diplomats to be here. And city residents traveling abroad don't think twice anymore when they see a logo of some hometown corporation—McDonald's, Motorola, Boeing, and the Bulls, to name a few. We expect them to be there too.

The curiosity of the native Chicagoan might have been aroused recently when two candidates for the office of governor of the Mexican state of Michoacan campaigned for votes here. Then again, Chicagoans are accustomed to candidates trolling far and wide for votes, sometimes even into the afterlife, and thus the Mexican campaign may have appeared more like Cook County politics than anything particularly foreign. Similarly, the globalization of crime seems not so new here. Yes, we have ethnically varied criminal networks, but we've had those before. We have immigrants exploited in the workplace, but that too is not new. The exploiters may have changed and the number of exploited may have increased, but the act is an old one.

We're a tough crowd. We don't impress ourselves. We've become an economic and cultural powerhouse, a commercial and artistic center of growing international importance. Mayor Richard M. Daley created World Business Chicago to promote the city to business investors from all over the world and to ensure that foreign trade delegations connect with the right partners in Chicago. Foreign delegations routinely stop by city hall for a chat, where they may board elevators with German architects filing their drawings, Irish contractors applying for building permits, or Italian restaurateurs petitioning for liquor licenses. Globalization touches all of our lives daily, sometimes hourly. Most of us take no notice at all…

## Global Before "Globalization"

Chicago's interaction with the world began long before "globalization" became a buzzword, embraced by some and reviled by others. From its inception in the 1770s as a fur-trading post founded by Jean-Baptiste Point du Sable, an immigrant from Sainte-Domingue (Haiti), Chicago has been a place where cultures, languages, and traditions have mixed.

Here, Native Americans intermingled with settlers from France, Great Britain, and Germany. Rather than being hurt by being situated in what was then the western part of the American territories, the outpost profited from its location at the mouth of a river flowing into the largest body of water in the region. It was this fortuitous location that helped transform a fur-trading outpost into a national hub for transportation. Transportation brought immigrants, and those immigrants brought skills, and those skills have built a metropolitan area that is home to more than eight million residents.

The 1893 World's Columbian Exposition in Chicago set in motion the city's transformation into the gleaming, bustling metropolis it is today. The exposition's Chicago organizers staged the grandest and most memorable world's fair ever held. They broke new ground in showcasing each country – the exhibits were designed by the members of each exhibiting country and not by Americans. As a result, each exhibit represented its country's particular sensibility and how its people saw themselves – rather than how Americans saw them. Chicagoans were thus infected with new ideas and perspectives. The Ho Ho Den building in the Japanese Village, for example, profoundly influenced Frank Lloyd Wright, and he incorporated elements of the building's design in his renowned Prairie style of architecture. Nearly three decades later, the Japanese hired Wright to design the Imperial Hotel in Tokyo, completed in 1922—a neatly closed loop of Chicagoans influenced by the world and the world influenced by Chicagoans.

That pattern repeated itself in industry, science, religion, and the arts in the decades that followed. Fifty years after the exposition, within a mile of the site where Wright had been inspired, a team of physicists led by the Italian refugee physicist Enrico Fermi created the world's first self-sustaining nuclear reaction. The experiment, staged under the football stadium at the University of Chicago, redefined energy development, altered the terms of international conflict, and changed the course of diplomacy around the world.

A hundred years after the exposition, the World's Parliament of Religions, one of the enduring legacies of the Chicago fair, marked its centennial by forging a consensual document entitled "Towards a Global Ethic." Commonly referred to as "The Chicago Declaration," the document is a pledge to work for a just social and economic order, for mutual understanding among peoples and nations, and for a recognition of the interdependence of all living things.

## Global Chicago at Work

A glimpse into the life of Chicago and its citizens during one spring month in 2002 shows the international dimension of everyday activities of individuals from all walks of life.

On a typical day in May, Robert Langlois, director of international relations at Motorola, walks into his office in Schaumburg at seven in the morning. "I get in early so that I have a few hours of overlap with my colleagues working in Europe, Africa, and the Middle East," he says.

On this particular morning, Langlois checks his e-mail and responds to a message from a colleague at the company's production facility in Israel. He calls the Moscow office to talk about the sale of Motorola pagers. He then calls Cairo and talks with the country manager for Egypt. At 10:30 A.M., he leaves his office for downtown Chicago, where he attends a luncheon for the vice president of Botswana. After lunch, he calls on the South African consulate to discuss that government's order of Motorola walkie-talkies. He ends the day by giving a talk on the international business climate to a group of young professionals.

In the Loop offices of Perkins and Will, one of Chicago's most respected architectural, interior design, and planning firms, William Doerge and Ralph Johnson have spent a good portion of the same day negotiating the timeline for construction of a university in Luanda, Angola. Eighteen of their colleagues in the Chicago office work on the project, while five others are in Mumbai, India, where they are retrofitting an existing concrete structure to accommodate a hospital. A dozen other international projects are in various stages of planning and completion. The firm, which is accustomed to exporting expertise, has no hesitation to import it as well. Consultants from Britain advised Perkins and Will on the design of two green "sustainable" projects—a middle school in Bloomington, Indiana, and a courthouse in Los Angeles.

While Perkins and Will is planning for the Angolan university, Flying Food Group is dispatching meals all over the globe. FFG was founded in Chicago by Sue Ling Gin in 1983, and it now caters meals for twenty-eight international airlines that fly out of Chicago's airports. During the month of May, the O'Hare kitchen alone made 183,598 meals. Says Gin, "Flying Food Group is a global company not only in its sales, but in its people. The 1,800 people who work for us come from all over the world, so we are truly global from production to sales to end users."

Minority-owned Blackwell Consulting Services, Inc., has a similarly international work-force. Blackwell employs natives of Cuba, Russian, India, Ireland, and Venezuela to advise clients on management and information technology, and this May they are laboring on a project for a local client, Waste Management. "Our clients call us the League of Nations," says Bob Blackwell, founder and CEO of the Chicago-based firm. "Our employees come from around the world and each person brings something different to the team. We do better work because of our diversity."

## Medicine and Science

In early May, Dr. Robert Murphy, who works in the infectious diseases lab at Northwestern University, is preparing to leave for the 2002 HIV/AIDS conference in Barcelona. One of the world's leading HIV/AIDS treatment researchers, Murphy is the only non-French citizen to serve on France's Conseil d'Administration, Objectif Recherche Vaccin SIDA, a committee for the discovery of a therapeutic AIDS vaccine. Working with Dr. Toyin Falusi, a Nigerian who directs HIV/AIDS clinical research at Cook County Hospital, Murphy recently established the Nigerian Adult Clinical Trials Group (NACTG) in Ibadan, a city sixty miles north of Lagos, Nigeria. The goal of the Nigerian project is to set up an AIDS treatment infrastructure to be run by Nigerians for Nigerians. To that end, AIDS specialists from Chicago will spend two weeks in Nigeria and their Nigerian colleagues will spend three weeks at three Chicago hospitals. Murphy will head to Masai country in Kenya where he is helping a local doctor upgrade a general clinic so it can treat HIV/AIDS patients.

While that AIDS treatment infrastructure is being planned on the city's north and west sides, Dr. Olufanmilayo Olapade, another native of Nigeria, is working on the South Side. Olapade directs clinical and laboratory research program in cancer genetics at the University of Chicago's School of Medicine. She is investigating why black women develop breast cancer at younger ages and why they suffer higher mortality rates from cancer than other population groups. Her research in Chicago and Nigeria will eventually examine the genetic material of 100,000 women who developed breast cancer before the age of forty-five.

At the Field Museum in May 2002, Debbie Moskovitz, director of the museum's Environment and Conservation Program, is talking on the phone with Alaka Wali, curator of the museum's Center for Cultural Understanding and Change. Wali is in Peru meeting with residents of Tocache, a town in the Huallaga Valley, and with staff from local nongovernmental organizations (NGOs). To ensure the protection of the Parque Corillera Azul, created through the collaboration of the museum, the government of Peru, and Peruvian conservationists, Wali and her team want to help Tocache residents find ways of sustaining their livelihoods while minimizing ecological damage to the buffer zone that surrounds the park. Wali tells Moskovitz that she began to make real progress in Tocache after the mayor realized that his cousin was a volunteer for the Field Museum.

## Art

At the Cultural Center of Chicago, Mike Lash, the director for the City of Chicago's Office of Public Art, is on the phone with Sylvie Fleury, an artist in Geneva, Switzerland. Fleury is a Swiss national who has agreed to do a project sponsored by the city, Tiffany's and Sears, where she will explore consumerism in a series of photographs and paintings.

For Millennium Park, Chicago's ambitious scheme to turn its lakefront park into a major cultural attraction, Lash's department has recently approved two other major pieces from European artists. A metal sculpture by Anish Kapoor, a London-based artist, will measure forty-seven feet by thirty-three feet by sixty-six feet and will be the largest noncommemorative piece of art in the world, weighing more than a hundred tons. The new park will also feature a fountain designed by the Spanish artist Jaume Plensa with LCD screens that will project images of Chicagoans.

The city's willingness to embrace the unorthodox in art is not new. "In the nineteenth century and the beginning of the twentieth century, Chicago art patrons had an appreciation for European artists, such as the impressionists," says the cultural historian Tim Samuelson. "Chicago art patrons were not constrained by the East Coast and European orthodoxy, and so they collected impressionist paintings before the rest of the East Coast and European art collectors came to value it. This was a reflection of the pioneering, open-minded attitude that characterized Chicagoans from the start. It was because of this openness that there are so many famous impressionist paintings at the Art Institute."

This pioneering spirit and the willingness to embrace new ideas is alive and well, as evidenced by Art Chicago, one of America's largest international contemporary art expositions. Two hundred six galleries from twenty countries exhibited work at the five-day festival in May 2002, the tenth anniversary of the event.

May is also a busy month for Carlos Tortolero, the founder and executive director of the Mexican Fine Arts Center Museum in Pilsen, a neighborhood in Chicago where many Mexican immigrants have settled. He spends a week in Mexico finalizing which pieces would appear in an upcoming exhibition of artwork from the Museo de Arte Carillo Gil, meeting with officials from the Instituto Nacional de Antropologia y Historia (INA) regarding an exhibition of clothing from the pre-Columbian period to the present, and planning for an exhibition of art from the Gelman Collection planned for January thrugh April.

"Much of my work is creating bridges between Mexico and the U.S.," he says. "While I was in Mexico City, I also met with the director of INA and discussed a possible collaboration over an amnesty program which would allow historical artifacts trafficked into the U.S. to be returned anonymously, displayed in the museum, and then repatriated to Mexico."

## Music and Dance

The Chicago Symphony Orchestra (CSO) has its home in Symphony Center, located across Michigan Avenue from the Art Institute. Considered an orchestra with few peers, the CSO is an unofficial ambassador of Chicago to the world, while also bringing the world to Chicago. Daniel Barenboim, the CSO's artistic director, hails from Argentina, was educated in Europe, and has lived in Israel.

In May 2002, Barenboim is preparing for the Fourth Annual West-Eastern Divan Workshop, a program he created to bring together seventy gifted young musicians from Isarel and Arab countries for three weeks of intensive musical training. The program is unique in its format and makeup. The participants would otherwise never interact. Held on the campus of Northwestern University in 2001, the workshop will be in Seville, Spain in 2002.

Chicago's vibrant jazz scene also draws world-class performers to the city. The Empty Bottle's Annual International Festival, held every April, brings internationally known musicians to play alongside local jazz artists. The festival is directed by John Corbett, a Chicago producer, writer, and musician, who has created numerous collaborations between European and Chicago-based musicians. While the CSO's Barenboim prepares for his Divan, Corbett is in Europe organizing the program for the 2002 Berlin Jazz Festival, for which he is artistic director. He is a good example of the large number of musicians who call Chicago home while collaborating with artists all over the world.

Dance in Chicago is also a global importer and exporter of ideas and personnel. In May, while dancers from Burkina Faso are performing at Columbia College in Chicago, the Hubbard Street Dance Company is touring the United Kingdom. Twenty-five percent of Hubbard's world-renowned company members are from outside the United States.

# Why the Fuss?

At this point, the true Chicagoan might say, "Yeah, so what's the big deal?" Paul O'Connor, executive director of World Business Chicago, puts it like this:

> "We invented the skyscraper, split the atom, made our river flow backwards, created a lakefront from scratch, figured out the transistor, drew all the railroads to us, pioneered and continuously dominated commercial air travel, broadcast the world's first all-color TV station, built the number-one manufacturing city of America, invented risk management markets, won more Nobel Prizes than any city on earth, communicate more data on a daily basis than any other city on earth, threw away more basic industries than most other cities ever had, you know, like, hog-butcher, stacker of wheat, steel capital of America. Should we tell anyone?"

Well, the answer is yes, we should. Being known as a global city is an economic and cultural asset. It helps attract corporations of Boeing's magnitude. It reminds us and our friends around the world that we are no longer a city defined by a manufacturing and industrial base, that we have a history of transformation, that we welcome new ideas, new markets, and new kinds of business opportunities. Being a beautiful city with twenty-nine miles of lakefront is not enough to guarantee our future. We must continue reinventing ourselves and keeping pace with global opportunities

# Can Chicago Make It as a Global City?

By Janet L. Abu-Lughod

*Chicago is a global city and has been since the 19th century, but its transition has not been even. Can it make it as a vital, growing, commanding center in the new configuration of the global economic system?*

*In this paper, based on a presentation made in November, 1999, Abu-Lughod argues that Chicago's future is shaped by local, regional, national, global forces. It must overcome its racial discrimination and the city/suburban split if it is to make it as a global city in the 21st Century.*

Is Chicago an international city? Of course it is. It has been ever since the second half of the nineteenth century: (1) when it was British bond investments that funded the rail lines to open the prairies and the west to the New York port; (2) when midwest corn and wheat began to supply Europe's bakeries; and (3) when new techniques of curing and refrigeration permitted the delivery of Chicago's meat to distant and even foreign markets.

And talk about a cosmopolitan population! Recall that at the turn of the century, four-fifths of Chicago's residents had either been born abroad or were the children of those who had. Attracting international capital, offering banking and financial services to tributary cities and towns, producing goods for export, and drawing diverse immigrant labor are all characteristics of a dominant global center.

Is Chicago now a global city? Of course it is. It has all the contemporary earmarks: high tech, producers' services, the MERC, and the busiest airport in the country, even though its attractiveness to migrants now trails Los Angeles and New York.

Nonetheless, Chicago is a city that for half a century first denied and then succumbed to "rustbelt anxiety," at best whistling in the dark. And especially after the census ignominiously demoted it to "third city," it has been the object, inter alia, of a glossy (even hysterical) Chamber of Commerce report in 1992, boasting that, like any third world country or depressed American city, it was prepared for a race to the bottom: Comparing the city to its "rivals" (especially New York and Los Angeles), the Chamber propaganda stresses that Chicago has lower wages, congestion, lower rents for office space, lower utility rates, corporate and individual, and a more "cooperative" administration.

While the slick brochure does not spell out the implications of these advantages, it is evident that lower wages and lower taxes can only mean more poor people and fewer funds to assist them. More recently, a similar anxiety shows through the Commercial Club's Plan to "fix" the metropolis by the year 2020, a report stronger on analysis than prescription.

There are good reasons for anxiety. But if the causes of a problem are not realistically diagnosed, proposed solutions may prove ineffectual. In present discussions of Chicago's future, it has become fashionable both to blame the global system for generating problems at the local level (a la Bill Wilson), but, paradoxically, also to lust after even globalization as the panacea (a la Chamber of Commerce). However, simply invoking the buzzword "global" neither advances the analysis of decline nor offers an easy way out.

I want to take a dispassionate look at the realities of Chicago's uneven development and possible stagnation, and to suggest some radical solutions that may be only tangentially related to "making it as a global city," although they are essential to making it "a city that works"…

But first, what do we mean by these new terms: globalization and global cities? I take a somewhat deviant position. From an historical point of view, the present phase of globalization is just a continuation, albeit at a faster pace and via new technologies, of what has been going on for much of human history. In its most literal sense, globalization simply refers to an ongoing process whereby larger and larger portions of the world have become increasingly linked to one another via material exchanges of resources, commodities and currencies, as well as through a widening of the geographic range over which populations move, whether temporarily or permanently. Inevitably, this process not only entails more "integration" on the economic and political levels, but also permits more contact on the symbolic and cultural levels, either directly or indirectly…

A global city is therefore simply an urbanized node through which disproportionate fractions of national and international interactions flow. Such flows are also neither symmetrical nor equally rewarding. Indeed, the enormous scale at which globalization now operates often camouflages clear lines between causes and effects, as capital and labor move with increasing freedom not only across national borders but beyond metropolitan boundaries as well.

Being designated as a "global city," then, gives no assurance of special rewards. Degrees of economic, political and cultural dominance help to distinguish more powerful from less powerful global cities. But even within the class of dominant global cities, the effects of globalization vary, not only between global city regions but also within them. Paradoxically, because globalization often flows through the increasingly disembodied cyberspace of information and high finance, its advantages do not necessarily fall directly on the physical ground that lies beneath their electronically flashing nodes and circuits.

There is, then, no contradiction between the proliferation of transactions in cyberspace, such as those that flow through the computers of the MERC, and the evisceration of localized functions. This disengagement means that even a healthy growth in command functions cannot protect those parts of the system (whether highly localized, at the national level, or at the global level) that are "out of the loop." Such marginalized zones can now be found in Bangladesh and many parts of the African continent, in Manchester and Sheffield, England, in downtown Detroit, in South Central Los Angeles and in the south and west side areas of Chicago!...

My book, *New York, Chicago, Los Angeles: America's Global Cities*, compares America's three largest global cities: New York, Los Angeles and, with reservations, Chicago. The book emphasizes differences, tracing over time the ways specific technologies, economic functions, geographic sites, demographic compositions, and cultural responses have shaped these three particular urban regions. It argues, moreover, that even the same forces emanating from the global system at any given time always interact with active agents on the ground who operate within distinctive political cultures that have been honed over long periods of time.

So it is easy to answer one question implied in part of the title of my talk. Of course, Chicago is a global city. It always has been. But the answer to the second part of the title: "Can Chicago make it as a vital, growing, commanding center in the new configuration of the global system?" is not so evident.

And here I am going to take an unpopular position. I think Chicago will continue to lose ground unless it diagnoses its strengths and weaknesses more realistically, and works not with some mythological "force" such as globalization, on which it can blame all its problems and through which it can dream of salvation, but on the energetic grittiness of its special history and people. I begin with the premise that Chicago's future is shaped by local, regional, national, global forces, and failure to attend to all four simultaneously cannot yield adequate policies.

There is an old prayer that I quote inaccurately. "God give me the strength to accept what can't be changed, the energy to alter what can be changed, and the wisdom to know the difference." That is how I propose to organize my talk.


## What Can't Be Changed: Chicago's Location in Geographic Space

Chicago is where it is, in the heartland of the subcontinent, a region whose population growth rate now falls below average. Even though O'Hare's boast that it is "the busiest air terminal in the country" is not to be dismissed, it must be acknowledged that the vast midwestern and plains hinterlands of Chicago have not been growing as before, and indeed, the population in many of its parts has actually been in decline.

To some extent, the demographic "failure to thrive" of the midwest, Chicago's service area catchment zone, has had serious repercussions on the city's economic health, repercussions that compound those caused by the shrinkage of heavy industry. Thus, not all of Chicago's problems stem from specifically local causes, such as post-Fordism or even Chicago's contentious race relations, although the effects have been experienced most severely by poor people of color.

In the four decades between 1950 and 1990, the population of the larger Chicago region grew by only 40 percent (well under its rate of natural increase). The city itself lost one-fourth of its population and the number of suburban Cook County's residents virtually stagnated. True, the population in the other five collar counties almost tripled, but this was insufficient compensation. The New York CMSA—and especially the Los Angeles CMSA whose population almost doubled in the 30 years between 1960 and 1990—have been growing faster; much faster because their hinterlands have been.

Reflecting the Januslike position of the contemporary US as both an Atlantic and Pacific power, and eventually, the greater integration of North America with the Caribbean and the Latin American continent, the three seacoasts of the US have become increasingly important magnets for internal migrants. In recent decades the population of the United States has been decanting toward the coasts, not only in the older directions of east and west but now, southward as well...

The "hollowing out" of the continent has been achieved not only through low rates of natural increase and heightened internal emigration from the Great Plains but, increasingly, through the recently enlarged streams of immigrants from abroad whose "ports of entry" remain the coastal cities. Chicago is no longer the magnet for immigrants that it once was. By 1990, despite the great burst of immigration to the US since 1965, only 11 percent of the residents of the Chicago CMSA had been born abroad, compared to two and three times that percentage in New York and Los Angeles. The recent demographic recovery of the New York urbanized region and, even more so, the growth of the Los Angeles megalopolitan region are clearly attributable to the heightened immigration from abroad that resulted not from changes in local policies but national ones.

How do these larger demographic trends affect Chicago? For one, Chicago's "central place" function as chief market for the midwest is undermined. Furthermore, because Chicago is far from the coasts; it benefits less from the new larger scale of global exchanges that move via sea or air. Chicago's rank among American ports is low: 59th in 1990. The ports of New York take in 15 times more raw tons of freight than Chicago and export 7 times as much weight; Los Angeles's ports export 11 times as much tonnage as Chicago. Even in air freight, Chicago handles only a small fraction of international commerce.

Thus, because of its location, Chicago can be neither the prime gateway to Asia that now makes the ports of Los Angeles engines for that city/region's growth, nor the gateway to Europe and Eastern Europe that underlies New York's dominance in international trade and traffic. Flows through cyberspace can supplement, but will never supplant, the movements of people and material. (In any case, cyberspace marketing is now done in back offices in small cities of the plains and Rockies.)

The Chicago region has also fallen behind the other two in attracting foreign capital and employment in foreign-owned firms. The value of direct foreign investment in Illinois is less than half that invested in either New York/New Jersey or California, and foreign firms are generating many fewer jobs here than elsewhere.

While size isn't everything, it is something, especially in national politics. The Chicago region's relative demographic losses have weakened its voice in Washington, an increasingly important force underlying the economies of states located in what Ann Markusen has called the "defense perimeter." She has shown how little money the Department of Defense actually spends on research and development, innovative weaponry, or even production in the Illinois/Chicago region. Whereas in 1951 Illinois was still near the middle rank of the 18 states she studied as measured by "Per Capita Prime [Defense] Contracts Relative to U.S. Average," by 1984 Illinois had dropped to the very lowest rank in defense contracts, below the remaining midwest states on their list, such as Wisconsin, Michigan, Ohio, and Indiana.

In contrast, California continues to grow in strength and New York, New Jersey, Connecticut, and Massachusetts still retain their attractiveness to defense investments. Chicago has not…Plant closings and reductions in the industrial labor force had already appeared in the Chicago region as early as the late 1940s, and these reductions persisted throughout the prosperous 1950s and mid-1960s, a period when the US still monopolized the world's production. Such losses not only preceded the recent phase of globalization and the "shift" to the services but have continued into the 1990s in parts of the region!…

Even though some of this deficit has been compensated by a growth in services, not much of that growth has been in the much-touted (i.e., high paying) services that are hallmarks of the "new globalization: FIRE (finance, insurance and real estate) and producers' services, for example. Between 1974 and 1985, the number of FIRE jobs in the Chicago region increased by only 7 percent, whereas they grew by 21 percent in New York and 63 percent in Los Angeles.

True, there was one exception. Chicago was able to "capture" some share in "the new economy" after the 1973 recession by innovating in the upper circuit of arbitrage and financials via the remarkable transformation in the Chicago Mercantile Exchange. By a bold stroke of anticipating a global market for financial futures and currency options, the then-foundering Chicago Mercantile Exchange was the first to grasp this opportunity which, by 1995, came to account for some 90 percent of its contracts. However, because the market is international and unregulated, the MERC is already seeing some of its base erode through competition from private deals and unregulated non-US exchanges. But even if the MERC had retained its monopoly, one must acknowledge that very few persons are employed in this and the other new sectors of the global economy, and what is worse, their multiplier effects are very narrow. Few of the profits of these "global" operations filter down to the local population. Furthermore, in comparison to New York (which moved almost directly from pre-Fordism to post-Fordism), and Los Angeles (which has grown more Fordist and industrial with time), the increases in producer services and high tech R&D in Chicago have lagged considerably behind those two competitors. In short, globalization is saving Chicago.

## What Can Be Done?

Some other midwest cities have faced similar losses and yet appear to be thriving. Why? Industrial production continues and expands. Connections to the global system and the knowledge industry increase. What handicaps does Chicago face that these do not?

And here I am going to be very blunt. In prosperous times, Chicago could afford to be profligate with its space and people. It could afford to leave its contradictions unresolved and its confrontations raw. J. W. Sheahan, writing in 1875, suggested that Chicago, instead of trying to resolve its divisions like the cities of the East Coast and Europe, had made its conflicts the basis of its identity. "Divisions that might paralyze other places provided the very condition for Chicago's existence."

I contend that these divisions no longer work, if they ever did. They now sap the city's vitality. Today, new ways must be found to fully utilize its space and people, ways that will not only adjust to the city's diminished role in the global system but also build upon its formidable local strengths. Perhaps, if this opportunity is seized, a new healthy basis for the region's economy and social life can be forged.

But to do that, Chicago's historical racism must be acknowledged as a "luxury" this city region can no longer afford!

Two "facts" must be faced honestly. Enormous sections of the city now lie "fallow," denuded of their industries and businesses. What a waste of sunk investments and potential resources! It is not that all growth has ceased, but that it has been taking place exclusively in the Loop, in Edge City or the outlying portions of the collar counties, especially along the almost exclusively white growth corridors to the northwest and, leaping over inlying urban quarters, in suburban sections of the southwest's growth corridor.

Second, Chicago's metropolitan region remains one of the most, if not the most, segregated places in the country. Not only does the region demonstrate the greatest inequality between its wealthy (white) and poor (minority) areas and suburbs, but the gap has been widening precipitously. Hyper segregation in housing, as Doug Massey has clearly shown for Chicago, underlies the increased poverty and isolation of minorities not only from jobs but from hope....

The combination of these forces means that not only land but whole fractions of Chicago's regional labor force also lie fallow. The underutilization of their labor power drags Chicago's growth down and saps its vitality as production center, market place and provider of desperately needed local infrastructure and services.

To claim that such inequalities are new and an inevitable product of globalization is false and self-serving, because it denies the local and long-term causes of this situation. And, in my mind, it is the failure of proposals for rescuing Chicago such as those advocated by the Chamber of Commerce report or even the Commercial Club's 2020 Plan to acknowledge the historic evolution of this situation and to advocate real, but hard and long-term correctives, that I want to address in the time left to me. Neither of these two reports, nor, for that matter, most other business analyses of Chicago's economic future, take seriously or even cite the penetrating analysis of racism by critics such as Greg Squires, or scholars associated with the Chicago Urban League and Metro Chicago analyses that demonstrate the systematic disinvestment in the people and places that now lie fallow in the region.

I am not claiming that all of the resulting inequalities in the Chicago region are due to racism, just as I have argued that not all of them are due to "globalization." Many are attributable to more national causes: increasingly unprogressive income tax rates, the obscenely high and hidden compensations paid to CEOs who "downsize," the atrophy of union strength and its substitution by flexible production without fringe benefits, the reforms to welfare without the accompanying substitute services to mothers, and the politically gated suburban communities that beggar their neighbors. All of these "choices" affect the growing gap in income and wealth distribution not only in Chicago but in New York and Los Angeles, as well as other places.

But Chicago's situation is extreme because of the very long time during which the conditions of the minority poor have not only been neglected but perversely exacerbated. Chicago's race problems cannot be simply explained on the grounds of numbers. Taken as a whole, the region has no higher a percentage of minority residents than the New York region: black non-hispanic residents constitute slightly under a fifth in both CMSAs and black hispanics are more numerous in New York than in Chicago, and combined minorities are even higher in Los Angeles.

However, neither New York nor Los Angeles has the same degree of cleavage as Chicago between the central city and its politically powerful "white" collar counties. And it is cleavage, which was the result of racism that stands in the way of a solution....As early as the 1919 riot, when African Americans constituted only a tiny percentage of the total population, racism had become the organizing principle of Chicago life, whereas in the political cultures of New York and Los Angeles, it was only one theme among many others.

Given this long history, I think white Chicago owes reparations and an investment in healing that can belatedly compensate for the pain, suffering, and demoralization it has created. And I also believe that if Chicago is to make it as a global city, it must make this investment its highest priority.

## What Policies Are Needed?

My reading of the 2020 Plan is that its programmatic suggestions are both too and little too late. Let me first address the latter because I want to end with the former. Too Late: There is absolutely nothing wrong with Adele Simmon's section that strongly advocates investing heavily in educating the young, paying special attention to underserved minority children. But this approach, even in the unlikely event that it were to receive overwhelming support and generous funding and that it achieved spectacular success, would not, in itself, either bind the city and collar counties into an integrated economic unit nor bind its populations into a common community. It is a necessary but not a sufficient cure. That is because education is very long term! And in the meantime, shorter-term payoffs are essential. If conditions of material deprivation, isolation, and hopelessness are allowed to persist through the present generation while we wait for the kids to grow up, even the best and brightest of the next generation may not be able to resist demoralization. Motivation requires real evidence of opportunity not in promises but on the ground. Unless massive reinvestment in the present is undertaken simultaneously, better math courses and computer literacy will not save us.

## Too Little and in the Wrong Places

Conservative reformers are fond of dismissing solutions that merely "throw money" at problems (although they tend to overlook the fact that the systematic withdrawal of funds is the most basic cause of problems) I agree, especially when only modest amounts are appropriated in relation to needs and when such investments are accompanied by unrealistic expectations of stunning and rapid results. They are bound to disappoint. Nickel and dime investments may yield an occasional bonanza in the stock market lottery, but they will make little dent on the task that really needs to be done, which is nothing short of rebuilding the fallow land and integrating its displaced labor. The long-accumulating deficiencies in large minority areas of Chicago cannot be repaired in a few years nor can we expect modest "incentives" to make philanthropists out of investors.

No. Given at least half a century during which jobs, hopes, and values have been drained from the African American and Latino hyperghettos of the south and west sides, only massive investments right now and continuing for many years can begin to repair the damage.

I am not here to tell Chicago how to do this, although redistributing the wealth of the entire region to replace the jobs that have been drained from the south and west sides of the city seems to me to be an indispensable starting point. That means breaking down the imaginary line between Cook County and the collar counties physically, politically, legally, and financially. Unless this can be achieved, the resources will be insufficient and the potential gains from both local and global sources of strength will continue to elude us.

Chicago's early history tells us that its ability to harness the labor and the "will" of its people was the basis for its past prosperity. It is time to do that again. The "living with contradictions" that Sheehan thought was Chicago's unique way of dealing with its social cleavages is no longer working. The contradictions must be acknowledged and resolved. The entire region can only harness its untapped power in a climate of hope. And hope requires not only preferential education but also the breaking down of the powerful spatial barriers that racism has consciously built into the region and that continue to deny opportunities to most of its minorities. Here we are, in the Harold Washington Public Library, a stunning building surmounted by what I take to be copper phoenixes that ever present image of hope in Chicago. More than ever before, this city needs hope and the realistic will to overcome its inequalities. That will require honest acknowledgement that a city cannot prosper with so large a fraction of its terrain and people underutilized and unintegrated into the spatial and economic fabric.

Most causes of growth and decline do not originate from global forces and most solutions to decline require careful attention to more localized causes. It will not be easy, but its payoffs will not only change Chicago into a region that "makes it" but one that "makes it globally."

# Economic Restructuring: Chicago's Precarious Balance

## By David Moberg

*Although Chicago has a diverse economy, it remains trapped in a precarious balance. In this article, David Moberg argues that for Chicago to succeed in a global world it must address economic inequality among individuals and communities. This can only be accomplished through regional cooperation and planning.*

After spurring cities across the country into a bidding war for its favors, Boeing Corporation announced, in March 2001, that it was moving its corporate headquarters from its long-time Seattle home to downtown Chicago. Although $56 million in public subsidies brought only 450 jobs, Chicago political and business leaders celebrated the capture of the nation's leading exporter and iconic global corporation as proof of the city's intrinsic attractions as a world corporate center. [1]

On the other hand, relatively little fanfare erupted when Brach's Confections Inc. announced two months earlier its plans to shut down the world's largest candy manufacturing plant at the end of 2003. It was easy to see the loss of roughly 1,000 jobs on Chicago's still-poor West Side as an episode in the oft-told "Rust Belt" story of a fading industrial past giving way to a postindustrial service and knowledge economy. The company's transfer of production to Mexico followed more than half a million other manufacturing jobs that, over the decades since World War II, had largely moved out of the central city to the suburbs, to the South, and to foreign countries. [2]

But what looks like a paradigmatic tale of the emergence of a new Chicago economy is not so clear and simple. After all; both Boeing and Brach's are manufacturing companies. Globally, manufacturing obviously has not died. Neither has it all migrated. At the time

Brach's was closing, metropolitan Chicago had the largest number of manufacturing jobs of any U.S. metropolis. Despite other shutdowns, it was still the candy capital of the country, and even without its once-famous stockyards by far the national leader in food processing.

Brach's was a local icon, cited by *Industry Week*[3] as one example why Chicago was the premier location for manufacturing in the United States. But, starting in 1986, Brach's was subjected to a wave of corporate buy-outs and spin-offs that imposed shifting and disastrous marketing strategies. Despite many years of both pressure and assistance (including $10 million from the city), community groups and the workers' union could not persuade the changing cast of owners and managers that they could succeed by improving technology and training workers rather than pursuing cheaper workers (and sugar) across the border.[4]

Attracting Boeing was a public relations coup, but it also raised troubling questions. If the subsidy wasn't critical, as a key Boeing executive said, what did the outsized enticement say about Chicago's confidence in its own merits? Might the $56 million have been better spent on improving schools, fixing infrastructure, training workers, or enriching cultural life? Ultimately, Boeing generated far fewer ancillary economic benefits than projected in the rosy, never-released analysis justifying the public subsidies. Another Chicago corporate giant, Arthur Andersen, had prepared the analysis not long before that one-time symbol of Chicago's strength in business services folded in the aftermath of the Enron debacle.[5]

The city's roster of corporate headquarters remained mixed, despite optimistic projections that Boeing heralded the beginning of a new era. Starting in 1998, Chicago had lost a string of headquarters, such as Amoco, Ameritech, and Inland Steel, mostly to corporate takeovers.[6] In January 2004, J. P. Morgan Chase & Co. bought Bank One, depriving Chicago of the headquarters for its largest bank. Also, corporate headquarters were nearly as likely to be in the suburbs as in the central city.[7]

Nevertheless, both suburbs and city could take comfort in the dramatic growth of business services, such as architecture, personnel, and consulting firms, which provided specialized assistance to the corporate managers of far-flung empires.[8] In one of the nation's fastest-growing employment sectors, with moderately above average salaries, metropolitan Chicago was either first or second nationally in the number of business service workers, depending on who's counting (World Business Chicago or the Harvard Cluster Mapping Project), and many of those jobs were in the city.

Also, despite its lingering Rust-Belt image, metropolitan Chicago had the largest concentration of high-tech workers of any urban region in the country (and tied with Washington, D.C. for the greatest number of information technology jobs). The city ranked considerably lower in the proportion of all workers in high-tech and in the ratio of high-tech manufacturing to services (whereas cities like San Jose and Seattle ranked at the top), and it lagged on measures of innovation and rate of growth.[9] But Chicago's history as an electronics and telecommunications center left a legacy of companies, research institutions, and skilled workers that could be a foundation for growth.

The wired world, analysts like Saskia Sassen have argued, does not eliminate the need for personal contacts among the decision-makers, professional advisors, and technical elite of the business world. Consequently, certain key cities-especially in their traditional cores-were likely to be centers of corporate control for the global economy.[10] Yet, just as cities like Chicago were gearing up to compete for global-city status, growing indications hinted that many highly skilled, business professional jobs—computer programmers, software engineers, architects, securities analysts, and others—could be outsourced to India, China, and other lower-wage locations, as were the manufacturing jobs before them.[11]

## Chicago: Regional Capital with a Global Reach

So what, if anything, do Boeing and Brach's reveal about the new Chicago economy? First, Chicago is increasingly globalized, shaped for both good and ill by the force of global markets in goods, services, capital, and labor and by the strategies of global corporations. Workers at factories like Brach's got the short end. Many new business professionals are winners—at least for the moment. However, ultimately, globalization and related factors, such as a declining union movement, contributed to growing economic inequality and insecurity.

Chicago will have to adapt to the constraints and opportunities posed by globalization, but it is not a "global city" that can be reasonably confident of a controlling position like that enjoyed by New York, London, and Tokyo. Despite the growing presence of foreign multinationals, significant trade, and a renewed and varied influx of immigrants, metropolitan Chicago remained, in the early twenty-first century, a strong regional capital with a global reach. Its best opportunity to extend its global importance may depend as much on the health of the wider Great Lakes region as on the steps both the city and metropolitan Chicago take locally to shape their economic future.

It is not simply greater global interconnectedness that is shaping Chicago and other cities or that defines most contemporary conceptions of a "global city."[12] Rather, contemporary globalization embodies a distinctive set of rules for an economic game that are heavily influenced by global corporations. With different rules, such as stronger worker rights around the world, an end to U.S. farm subsidies, the cancellation of most less-developed country debt, or a "Tobin tax"[13] on currency, and financial transactions, Chicago would still be a globalized city, but one with different opportunities.

More broadly, the Boeing and Brach's cases both underscore how market relationships have intensified and penetrated more deeply into social and economic life, a political and economic process driven partly by globalization. For example, deregulated financial markets spurred the market in corporate control, which subjects to the solvent of financial calculations ties that might have bound parts of corporations together or business facilities to a particular location. Cheap transportation and communications provide technical means for a geographic dispersal of factories and offices, but a distinct business strategy, often shaped by short-term profit horizons, is the driving force behind the often frenzied relocation of operations. Just as Brach's can be easily detached from Chicago, other corporate centers of control, like Boeing's head office, increasingly separate themselves from the gritty reality of the enterprises they manage and the cities or nations where they have headquarters. While the corporate centers retain control over dispersed and contingent empires,[14] managers devote much effort to managing risk—such as through the Chicago futures markets—and, above all, to shifting risk to employees, contractors, governments, and the general public.

There are implications for cities like Chicago in these intensified trends. One economic rationale for cities is that they provide agglomeration advantages, such as large labor pools, nearby suppliers, easy transportation, ready customers, and a climate of both cooperation and competition that generates useful information. A variety of networks of businesses develop, including both industrial districts made up of small firms, such as the old printers' row or garment districts in Chicago's Loop outskirts, and those networks fanned around a government institution or a dominant corporation, the most common pattern in Chicago as it industrialized. These relationships often made businesses more efficient, but in the process they created a kind of "stickiness" or reason to stay in place.[15] Even ownership made a difference. A privately held business run by owners who live in the same area, or a worker-owned business, is likely to be less mobile than publicly held nationals, which were disproportionately quick to relocate out of both the city and the country.[16]

In the newly globalized world of intensified market relations, capital becomes ever "slippery."[17] The capitalist ideal of liquidity is exemplified in the global financial markets, but both people and places can suffer from an excess liquidity of investment and employment. Stickiness can yield economic benefits, for example, through stimulating businesses to increase productivity by building on human skills, cooperative community relationships, or technical innovation to cut costs rather than fleeing to lower-wage locations.

\* \* \*

## Challenges to Chicago's Future as a "Global City"

Saskia Sassen, the influential urban sociologist, argues that global cities have a new role as producers of services, such as the work of lawyers and financial specialists, for the demanding task of managing global corporate empires. These services thrive on face-to-face interaction among business and professional people in city centers, which is more effective than communication at a distance by telephone or the Internet.[18]

At first blush, this certainly seems to be happening in Chicago, with its expansion of business services, construction of new Loop office buildings, recycling of older office buildings into downtown condominiums, and the creation of new and more affluent residential neighborhoods near the Loop.

By most accounts, Chicago clearly ranks among the second tier of global cities, in the company of cities such as Hong Kong and Frankfurt. Some economic strategists envision a "global Chicago," with a central city featuring more of both multinational corporate headquarters and related financial, professional, and service firms. But even the relatively flush decade of the 1990s contained some worrisome signals.

First, while Chicago pursues corporate headquarters and their elite business service partners for the city center, corporate headquarters have been shifting to suburbs and "edge cities." Consequently, Sassen argues that "'the center' now has many centers, as the business activities associated with downtown spread into the suburbs."[19] But if "instant cyber-touch" permits this redefinition of the center for corporate headquarters, businesses serving global corporations may also not be a reliable engine for central city employment growth.

Second, a detailed analysis of Chicago's economy during the 1990s raises questions about the quality and quantity of future growth. For example, personnel supply services constitute by far the largest business service category and the category with the largest increase during the 1990s. But this industry includes not only executive recruiters and global giants, such as Manpower, but also proliferating day-labor agencies, like Laborama or Ready Men, which are concentrated in Latino neighborhoods. While about a fifth of temporary workers are professionals, most temp jobs are low-wage, degraded versions of former full-time office and laborer jobs.[20]

Some higher-end corporate service jobs, such as engineering and architectural services, research and testing services, and advertising, grew slowly or even declined during the 1990s. A dramatic decline even occurred in sectors that serve global corporations, such as legal services (down by 25 percent, for a loss of more than. 8,000 jobs) and depository institutions (a 17 percent loss, typically in banks). However, employment doubled at non-depository financial institutions, which include currency exchanges and payday loan offices—unlikely servants to global business.

During the 1990s, security and commodity brokers increased by nearly half, a byproduct of the stock bubble, but the subsequent bust almost certainly reduced those numbers, at least temporarily. Job prospects are at risk as the city's futures, options, and stock exchanges face both rising global competition and a shift from the open outcry system—and its face-to-face interactions—to electronic trading. Overall, employment in the broad category of finance, insurance, and real estate, as a share of total employment, declined after the stock bust—at a rate slightly faster than the national average-in both the city and the metropolitan area.[21]

Third, corporations will likely subcontract more managerial activities, thus generating demand for public relations, data management, and other business services. But, as economist David Gordon argued, for decades, corporations in the United States have had a much higher ratio of managerial to non-managerial workers and greater workplace conflict than that of competitors from countries like Germany, Japan, and Sweden.[22] Those more cooperative economies performed better in terms of investment, productivity growth, inflation, and unemployment. If U.S. corporations maintain high managerial burdens, then workers are more likely to lose jobs or income in a competitive global economy. But if corporations turn more cooperative and efficient, then the need may be reduced for some business services on which Chicago depends.

Fourth, many of the jobs that strategists hope will grow rapidly in the new global Chicago are now being performed at a fraction of the cost by well-educated workers in India, China, Russia, and other newly industrializing or transition countries. Management consultants—a business service growth industry in Chicago—now tell businesses that they must relocate both blue and white-collar work to China and elsewhere if they want to succeed.[23]

## Challenges to the "High Road" Adaptation to Globalization

The new challenge of globalization strikes at the heart of even the more progressive strategies of adaptation to global competitive pressures and capital mobility, such as educating workers to perform higher-skilled, better-paying jobs even as lower-wage workers in developing countries do tasks like sewing clothes or assembling automobiles. But millions of educated workers in both the rich and poor countries are up the same skill ladder, applying downward income pressure even on those jobs that may remain in the United States.

Inspired by the success of Silicon Valley, Chicago strategists have also longingly looked for salvation from manufacturing losses through the development of high-tech industries, as biotechnology, business software, nanotechnology, or advanced manufacturing and materials. But metropolitan Chicago's large pool of science and technology workers is distributed throughout a wide range of both "new" industries, from pharmaceutical companies (such Abbott Laboratories and Baxter Pharmaceuticals) to electronics firms (such as Motorola or Tellabs), and "old" industries, from steel mills to machine tool and fastener makers. Indeed, Chicago ranks quite low in high-tech specialization and just below the national average in the number of patents per employee.[24]

Metropolitan Chicago has also not been especially hospitable to new technology businesses. Very little venture capital is available. The region's universities and research centers have, until recently, done little to link research to local business development.[25] Also, the required critical mass of workers has rarely existed in any particular emerging high-tech industry to create an environment of intellectual exchange, cooperation, public institutional support, and competition that can stimulate the growth of new companies in a geographic region. The symbol of the region's high-tech slipups is Marc Andreessen, who developed the computer code for an Internet browser as a student at the University of Illinois but had to go to California to find venture capital to launch his business, Netscape. Also, the local giant, Motorola, has faltered, losing an early lead in the cell phone business. In 2003, it closed its five-year-old, $100 million factory in the collar county town of Harvard, where 5,000 workers once were making and distributing cell phones. Now that building may become an indoor water park, an unwelcome symbol for the region's high-tech hopes.[26]

Many urban economic development analysts argue that innovation is nurtured by the clustering of businesses in a particular industry, whether around a dominant firm or as a district of small businesses. Chicago has a large number of highly concentrated clusters of related businesses, making goods for trade rather than for local consumption, in which the metropolitan area's share of national employment is greater than its share of the national work force. But Chicago is not known for one or two hallmark industries, such as computers and aerospace in Seattle, finance in New York, or entertainment in Las Vegas. Local leaders are proud that Chicago is, according to one study, the most diverse urban economy in the nation. While diversity helped Chicago rebound from the 1980s manufacturing collapse, it is no guarantor of future success. The varied cities following Chicago in the diversity ranking are questionable models: Little Rock, Baltimore, Salt Lake City, and Buffalo.[27]

Indeed, in most of Chicago's strongest industrial clusters, the metropolitan area was losing share throughout the 1990s, not an indication of growing strength. According to the Cluster Mapping Project of Harvard University's Institute for Strategy and Competitiveness,[28] Chicago gained national share among its most concentrated clusters only in the processed food industry and the education and knowledge cluster. Chicago remained the leading metropolitan area for employment in metal manufacturing, food, plastics, communications equipment, production technology, lighting and electrical equipment, heavy machinery, and medical devices. It also had a very high relative concentration in other clusters: transportation and logistics (second among all metropolitan areas), publishing and printing (second), distribution services (third), chemical products (second), business services (second), and financial services (third). Yet, at the same time, it was losing national share in all those clusters, suggesting that they were not serving as the needed seedbeds of innovation and superior economic growth.

The focus on diversity leaves unanswered a big question: What will be the engines of both job and income growth for the Chicago region? The strongest sectors have been lagging behind national averages in employment growth. Many of the biggest corporate pillars-United Airlines, McDonald's, Allstate, Sears, Motorola, and even the new star, Boeing-are experiencing hard times for varied reasons. Outside takeovers continue to undermine the city's position as a corporate decision center. Chicago's big-business exhibition and convention business faces Sun belt competition (Orlando and Las Vegas), economic doldrums, and *post-9/11* travel jitters. Even a rapidly growing local film industry has been undercut by the industry's shift to foreign locales: Toronto often serves as the backdrop for television shows or movies supposedly set in Chicago, according to a *New York Times* report.[29]

At the start of the new century, neither high-tech nor financial industries are poised to be the new drivers of a growing economy. Despite efforts to retain manufacturing and upgrade workforce skills and technology, manufacturing is unlikely to yield job growth. Business services, perhaps even education, have promise but also vulnerabilities. In all those sectors, a base exists that could be developed, but it seems likely that, in 2020, Chicago's leaders will still be touting diversity rather than a new job-generating champion.

# Inequality: The Economic and Social Threat

The economic challenge for the city is not simply to create jobs, but to generate adequate income from good jobs. In the competition to attract businesses, pressure always exists to sell a city as offering cheap labor, but the prospect of earning low incomes does not attract talented people. If workers earn more, they can invest in their homes, buy goods and services for local consumption, and strengthen their communities, making the city even more attractive. An economically thriving population can afford to pay for the schools and infrastructure that make the city more livable and businesses more productive. But raising average incomes is not enough. The metropolitan area will be more likely to thrive if there is greater economic equality among individuals and among communities. Urban regions with higher economic inequality typically grow more slowly, hurting both central-city and suburban residents.[30]

Inequality has grown both among different geographical communities within the metropolitan region and among households. From 1989 to 1999, an increase occurred in the percentage of families in the metropolitan area in the lowest quintile of national income and in the highest quintile, but a decrease occurred in the broad middle-income quintiles.[31] By 2000, household income was more unequal in metropolitan Chicago than in the nation as a whole. Among the central cities of the 40 largest metropolitan areas, the city of Chicago ranked fifteenth in income inequality in 1999.[32]

But metropolitan Chicago scored even worse in the contrast between poverty levels in the city and its suburbs. With its central-city poverty rate 3.5 times the poverty rate in the suburbs, metropolitan Chicago was the eighth most unequal urban region in terms of poverty level.[33] The suburbs are richer than the city largely because many suburbanites work at well-paid jobs in the city, even though suburban corporate headquarters also increasingly provide high-paid jobs.[34] Suburban workers prosper disproportionately from the higher wages in the city, but they pay local taxes to support communities that escape much of the costs of social inequality.

Sassen argues that increasing inequality is "built into the new growth sectors" of global cities.[35] That is partly because of the intrinsic effects of competition in the global labor market, but it also reflects the lack of unionization in many growth sectors. Although Chicago has long been a union stronghold, unions represented only 19 percent of metropolitan area workers in 2002, more than the 13 percent nationally, but a decline from the 22 percent of workers in unions during the mid 1980s. Yet, unions representing janitors and hotel workers have recently won significant gains for these workers, suggesting that current levels of inequality are not intrinsic to the new economy.

Just as inequality exists among workers and families, the disparities among geographic communities, including individual suburbs and city neighborhoods, are deepened by the exodus of manufacturing from the central city and by suburban sprawl. Because of persistent discrimination and the historically high degree of racial segregation in Chicago, the mismatch between the skills of black inner-city residents and service and manufacturing jobs in the suburbs is particularly severe.[36] Sprawl also has created huge public and private external costs-such as traffic congestion and environmental destruction-and shifted public spending away from modernizing inner suburb and city infrastructure. On balance, the social costs of sprawl have roughly equaled the private benefits. Sprawl thus transfers income from low—and middle-income workers to upper-income business owners, especially if one takes into account the state's highly regressive taxes.[37] Suburban growth thus made it harder, even if the good will existed, to reduce racially based economic inequalities and to resolve the racial contradiction in post-war Chicago urban development.

Although businesses that sell goods and services outside the region typically have a disproportionate effect on the region by stimulating the growth of related jobs, roughly two-thirds of all jobs provide goods and services for local consumption.[38] These local businesses, from grocery and hardware stores to restaurants and theaters, affect both the economic vitality and livability of the diverse micro-economies within the broader urban region, from depressed and depopulated communities like Lawndale on the city's West Side to wealthy Kenilworth in the north suburbs.

Although the influx of new immigrants to Chicago has strengthened many neighborhood economies, the central city overall is undersupplied with retail stores. Many businesses fled—just as banks deprived the same neighborhoods of credit—because they did not want to serve black neighborhoods. By the late 1990s, the federal government estimated that Chicago had a "retail gap" of $9.9 billion, second only to New York. But, because land is scarce and the "big box" store has emerged as the retail model, initiatives by retailers to replicate their suburban-style stores often conflict with the need to preserve manufacturing jobs. After concluding that the city gained more economically from manufacturing than from retail or residential development, Mayor Harold Washington protected several key manufacturing districts from real estate speculation.[39] Also, anti-union discount retailers, such as Wal-Mart, put downward pressure on wages and benefits and are likely to lead to a net loss of jobs.[40] In 2004, community and labor critics of Wal-Mart proposed that future "big box" retailers meet certain minimum standards on wages, hiring, and other policies.

## Creating an Economically Coherent Region

Beyond such problems as the mismatch between job location and willing workers or the inequities of tax revenue among different jurisdictions, this dispersal of jobs through a large number of competing municipalities unravels the metropolitan areas economic coherence. As major firms or factories moved out, small businesses whose fates had once been linked to them failed, followed, or adapted to a more national market. A few local businesses still benefit from their proximity to one of the remaining giants, and some local suppliers to big corporations such as McDonald's have expanded their national or global operations.[41] Ford is also creating a new supplier park close to it's South-Side assembly plant.

Businesses now rely on ties within the Midwest or Great Lakes region much in the way that they once looked to links within the city or metropolitan region. During the 1990s, the average firm in the Chicago region relied much more on external customers and suppliers than in previous decades. But, despite the growing importance of international trade, especially with Canada and Mexico, Illinois companies' trade with other states is roughly four to five times larger than trade with other countries.[42]

Chicago could thus gain greatly from a strategy to develop the region: strengthening the manufacturing base, providing business services, and developing new high-tech firms that complement the region's needs. This refocusing of the region's economic ambitions does imply two strategic changes.

First, the political will would be necessary for the entire region to stop its low-road tragedy of attempting to compete in the world—and often among the states and cities of the region—by offering cheap labor, lower taxes, and direct public subsidies. Instead, a commitment to a high-road regional strategy is necessary, one that emphasizes research, education, skilled workers, high wages, innovation, and productivity.[43] Trying to pursue both is impossible. The low road continually undermines the potential for the high road.

For the region to be more economically integrated, it needs a dramatic increase in infrastructure spending designed to increase regional efficiency, such as upgrading existing streets, expanding public transportation, and making Chicago the hub of a high-speed rail network. Despite substantial infrastructure investment in Chicago during the 1990s, key areas were neglected (such as upgrading the city's intermodal freight capacity), and public investment was often misguided (especially tax increment financing for Loop businesses).[44]

Before Chicago can hope to implement a vision of an integrated Midwestern region, it must first confront the political and economic conflicts within the metropolis itself. Part of the business elite, as well as many neighborhood groups and labor unions, now recognize the need for a regional approach that includes control of sprawl, balanced growth, improved energy and transportation efficiency, a strengthened manufacturing sector, and enhanced education and training.

Ultimately, regionalism will only work effectively if strategies are also implemented to share tax revenues throughout the region, starting with state efforts to equalize funding for public schools, but including more regional tax sharing as well. Growing disparity among local governments' capacity to raise revenues feeds on itself in a spiral of growing inequality. From 1980 to 1993, 26 suburbs (mainly black and poor to start with) lost tax base by as much as 36 percent, but the tax base increased by more than 48 percent in 77 suburbs (mainly white and affluent).[45]

Regionalism—whether it spans metropolitan Chicago or the Midwest—will be most successful if leaders can unite a divided metropolis around a vision of self-consciously creating good jobs and communities for all, rather than relying on the trickle-down effects from an increasingly unequal region. Chicago was initially "the city of the [nineteenth] century"[46] partly because it embodied a vision of both the city and its industries opening up the Great West. It was driven with class conflict, but it had a vitality that was captured in the classic odes to Chicago by Carl Sandburg, who was a keen socialist critic of the city. Chicago in this era was rough-edged, but it was also coherent.

## The Future of Chicago in a Global Economy

In the decades after World War II, Chicago lost much of that vitality, as people and jobs, especially in manufacturing industries, moved to suburbs not integrated within one metropolitan area, and as racial discrimination divided the central city and fed the suburban exodus. As businesses moved out or simply folded, the metropolitan region became less politically and economically coherent as well. Inequalities grew, among individuals and communities, and these inequalities undercut the economy of the entire region.

The form that globalization took exacerbated the tensions within the urban region, putting severe pressure on traded-goods manufacturers, but opening new opportunities for corporations to move production to meet short-term performance goals. Globalization reinforced the trend toward the dominance of financial interests and the transformation of corporate power into remote strategic centers distanced from routines of production, whether of candies or airplanes, and from the communities in which they operated.

These tendencies towards a less coherent and less egalitarian metropolis deepened even during the 1990s, but after a horrendous previous decade of manufacturing job losses and economic hardship, there was a tenuous recovery of both economic and population growth. Surviving manufacturers had reorganized and reinvested to survive, new business service firms were expanding in the central city, and a renaissance occurred around the Loop and even in some outlying neighborhoods. New efforts were made to exploit Chicago's historic advantages and economic legacy, to enrich the amenities of community and cultural life, and to give new focus to the neglected needs of deprived communities and of the region.

A growing awareness has arisen of Chicago's economic role in the wider world. With the forces of globalization nibbling away at highly skilled white-collar jobs, as well as both skilled and unskilled blue-collar jobs, it is becoming difficult to make increasingly slippery jobs stick in the city or metropolitan area. Local government can foster supportive cultures among businesses in common industries and professions, guarantee adequate infrastructure, and improve education and both basic and advanced job skills, but it needs more progressively generated revenue from regional, state, and federal governments. Local government can also encourage management cooperation with workers and an organized voice for workers themselves, but Chicago's economy could benefit as well from closer cooperation with universities and research centers and from a greater variety of investment and credit, including both more venture capital and more neighborhood capital (such as lending by community-oriented development banks).

If Chicago is to become a global city, it is likely to do so by first becoming an integrated metropolis that serves as the capital of a more integrated Midwestern region. Globalization is full of contradictions for Chicago, destroying and creating opportunities, generating inequalities, and encouraging a less parochial outlook while ungluing local ties that bind. Chicago's hold on the business service firms that cater to the needs of global corporations, as well as the headquarters of many of those corporations, will depend on the health of the Midwest region and the quality of life in the metropolitan area. In the end, local government can have little effect, even with its most generous subsidies and tax breaks, on the shifting winds of globalization and markets for corporate control. It may achieve most on the skills of its citizens and of the quality of life in the region.[47]

Far from being a Rust Belt relic, high-tech incubator, or global city, the new Chicago economy is precariously balanced, retaining a diminished but transformed legacy of industrial greatness and expanding its potential as a center of high-skilled services. Chicago is the globally important capital of a region larger than nearly all other national economies, yet it lacks metropolitan political and economic coherence. It also lacks the commitment to renewal that would create a more integrated, egalitarian region. Those shortcomings are as much a threat to the region's economic future as are the shifting winds of national politics or economic globalization.

## Notes

1. Ginsburg, Robert, Xiaochang Jin, and Sheila McCann. E.J. Brach: A Misadventure in Candyland. Chicago: Midwest Center for Labor Research, 1994.
2. Verespej, Michael A. "The Atlas of U.S. Manufacturing." Industry Week. April 5, 1999.
3. Ginsburg, Robert, Xiaochang Jin, and Sheila McCann. E.J. Brach: A Misadventure in Candyland. Chicago: Midwest Center for Labor Research, 1994; Langly, Alison. "Swiss Maker of Chocolate Will Acquire Brach's Candy." New York Times. September 2, 2003.
4. McCourt, Jeff and Greg LeRoy with Phillip Mattera. "A Better Deal for Illinois: Improving Economic Development Policy." Washington: Good Jobs First, 2003.
5. Looking only at the biggest companies, Chicago's share of corporate headquarters dropped by 40 percent over two decades. But, by other measures, the metropolitan region was second to New York and growing (counting corporations with 2,500 or more employees) or in fourth place and declining (counting corporations with more than SOD employees) (Klier and Testa 2001; Strahler 2003).
6. "Special Report: Top 100 Companies." Chicago Tribune. May 18, 2003; Economic Focus. World Business Chicago: November, 2002.
7. An increase of 42.7 percent occurred in professional and business services employment (NAICS code 54) in metropolitan Chicago from 1990 to 2000, according to U.S. Census Bureau figures compiled by Glen D. Marker, Director of Research, World Business Chicago.
8. Markusen, Ann, Karen Chapple, Greg Schrock, Daisky Yamamoto, and Pingkang Yu. "High-Tech and I-Tech: How Metros Rank and Specialize." Minneapolis, MN: The Hubert Humphrey Institute of Public Affairs, 2001.
9. Sassen, Saskia. "A Global City." In Global Chicago, C. Madigan , ed. Urbana: University of Illinois Press, 2004.
10. Engardio, Peter, Aaron Bernstein, and Manjeet Kripalani. "Is Your Job Next?" Business Week. February 3, 2003.

11. Sassen, Saskia. "A Global City." In Global Chicago, C. Madigan , ed. Urbana: University of Illinois Press, 2004.

12. Named after economist James Tobin, who first proposed it, a very small tax on international financial transactions could dampen speculation and some of its destabilizing effects (ul Haq, Kaul, and Grunberg 1996).

13. Harrison, Bennet. Lean & Mean: Why Large Corporations Will Continue to Dominate the Global Economy. New York, NY: The Guilford Press, 1994.

14. Markusen, Ann. "Sticky Places in Slippery Space: A Typology of Industrial Districts." Economic Geography 72:294-314. 1996.

15. Squires, Gregory, Larry Bennett, Kathleen McCourt and Philip Nyden. Chicago: Race, Class and the Response to Urban Decline. Philadelphia: Temple University Press, 1987.

16. Markusen, Ann. "Sticky Places in Slippery Space: A Typology of Industrial Districts." Economic Geography 72:294-314. 1996.

17. Sassen, Saskia. "A Global City." In Global Chicago, C. Madigan , ed. Urbana: University of Illinois Press, 2004.

18. Ibid.

19. Peck, Jaime and Nik Theodore. "Contingent Chicago: Restructuring the Spaces of Temporary Labor." International Journal of Urban and Regional Research, 25 (3):471-96. 2001.

20. Economic Report of the President. Washington, D.C.: U.S. Government Printing Office, 2004; SOCDS: State of the Cities Data System. Http://socds.huduser.org.

21. Gordon, David. Fat and Mean: The Corporate Squeeze of Working Americans and the Myth of Managerial "Downsizing." New York, NY: The Free Press, 1996.

22. Engardio, Peter, Aaron Bernstein, and Manjeet Kripilani. "Is Your Job Next?" Business Week. February 3, 2003; Goodman, Peter. "White Collar Work a Booming U.S. Export." Washington Post. April 2, 2003; Roberts, Dan and Edward Luce. "As Service Industries Go Global More White Collar Jobs Follow." Financial Times. August 19, 2003; Uchitelle, Louis. "A Statistic That's Missing: Jobs That Moved Overseas." New York Times. October 5, 2003.

23. Markusen, Ann, Karen Chapple, Greg Schrock, Daisky Yamamoto, and Pingkang Yu. "High-Tech and I-Tech: How Metros Rank and Specialize." Minneapolis, MN: The Hubert Humphrey Institute of Public Affairs, 2001; Porter, Michael E. n.d. Cluster Mapping Project. Harvard Business School, Institute for Strategy and Competitiveness. Http://data.isc.hbs.edu/isc.

24. Johnson, Elmer W. Chicago Metropolis 2020: The Chicago Plan for the Twenty-first Century. Chicago: University of Chicago Press, 2001.

25. Tita, Bob. "A White Elephant Tramples Harvard." Crain's Chicago Business. May 5, 2003; Tita, Bob. "Trying to Make a Splash with Harvard Water Park." Crain's Chicago Business. July 21, 2003.

26. Moody's Investor Services. "CMBS: A New Economic Diversity Model for a New Economy. June 9, 2003.

27. Porter, Michael E. n.d. Cluster Mapping Project. Harvard Business School, Institute for Strategy and Competitiveness. Http://data.isc.hbs.edu/isc.

28. Bernstein, David. "Films Flee the Loop, but Chicago Fights Back." New York Times. April 9, 2003.

29. Dreier, Peter, John Mollenkopf, and Todd Swanstrom. Place Matters: Metropolitics for the Twenty-first Century. Lawrence, Kansas: University of Kansas Press, 2001; Moberg, David. "Separate and Unequal." The Neighborhood Works. August/September 2001.

30. SOCDS: State of the Cities Data System. Http://socds.huduser.org.

31. Rodgers, Angie and Ed Lazere. "Income Inequality in the District of Columbia is Wider than in Any Major U.S. City." Washington, D.C.: D.C. Fiscal Policy Institute, 2004. www.cbpp.org.

32. Ibid.

33. Dreier, Peter, John Mollenkopf, and Todd Swanstrom. Place Matters: Metropolitics for the Twenty-first Century. Lawrence, Kansas: University of Kansas Press, 2001.

34. Sassen, Saskia. "A Global City." In Global Chicago, C. Madigan , ed. Urbana: University of Illinois Press, 2004.

35. Wilson, William Julius. The Truly Disadvantaged: The Inner-City, The Underclass and Public Policy. Chicago: University of Chicago Press, 1987.

36. Persky, Joseph J. and Wim Weivel. "Introduction." In Suburban Sprawl, W. Wievel and J.J. Persky eds. Armonk, NY: M.E. Sharp; Chicago Case Study Working Group of the Great Cities Institute. Metropolitan Decentralization in Chicago. Chicago: Great Cities Institute, University of Illinois at Chicago. 2001; Gardner, Matthew, Robert G. Lynch, Richard Sims, Ben Schweigert, and Amy Meek. "Balancing Act: Tax Reform Options for Illinois." Washington: Institute on Taxation and Economic Policy, February 2002.

37. Porter, Michael E. n.d. Cluster Mapping Project. Harvard Business School, Institute for Strategy and Competitiveness. Http://data.isc.hbs.edu/isc.

38. Clavel, Pierrre and Wim Wiewel, eds. Harold Washington and the Neighborhoods: Progressive City Government in Chicago 1983–1987. New Brunswick, NJ: Rutgers University Press, 1991.

39. Mehta, Chirag, Ron Baiman and Joe Persky. "The Economic Impact of Wal-Mart: An Assessment of the Wal-Mart Store Proposed for Chicago's West Side." Chicago: University of Illinois at Chicago, Center for Urban Economic Development, March 2004.

40. Gupta, Sapna. "The Global Corporation: McDonald's, A Case Study." In Global Chicago, C. Madigan, ed. Urbana: University of Illinois Press, 2004.

41. Hewings, Geoffrey J.C. n.d. "Infrastructure and Economic Development: Perspectives for the Chicago and Midwest Economies." 2004. www.chicagofed.org/newsandevents/conferences/ midwest_infrastructure/documents/hewings_infrastructure.ppt.

42. Swinney, Dan. "Building the Bridge to the High Road." Chicago: Center for Labor and Community Research. 1998.

43. PRAGmatics (Chicago). "Looking Into Tax Increment Financing." Summer 2002.

44. Chicago Case Study Working Group of the Great Cities Institute. Metropolitan Decentralization in Chicago. Chicago: Great Cities Institute, University of Illinois at Chicago. 2001.

45. Miller, Donald L. City of the Century: The Epic of Chicago and the Making of America. New York: Simon and Shuster, 1997.

46. Markusen, Ann. "Sticky Places in Slippery Space: A Typology of Industrial Districts." Economic Geography 72:294-314. 1996.

# Building Human Capital

## The Chicago Council on Global Affairs

*Chicago can grow its own educated workforce through educating students here or by attracting them to the metropolitan region with good jobs, amenities and a positive environment. It must be a top priority to improve our educational system, especially our public schools and community colleges. But we also need pro-business tax and regulatory policies, a top-flight communications infrastructure, public transit reforms, a transparent bureaucracy, and lifelong education. In the global era, public services—safety, schools, clean air—are keys to economic development and economic vitality.*

Cities are the places where people come together to trade goods, money, and ideas. This has been true for millennia. Cities grew as the arena in which artisans from tinsmiths to hatmakers gathered to compete and cooperate. With the Industrial Revolution, workers came from surrounding farms and from far countries to work together in factories and mills. Cities exist to reduce the distance between people who want to do commerce with each other.

Cities are people, no more and no less. The most successful cities are those that are richest in people—in skilled, smart, educated, diverse, innovative, hard-working, productive people. A city may have every other attribute—a deep harbor or splendid setting or glorious climate. But unless it also embraces a superlative workforce at all levels, it cannot call itself successful.

This has been true throughout history. It is ever more true today, in the global era. A global city is powered not by brawn, but by the brainpower of skilled and educated people who come together to trade ideas, to bounce innovations off each other, to be stimulated by the creativity of others. But a global city is not just the place that ferments this creativity. It also is the place with the workforce to take this creativity and turn it into products, exports, and services.

---

### Grads and Fads

Robert Weissbourd of RW Ventures was asked by the Study Group to research the main attributes of global economies. He found that skilled and educated workers drive the new economy. Some scholars say amenities—recreation, culture, restaurants—draw these workers to a city. But Weissbourd says the big draw is professional opportunity—good jobs in these workers' specialties and companies that provide these jobs.

"People want to go to places where there are other people like them," Weissbourd said, "so what you're looking to do is build a concentration of knowledge functions." This requires education, including lifelong learning, and a knowledge infrastructure, including a fiber-optic "backbone for businesses."

"What matters most," he said, "is having knowledge jobs. After that, amenities matter. If you have one economic dollar to spend, spend it on the economy. If you have ten economic dollars, then you can invest in culture."

---

Economists call all this "human capital." As the Harvard urban economist Edward Glaeser told our Study Group, "The comparative advantage of cities is determined by how smart, how trained, how innovative, how entrepreneurial the people are in that city. Very much of the success of Chicago as a global city depends on its attracting skilled people, keeping them and letting them innovate, letting them lead the city forward."

In this competition, the returns are mixed. The region is doing fine, but the city itself seems more successful in attracting people than keeping them.

The city of Chicago is an unrivalled magnet for young, creative people. Among all American cities, Chicago ranks first in the concentration of young people aged twenty-five to thirty-four living within three miles of downtown. For those with college degrees, it ranks second only to New York. In the 1990s nearly 100,000 more white non-Hispanics in their twenties moved into the city than moved out. Chicago, indisputably, is a young person's town, the sort of city with the buzz and pop that draw the young and the restless.

And then it stops. From 2000 to 2006 the city lost a net 62,700 people. Suburban Cook County lost another 27,000. A big part of the loss was white non-Hispanics over thirty years old. Clearly, those youngsters who came to Chicago in their twenties had decided to move to the suburbs when it came time to get married, settle down, and raise their kids. Beyond Cook County, the rest of the Chicago region grew by 501,000 between 2000 and 2006. This means sprawl. One of the twenty-five fastest-growing cities in the nation (and the only one not in the South or the West) is Joliet, which lies directly in the path of Chicago's urban

**Figure 1. Relative Preference for Close-In Neighborhoods.**

| Share of 25-to-34-year-old population within three miles of urban center divided by share of total population within three miles of urban center | | |
|---|---|---|
| **Rank/Metropolitan Area** | **Year** | |
| **Most Centralized** | **1990** | **2000** |
| 1. Chicago-Gary-Kenosha, IL-IN-WI CMSA | 1.39 | 1.79 |
| 2. Seattle-Tacoma-Bremerton, WA CMSA | 1.27 | 1.73 |
| 3. San Franciso-Oakland-San Jose, CA CMSA | 1.26 | 1.69 |
| 4. New York-Northern New Jersey-Long Island, NY-NJ | 1.30 | 1.62 |
| 5. Boston-Worcester-Lawrence, MA-NH-ME-CT CMSA | 1.28 | 1.61 |

Source: CEOs for Cities, The Young and the REstless in a Knowledge Economy, Joseph Cortright, December 2005

sprawl. It means more pressure on roads and rail from commuters. It means continued flight from Chicago's schools and high-cost housing. It also means lost income. The people who moved out of Cook County into its six immediate neighbors earn some $1.2 billion more per year than persons moving in.

If Chicago is to remain a global city and thrive in the global economy, it must stem this tide. It must keep the brains and skills that are the raw material of the global era in the city.

A city like Chicago can get this raw material, this human capital, in two ways. It can create it itself, through its educational system, from early childhood education through public

**Figure 2. Net Migration, 1990 to 2000, City of Chicago (by age).**

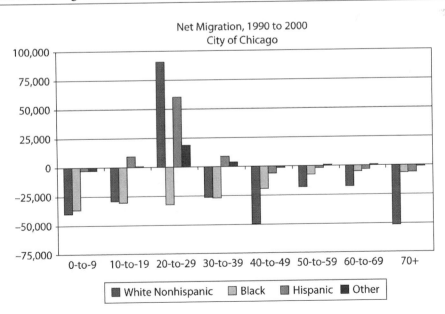

schools to colleges and on to the mightiest research universities. Or it can draw it from outside by becoming the kind of city where the best and the brightest want to work and live. A successful city does both. And, having done so, it needs to keep this human talent with the irresistible lure of a rich quality of life and stimulating work.

Brains, like hearts, go where they are wanted. No challenge is greater to Chicago's future success. The keys to creating, attracting, and keeping human capital are education, quality of life, good jobs, and diversity.

## Education

Mayor Daley has made the improvement of public education in Chicago his leading priority. In a recent speech he said: "I believe this city is in a global economy. It can compete only if we give every child an opportunity. We should have the best educational system in the country if we are going to compete in the global economy. This—the changing of the public school system—is the most challenging problem I have ever faced."

The mayor listed several goals that have also been singled out by educational experts to improve the schools. These include longer school days, longer school years, more teaching of foreign languages, better education in science and mathematics, better training for jobs and careers, better recruitment and training of teachers, more after-school and summer programs. Especially, he said, every child should have access to preschool learning and full-day kindergartens.

The dropout rate in Chicago city high schools, between 30 and 40 percent, is too high. Test scores in too many schools remain too low. Too few of Chicago's public school students, about 10 percent, eventually graduate from a four-year college. These statistics justify the mayor's alarm.

But behind this grim facade are signs of a regeneration of a public school system that was once derided as the nation's worst. One sign of hope is the very fact that the city has put its schools at the top of its agenda—a crisis that has festered for decades now has the city's attention. Another sign is a variety of successful programs and experiments going on across the city. The challenge may be less to invent new systems than to take the programs that are working and apply them across the system.

A few statistics stand out:

- Student participation in preschool has increased from 25,000 in 2002 to 32,000 in 2007.
- In 2001 only 38 percent of students met or exceeded the state test standard. By 2007 this was up to 64 percent. More than 71 percent of eighth graders passed the math portion, up from 64.7 percent in 2006. Nearly 78 percent passed the reading portion, up from 72 percent the previous year.

- In elementary schools, students in 183 schools were performing at only 20 percent of the national average in 1992. By 2005 that rate had reached 49 percent. Of these schools, 88 percent were in low-income neighborhoods.
- The number of students taking Advanced Placement examinations rose from 7,598 in 2002 to 12,652 in 2006.
- The Chicago Public Schools (CPS) system is recruiting teachers more vigorously, and more teachers want to teach in the CPS. In 2001 only 4,000 teachers applied for jobs, or about two applicants for each job. In 2006-07 there were 20,000 applicants, or ten for each position.
- The Advancement Via Individual Determination (AVID) program, designed to provide students with high-standard, college-preparatory strategies, has been implemented in forty high schools.
- The teacher vacancy rate dropped by 40 percent over the past two years. Since 2001 the number of National Board Certified Teachers in the CPS system rose from fewer than one hundred to 645.
- Nearly 75 percent of all kindergarten students are enrolled in full-day programs, up from 60 percent five years earlier.

Many experts and committed volunteers are working to make schools better. In the Consortium on Chicago School Research, the city has one of the best research teams in the country, providing schools with information about what works and what does not. A variety of programs, some in charter schools and some in regular schools, are bringing best practices—good principals, strong professional development, and parental involvement—to many schools. The Young Women's Leadership Academy, the Academy of Urban School Leadership, Fresh Start Schools, and Strategic Learning Initiatives (SLI) are all putting best practices in place in schools and the results show. In Little Village, five schools working with Strategic Learning Initiatives showed a sharp improvement in ISAT scores over a two-year period, compared with 220 Chicago public schools with similar family incomes. In the Little Village schools, students showed a 21-percent improvement in mathematics and a 12.5-percent improvement in reading, compared to improvements of 10 and 6 percent, respectively, in a comparison group of 220 Chicago public schools with similar family incomes. SLI recorded similar results in three schools in Pilsen and even more dramatic improvement in the Willa Cather School on the west side.

All are steps in the right direction. But this process needs to be accelerated and implemented across the system. Chicago students still spend relatively few hours in class—only 1,001 hours per year, compared with the national average of 1,161 hours and the 1,271 hours required by the New York City schools.

The same study that showed a sharp gain in reading achievement in 183 of Chicago's elementary schools also showed a lower gain—from 18 percent of the national average to only 29 percent—in an almost equal number of other schools with an equal number of students over the same period. Of these 183 schools, 94 percent were in low-income neighborhoods. In other words, improvement is real, but it is reaching only about half the city's elementary school students.

A global city needs people who speak multiple languages. The city is stressing the teaching of Mandarin in schools. The program, now nearly a decade old, embraces 6,000 students and should be expanded. But Chicago can do more to take advantage of the children of immigrants who already speak a second language at home but need formal instruction in grammar and writing before they can become fully proficient in their native language.

In addition, the state of Illinois is short-changing its students. The state provides only 37 percent of school funding, making Illinois forty-ninth out of fifty states. The foundation level per pupil is $5,334, which is $1,071 less than the level recommended by a state commission and less than half the $11,900 provided for the New York City schools.

## Recommendation:

Improving Chicago's public schools is an urgent priority, both to prepare all Chicago students to compete in the global economy and to persuade educated, middle-class parents to live in the city. Many dedicated Chicagoans—not only the region's mayors and educational experts, but teachers and administrators—are working hard and effectively on aspects of this problem. Rather than second-guess or duplicate their work, this report applauds their efforts and urges the city to maintain this sense of urgency. In particular, successful pilot programs need to be expanded to the entire system. The work needs the focused support of all citizens, including the business community.

Early childhood education in particular has been shown to confer long-term benefits and must be available to all children. Several well-designed and controlled program evaluations have produced estimates that every dollar spent on early childhood education returns $7 to $17 to the economy later on, a clear benefit to society.

The City Colleges of Chicago present a particular problem and a particular opportunity. These are seven separate colleges mandated to provide affordable education to Chicagoans who, for the most part, cannot afford the higher costs at other schools or who have family or job responsibilities that make other options impractical. The City Colleges have several purposes—vocational training, remedial education, adult and continuing education, developmental education (including English as a Second Language), and the preparation of students to transfer to full four-year colleges. Data showing how well the City Colleges of Chicago are fulfilling these functions are scant.

Enrollment in the City Colleges has dropped by one-third in the last decade, from nearly 180,000 students in 1998 to less than 115,000 in 2006. The majority of students attend

**Figure 3. Chicago Community Colleges Enrollment: Enrollment Trends.**

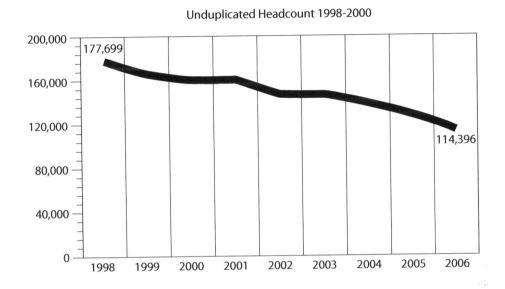

Unduplicated Headcount 1998-2000

**Figure 4. Chicago Community Colleges Enrollment: Enrollment by Mission.**

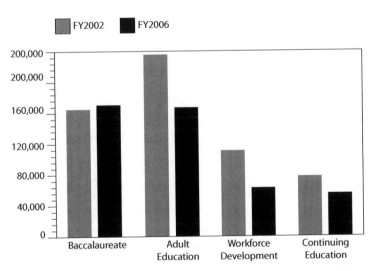

Source: CCC Office of Research and Evaluation, Enrollment Trend by Program Cluster, FY 2002—2006;
Unduplicated Enrollment Trend FY 1998–2001

part-time: Few have the freedom from family or job responsibilities to be full-time students. Despite this plunging enrollment, the colleges' operating revenue has risen by 26 percent since 2003 and continues to rise slightly.

Graduation statistics are the most obvious measure of success, but they can be elusive or even misleading. For instance, in 2006 a total of 1,120 of the 42,840 students enrolled in baccalaureate transfer programs received associate's degrees. This represents only about three percent of the full-time-equivalent enrollment. But not all students intend to earn degrees. The experience of other community college systems shows that students can improve their economic status significantly by completing only a handful of courses or gaining a certificate rather than going for a degree.

What is clear, though, is that the city has not focused on this City College system in any meaningful way as a gateway to good jobs—including entry-level jobs with a future—for its students. The opportunity is great. As one expert put it, "If the city has been successful so far without the colleges being a significant player, imagine what we could do if the colleges were firing on all cylinders."

Why is this important? First, the City Colleges should be the institution educating the workforce of a global Chicago, the human capital that turns ideas into products, exports, and services. A study by Northern Illinois University showed that a minority of jobs but a majority of good jobs will go to workers with an associate's degree or higher. Most future jobs, it said, will require only on-the-job training, but these same jobs will pay $35,000 per year or less. Of the good jobs, paying $40,000 to $80,000, no less than 71 percent will require an associate's degree or higher. City Colleges, in other words, are the gateway to the middle

---

### A Demand for a Middle Class

Globalization offers opportunity for Chicago's middle class, but only through workforce skills development. As trade rises, employment opportunities for moving goods also rise. But already, metro Chicago has nowhere near enough commercial truck drivers to meet demand. Freight railroads offer tens of thousands of jobs. Chicagoland is North America's distribution capital, with explosive growth in warehouse construction, plus needs for forklift operators, logistics personnel, supply chain workers, intermodal crane operators—solid, middle-class jobs all.

Our community colleges are the key to opportunity for underskilled people. The City Colleges of Chicago offer many programs, but the problem is one of scale. The system is not producing enough skilled workers. The same goes for other areas—health care, culinary arts, hospitality, advanced manufacturing. No City College program meets market demand. The possible result: Chicago cannot sustain economic growth and Chicagoans with third-world skills will be left behind.

Will we capture or fumble this opportunity of globalization?

---

class.

But beyond this middle-class focus, the City Colleges play a critical role as the largest provider of workforce development programs, or pathways to employment for Chicagoans wanting to earn a living wage. These programs—workforce development, certificate programs, and remediation—are important steps toward this goal. This stress on workforce development and certificate programs cannot be overstated. First-level jobs, even those paying $35,000 or less, can put people on a career path that leads later to more education and income.

The global economy is producing extremely well-paying jobs at the top and, as the Northern Illinois study showed, a large number of poorly paying jobs at the bottom. Chicago has plenty of both because it has plenty of people willing and qualified to take them. This economy also promises to create tens of thousands of solid jobs in the middle. Nursing is an example. There is great demand for nurses and other health-care workers, but City Colleges programs fall far short of meeting demand across the full spectrum of healthcare jobs. These jobs will be in Chicago only if there are trained and skilled people able to fill them. Some of these people will be trained by more expensive private schools like DeVry Institute. But employers everywhere look to community colleges to educate these workers. If they can't find them here, they will go to other communities or other states.

The demand for education is there. By definition, City Colleges' students are motivated—almost all must get to school before or after work because they want better lives, not because the state tells them to be there. For the 115,000 students, the City Colleges are possibly the last chance for economic stability. Many of these students are Hispanic or African American. Many—80 percent or more of those who test—need remedial education. The average student is thirty years old and trying to balance school, a family, and possibly a job. But with enrollment down by one-third in a decade, many of these potential students—and potential middle-class workers—are opting out or are opting for other, probably more expensive and less convenient options. Chicago employers would hire City Colleges' students if they were convinced that the colleges were turning out the workers they need. Some successful pilot programs exist, but they are too small so far to affect the overall picture.

## Recommendation:

Chicago's City College system needs thoughtful reform in both practices and mission. The city has made its public schools a priority, and is seeing progress. Now, the City Colleges need the same priority attention. The city, both its government and its private employers, must keep a clear goal in mind—to prepare Chicagoans who are ready for work and further education and to help businesses have access to well-prepared workers.

No city can be a global city without the educational resources and research provided by great universities. Chicago is blessed with such universities, but these schools and the city do not make maximum use of each other. Two universities—Northwestern and the University of Chicago—are globally renowned. But others—the Illinois Institute of Technology, DePaul, Loyola, the University of Illinois at Chicago, Roosevelt, Columbia,

Northeastern Illinois, and other schools—are just as important to the life of the city and the region. All boast intellectual resources that are an asset to the city and its businesses, which do not always use them.

This intellectual leadership is endangered, as it is in all American cities, by the enforcement of immigration laws that bar foreign students, scholars, and entrepreneurs from the United States or makes it difficult for them to work or study here. Chicago relies on immigrants in its health-care services, its education, its trading floors, its electronic and pharmaceutical companies, and in many other areas of intellectual and commercial life. In such areas as science and engineering, immigrants literally drive the local economy. Immigration policies that keep them away hurt the city.

### Recommendation:

The City of Chicago and its businesses must work with Congress and the administration to support immigration policies that welcome highly qualified immigrants—workers and students—including those who stay and those who visit.

## Quality of Life

Quality of life is an all-encompassing term that should be less controversial than it is. One school of urban studies holds that the future lies with "creative cities," the sort of places, rich in amenities, that draw the "creative classes" who hold the future of the global economy in their hands. According to this school of thought, these people settle wherever they choose and, once there, look for a job or, more likely, make their own jobs and create their own companies. These people prize recreation, vibrant entertainment, diversity, other creative people, a free-wheeling atmosphere in which their city becomes one great urban bistro where ideas and innovations leverage each other to build an economy. Cities like Boston, Austin, San Diego, Madison, and Raleigh-Durham fit this description. Indeed, all are doing well in the new economy.

Others say that this emphasis on amenities amounts to little more than counting bicycle racks and coffeehouses. What counts, they say, is what has always counted - good jobs that pay well but, more important, that enable skilled and educated people to use their skills and education to the utmost. Such people are usually comfortable with ethnic and social diversity, but what they really want is the more down-to-earth amenities like safe neighborhoods, good schools, and efficient transit systems.

For Chicago this may be an academic argument. The fact is that to be a global city, Chicago needs both good jobs and good amenities. Despite its beauty, Chicago lacks the mountains of Colorado or the beaches and balmy weather of California. It has always been

**Chicago's Universities are International Intellectual Resources**

- The University of Chicago boasts twenty Nobel Prize laureates who won the prize while on the faculty or for work done at the university. These include Milton Friedman (Economic Sciences, 1986) and Saul Bellow (Literature, 1976). Six laureates are currently members of the faculty.
- Two of Chicago's business schools—the Kellogg School of Management at Northwestern and the Graduate School of Business at the University of Chicago - are consistently ranked among the best in the nation.
- DePaul University's reach extends worldwide, with faculty teaching in Bahrain, Poland, Thailand, and the Czech Republic.
- Loyola University has been consistently ranked by U.S. News and World Report among the "top national universities" for its excellence in education.
- The Illinois Institute of Technology's College of Architecture is among the best architecture and design schools in the United States.
- The University of Illinois at Chicago's College of Urban Planning and Public Affairs is a nationally recognized innovator in research of the nation's cities and metropolitan areas.

**The United States Loses International Students to Great Britain and Canada**

The United States' visa policy is to "welcome citizens from around the world who genuinely want to visit, study, and do business here," but following the terrorist attacks of September 11, 2001, some changes in the laws governing visitor entry and exit were made. In addition to submitting applications and fees, students now need to undergo rigorous interviews that prove without any doubt that they intend to return home after their studies. The average wait time to get an interview ranges from thirty days (China) to seventy-two days (Brazil). This does not include the time required for special clearances and administrative processing. The number of students applying to American university programs has dropped significantly, and countries like Great Britain and Canada, where applying for student visas is easier, are receiving a wealth of international talent.

a place where people came to make money, and it remains that today. But in this global age, there is something to the argument that creative and innovative people want more than just a good paycheck. They do want a "quality of life" and all that it means.

This quality of life embraces everything from safe streets to great theater, opera, blues, and rock music. It includes clean air, good restaurants, youth-related activities, nice parks, affordable housing, buses and trains that run on time, professional sports, the excitement of ethnic diversity, good stores, and places to play. Chicago needs to stress all these amenities, but in truth, it has come a long, long way from its grim Rust Bowl days of twenty or thirty years ago.

Chicago has cultural strengths and cultural gaps. It is strong in classical music, jazz and blues, dance and theater, for instance. It has world-class museums, and its ten "Museums in the Park" are a unique public-private partnership, the best in the nation. But Chicago is outshined by other cities in filmmaking and in other realms of musical life. Chicago has a community of "indie" musicians - musicians who record and perform regularly but who do not enjoy national or international audiences. The music embraces rock, folk music, avant-garde music, and a wide variety of musical instruments. It is important for Chicago to nurture its musicians and to make them more visible. A recent University of Chicago study called Chicago "a music city in hiding" and said it trails smaller cities in profiting from its local music community. To remain a global city, Chicago needs its musical talent to stay in Chicago, and it needs musicians from elsewhere to come here.

Chicago also has the potential to be a major filmmaking center. Many films are made here, but they underutilize Chicago's stock of good actors trained in Chicago's live theaters and in its unsurpassed improv programs. Little postproduction work is done here. Chicago should focus on developing a critical mass of filmmaking talent and infrastructure, including matchmaking between the region's financial investors and film producers who seek nontraditional financing.

The city government understands the importance of amenities, and has responded with everything from flowers to Millennium Park to the championing of ethnic festivals and the Gay Pride Parade. Chicago is strong in theater, architecture, art, and music of all sorts. Once a meat-and-potatoes town, it has become one of the nation's culinary capitals. Many important areas of life—mass transit, education, the environment—are priority needs and are discussed in other sections of this report. But Chicago is on the right track in developing the amenities that make it a lively, exciting, and enjoyable place to live and work.

When high-quality workers want to be in Chicago, so will firms that need these talents.

# Infrastructure Development and the Tourism Industry in Chicago

By Costas Spirou

*In the context of the new economy and the role that amenities play as drivers of growth, Chicago competes with other cities to advance its urban tourism infrastructure. Chicago's substantial tourist infrastrcture in the form of museums, parks, stadiums, and convention centers produce a multitude of other related amenity services. This paper examines the role of structure and agency in relations to the investment and creation of tourism and infrastructure in Chicago. Investment in Chicago's tourist infrastructure has been shaped by political forces, civic groups, corporations and social/cultural trends.*

## Introduction

Urban tourism and policies that advance its promotion, as well as cultural planning that affirm past heritage and construct new destinations are increasingly becoming commonly used strategies in urban centers across the world. Cities pursue the creation and maintenance of comprehensive visions to assess current resources, induce the rebirth of existing cultural assets, develop new ones, invest in physical infrastructure and commit to related policies; all actions occurring within complex social, political and economic milieus.

\* \* \*

In this paper, I present the current development of urban tourism in Chicago and conclude with some reflections on the role of structure and agency, as well as on the unique issues that arise within this new economy. I do not subscribe to the position that the role of the consumer is the key factor in the tourism production process, almost singe-handedly determining the creation of this industry. While the consumer plays an important role, just as critical is the investment and creation of the infrastructure that occurs within a complicated set of circumstances, shaped by political forces, civic groups, corporate interests and general social trends. These, I believe, serve as the fundamental elements in the making of the tourism industry. The tourist experience is thus informed by an appropriate infrastructure and a positive image/perception, as the need to visit the "tourist bubble" is secondary and predetermined by the process of producing that desire itself.[1]

## Early Development of Tourism in Chicago

The Columbian Exposition of 1893 is considered to be one of the largest infrastructural investments ever made by Chicago. The Fair took place on the south side of the city, and Jackson Park and nearby Washington Park served as the 686 acre site for the exposition. The total cost for the event surpassed the $30 million mark and under the leadership of Daniel H. Burnham, more than 12,000 workers constructed 150 buildings of European architecture. Over 21 million tickets were sold and the attendance neared 28 million visitors. Because of the central location of Chicago, most of the visitors came from the midwest while a substantial number of attendees traveled to Chicago from Europe. The magnitude of the exposition was so monumental that it required the erection of hotels and apartments to house the influx of tourists.

During the Columbian Exposition of 1893, Chicago aimed to display its vitality and emerging position as both a railroad and a commercial center. The city was promoted to have rapidly embraced industrial and commercial progress, thus positioning itself on par with the older, established cities of the Atlantic seaboard. Chicago was also showcased as a community attentive to the social needs of its residents. It possessed hundreds of churches and places of worship, numerous charitable, benevolent and fraternal associations, some of the best libraries in the country, two universities, a college of law, seven medical and five theological colleges. Furthermore, City Hall expended considerable funds on education, from only $50,000 in 1855 to more than $4,000,000 in 1891. The promotion of Chicago and of the Fair was conducted by the first ever Department of Publicity and Promotion. It began its operation in 1890, and under the leadership of Moses Handy mailed thousands of promotional material daily across the world.[2]

Similarly, the 1933 and 1934 Chicago's World Fair, known as "A Century of Progress" was a monumental event, commemorating the city's one hundred year anniversary. This was a celebration of industrial and scientific successes. Through the theme of the Fair, "achievement and its promise", and with an attendance of nearly fifty million people, Chicago conveyed itself once again, as a city on the move, signaling its departure from a period marked by the economic disaster of the Great Depression, thrusting itself into a new era defined by advancement and progress.

Chicago engaged in an organized effort to advance its tourism and related business at the early part of the 20th century. In 1907 the Chicago Association of Commerce identified a subcommittee to work on attracting convention meetings to the city. Like Chicago, many other cities formed formal agencies out of loosely defined civic or business groups whose agendas centered on promoting and attracting tourism and related businesses to their respective locales. Convention and visitor bureaus were created across the country in San Francisco (1909), St. Louis (1909), Atlanta (1913), Kansas City (1918), Minneapolis (1927), Washington (1931), Cleveland (1934), New York (1935), Philadelphia (1941), Las Vegas (1960), New Orleans (1960), Anaheim, CA (1961), Orlando (1984) and Miami (1985). The Chicago Convention and Visitors Bureau (CCVB) was founded in 1943 and eventually expanding in 1970 to include the Tourism Council of Greater Chicago, forming the Chicago Convention and Tourism Bureau. The management and operation of the McCormick Place was added to the responsibilities of the CCVB in 1980.

**Figure 1. Dates of Origin Festivals and Events.**

| | |
|---|---|
| 1.  Tree Lighting Ceremony at Daley Plaza | 1913 |
| 2.  Venetian Night | 1957 |
| 3.  Chicago Air & Water Show | 1959 |
| 4.  Chicago Jazz Festival | 1979 |
| 5.  Taste of Chicago | 1980 |
| 6.  Chicago Blues Festival | 1983 |
| 7.  Chicago Gospel Music Festival | 1984 |
| 8.  Viva! Chicago Latin Music Festival | 1989 |
| 9.  Chicago Country Music Festival | 1991 |
| 10. New Year's Ever Fireworks at Buckingham Fountain | 1991 |
| 11. Bike Chicago | 1992 |
| 12. Race to the Taste | 1993 |
| 13. Mayor's Cup Youth Soccer Tournament | 1993 |
| 14. Chicago Winter Delights: It's a Cool Place | 1994 |
| 15. Celtic Fest Chicago | 1997 |
| 16. Chicagoween | 1998 |
| 17. Great Chicago Places & Spaces: Celebrating Chicago Architecture | 1999 |
| 18. Mayor Daley's Kids & Kites Fest | 1999 |
| 19. Mayor Daley's Holiday Sports Festival | 2000 |
| 20. Chicago Outdoor Film Festival | 2000 |

Source: The Mayor's Office of Special Events..

# A New Era of Tourism: Infrastructural Development Along the Lakefront

Following his election as mayor in 1989, Richard M. Daley brought an intense commitment to advancing culture and tourism in Chicago. Since then, the city has experienced a considerable construction boom of amenities along the lakefront, extensive efforts toward beautification and numerous festivals and related programming aiming to help grow the local economy. As Figure 1 indicates, Daley's commitment can be drawn from the fact that twelve from a total of twenty events managed by the Mayor's Office of Special Events have been instituted since he was elected into office, signifying the recent nature of these planning efforts.

In addition, during the last ten years, major, multi-billion dollar construction projects have adorned the lakefront including Navy Pier, Millennium Park, Soldier Field, the Museum Campus and Meigs Field.

In 1989 the city embarked on a plan that would redevelop its 3,300-foot pier just north of Grant Park. Completed in 1995, Navy Pier cost over $200 million and presented the public with many new attractions including the Chicago Children's Museum, a 32,000 square foot indoor botanical garden, a 15 story Ferris Wheel, street entertainment areas with outdoor stages, an IMAX theatre, retail concessions, restaurants, food courts, a skyline stage, a festival hall, a huge ballroom, and 50 acres of parks and promenades amongst others. The project proved to have a considerable impact on the nearby communities including the revitalization of housing in the adjacent neighborhood of Streeterville.[3] In the Fall of 1999, the complex was the recipient of a $27 million, 900 seat Chicago Shakespeare Theatre, significantly diversifying its overall use.[4] The Pier renovations have been so extensive that the location was unable to maintain its prior status on the National Register of Historic Places.[5]

The Pier is the most popular attraction in the City of Chicago. According to the Chicago Office of Tourism and the Chicago Convention and Tourism Bureau, the attendance exceeded 7 million in 1997. In 1999 that number increased to 7.75 million and in 2002 it neared the 8.4 million mark. In 2003, 8.7 million visited the pier generating $45.8 million and in 2004 the attendance surpassed 8.75 million, slightly behind the 9 million visitor peak attendance achieved during 2000.

June 2005 data from the Metropolitan Pier and Exposition Authority (MPEA) reveals that over 70 percent of the visitors to Navy Pier are local. Specifically, 39 percent come from the city of Chicago and 32 percent from nearby suburbs. The remaining originates from other US cities (25 percent) and from other countries (4 percent). Navy Pier has also proved to be a comprehensive entertainment center, capable of keeping travelers occupied for long periods of time. According to the same source, 44 percent of visitors spent 5 hours or more at the Pier with 52 percent averaging 3-4 hours at the location.[6] Today, Navy Pier is viewed by Chicagoans and tourists alike as a center of entertainment and recreation and a generator of substantial tax revenue for the city.

The Lakefront Millennium Project is the most recent, culturally-based development effort of the Daley administration. Mayor Daley announced in 1998 his plan for a major expansion of the park system along the lakefront. The new park, to be constructed on rail yard land, was estimated at $150 million with over $120 million to be generated from revenue bonds and the remaining funds to derive from corporate sponsors and private donations. On 16.5 acres the new space would include an outdoor performance stage, an indoor theatre, a skating rink, gardens, and concession stands. The Grant Park Symphony would perform at this new location and the city would utilize the amenities for other musical festivals. Proceeds from the two-level, 2,500 space parking garage, scheduled to be constructed underneath the park, would be used to pay off the bonds and the project would open in the summer of 2000.[7]

Within a year, the plan was substantially expanded to include additional amenities including a warming house and a restaurant for an ice skating rink, an increase of the planned indoor theatre seating from 500 to a 1,500-seat auditorium, a commuter bicycle center, a glass green house hall and an improved music pavilion design with good sight lines. This new plan also resulted in expanding the park to 24.6 acres. According to Ed Uhlir, Millennium Park Project Director: "Grant Park is Chicago's front yard. Sadly this 16-acre corner of the park has been a blight for too long. Millennium Park will remedy that with a plan that brings Chicagoans together on a year-round basis."[8]

The Millennium Park Project was hampered by cost overruns and delays. For example, initially scheduled to be completed in 2000, Frank Gehry's band shell opened in the summer of 2004. While early cost estimates required $17.8 million for the structure, the actual cost ballooned to $50 million. Initial projections for the flowing stainless steel bridge were around $8 million but surpassed the $13 million mark.[9] The cost of the entire park development reached $500 million when it finally opened in 2004. While earlier [in 1998], Mayor Daley in a letter to the people of Chicago described the Millennium Park as "an exciting new cultural destination for families and children, and an economic magnet for visitors and conventioneers" he later, indirectly acknowledging its development challenges, placed the project in a historical context by indicating that this is a "…civic project [that] marks the new Millennium as no other project ever before undertaken in the history of Chicago."[10]

The Millennium Park attracted 1.5 million visitors during its first year of operation and its popularity signals continued high attendance rates. More interestingly, though the opening of the park has brought about changes both in the surrounding area as well as in the public policy front. A new 90 story skyscraper to the north of the park, scheduled to be completed sometime in 2008, will include the upscale Mandarin Oriental Hotel. That project is just one of the many developments that will take place because of the allure of the park. According to Gerard Kenny, a Chicago real estate developer "The opening of Millennium Park made this [skyscraper project] thing go."[11] Similarly, the nearby Streeterville neighborhood is experiencing an unprecedented residential boom that includes the construction of 13 new highrises scheduled to be completed within the next five years. That will increase by one third the influx of new apartments and condominiums to the neighborhood, totaling 12,523 units.[12]

Local government officials also realized that the world class park has positively impacted the property values across the Loop. As a result, in the Fall of 2005 the city considered a new tax on the downtown area. The funds from this special property tax district, estimated at about $18 million annually, would support the $7 million operating and maintenance park budget. According to a city spokeswoman "This is a way of looking at keeping the downtown vital and making sure that it continues to be the attraction and destination that it is right now."[13] In early October of 2005, following vocal opposition by business leaders and property owners, Mayor Daley withdrew support of the tax proposal.

To the south edge of Grant Park, the development of the Museum Campus can be viewed as one of the most aggressive plans of Mayor Daley's culturally-driven redevelopment agenda during the last decade. The vision to join the grounds of the Field Museum of Natural History, the Shedd Aquarium and the Adler Planetarium and thus create a museum campus, required the re-routing of northbound, five traffic lane, Lake Shore Drive, which cut through and separated these cultural institutions. With the approval of a bond in 1994 for the expansion of nearby McCormick Place (Chicago's major convention center) funds were allocated for the South Lake Shore Drive project. At a cost of more than $120 million, the Metropolitan Pier and Exposition Authority carried out the project with city and state financial resources.[14]

After the completion of the relocation of Lake Shore Drive to the west, additional work was conducted to add 57 more area acres, including expansive greenways, massive landscaping, raised terraces, sidewalks and land bridges designed to cover the old multilane thoroughfare. To put into perspective the size of this project, consider that more than 120,000 cubic yards of dirt were displaced and the ground was lowered by as much as 22 feet to create a tiered lawn.[15] The purpose of the Museum Campus has been to create a destination place and increase the attendance of Chicagoans and tourists at the three museums.

Meigs Field and Soldier Field have also added to the infrastructural development and amenities necessary for further developing Chicago as a city of tourism. Meigs Field was a small airport along the lakefront providing business leaders with easy access to downtown Chicago. Following the end of a 50 year airport lease in 1996 with the Chicago Park District, Mayor Daley placed forth a proposal to create a 91-acre park at a projected cost of $27.2 million. The plan would link the park to the Museum Campus and would include botanical gardens, playgrounds, wetlands, a nature center and a sensory garden for the visually or hearing impaired. The island would be accessible by a ferry and a rubber-wheeled trolley. According to city projections the "superpark" would generate over $30 million a year in revenue from parking, concessions, souvenirs and other fees and it would draw more than 350,000 visitors annually. This environmental park would be fully accessible to the disabled as ramps would extend to the lake, fully accommodating those using strollers and wheelchairs.[16]

The plan faced political opposition by then Governor Jim Edgar, who argued that closing Meigs would negatively affect the transportation of the region. The state filed a lawsuit to take control of the property, eventually resulting in a compromise that would allow the airfield to remain open for an additional five years. Following that operation term the city would proceed with its plans to create a park on Northerly Island. In 2001 the State and the City agreed to keep Meigs Field open until 2006. Yet, the federal portion of the agreement did not pass, setting the stage for the March 2003, middle-of-the-night destruction of the runway. Large X-shaped markings were carved out in the center of the runway by city equipment, ending the history of the Field as an airport, and giving complete control of the space to the mayor.

In the summer of 2005 the Charter One Pavilion opened at Northerly Island, a 7,500-seat venue offering outdoor concerts and live entertainment to music fans.[17] Nearby Soldier Field, home of the Chicago Bears of the National Football League (NFL), has also become part of this culturally-based image advanced by Mayor Daley. Located adjacent to the Museum Campus to the south, Soldier Field opened in 1924 and since then it has been identified as an integral part of the city. The facility is owned and operated by the Chicago Park District and its major tenants, the Bears, have been leasing the stadium. The relationship between the city and the ownership of the team has been contentious, especially after 1986 when the team won the Super Bowl and began to argue against the antiquated Soldier Field, advancing pressure for a brand new facility with a large number of luxury skyboxes.

As the team explored multiple options both in the city, the suburbs and even in neighboring Indiana, Mayor Daley continued to support the Soldier Field choice. Stadium development has proven capable of reshaping urban space even at the neighborhood/community level.[18] Because of its lakefront location and its proximity to the Museum Campus a new facility would complement the city of culture theme.

In the summer of 2000, following many years of "battles" over locations and financing, Bears officials and Mayor Daley settled old differences and jointly began to promote an ambitious proposal for a new stadium that included substantial redevelopment of the surrounding areas. The Mayor would also take another step in his campaign "to restore the Lakefront", a central piece of his administration's ongoing effort to improve Chicago's downtown and near downtown public spaces.[19]

The cost of the Soldier Field renovation surpassed the $680 million mark, with the Bears contributing $200 million, and the remaining financed by Chicago's two percent hotel-motel tax. The Illinois Sports Facilities Authority (ISFA), an agency created to oversee construction of another Chicago stadium, the New Comiskey Park in the late 1980's, issued bonds to cover the city's share of stadium construction costs. The physical plan specified a new football stadium set within, though also rising substantially above, the classical colonnades crowning Soldier Field's east and west facades. Extensive underground parking has been added and surface parking areas to the south of the stadium were landscaped, adding more that fifteen acres of green space to the lakefront.

Overall, 1,300 trees of 45 different species were planted, a sledding hill was configured and a children's garden has been created.[20] The new facility opened in 2003, and is in concert with the city's larger vision of keeping Soldier Field as part of the lakefront, positioning it as an additional piece to the available entertainment venues along Chicago's front yard.[21]

Daley's commitment to advancing the tourism industry has persisted over the years through the above mentioned infrastructural developments. At his last inaugural address, he reaffirmed this position: "And we must continue to enhance the competitive advantage of our tourism and convention industry, which attracts thirty million visitors to Chicago each year, pumping some $8 billion a year into the Chicago economy.[22]

## Complementing the New Infrastructure with Urban Beautification

In the last few years visitors and locals alike have been impressed by the rapid transformation that the city has undergone especially in the area of beautification.

The assessment below by Steve Berg is typical of the one that many have of the city. Specifically:

> To me, Chicago was always heavy on bulk and incapable of charm. But this impression is badly outdated. No corner gas station is safe from decorative lamp-posts and baskets of drooping geraniums. No surface parking lot can escape a border of wrought-iron fencing and leafy canopies of newly planted trees.[23]

A key program that has been promoted in City Hall is Mayor Daley's GreenStreets Program. Founded in 1990, the program is directly aiming to establish hundreds of thousands of new trees in Chicago through distribution, planting and education programs. Additional goals of the program include preserving and maintaining existing trees and improving the overall physical environment of the city. The program distributes grants to community based efforts and tree seedlings for planting to residents. Funding from municipal and federal government sources surpassed the $1 million mark annually in the early 1990s, and since 1997 over $2.4 million has been budgeted with $497 thousand allocated for 2003. In recent years the program has been expanded to provide residents with mulch services and has included the installation and maintenance of hanging flower baskets and antique light poles. As part of the mayor's efforts to further enhance the aesthetic quality of the areas located throughout the downtown Loop, River North and Printers Row in 2001, 950 hanging baskets were installed in city streets.[24]

Mayor Daley has repeatedly outlined his belief that urban beautification programs can increase residents' quality of life. During a keynote address to the Urban Parks Institute's "Great Parks/Great Cities" Conference in New York City, the mayor noted:

This is quite a wide variety of amenities—everything from fiberglass cows to playlots—but they all have this in common: they improve the quality of life. And I believe very strongly that the cities that pay attention—really pay attention—to quality of life will be the cities that thrive in the 21st century. Part of this is psychological. Cities are vibrant and exciting, but they also can be overwhelming and intimidating. Trees, flowers, a small park, even a sidewalk bench can soften the rough edges of a city, calm your nerves and make you feel a little more in control of things.[25]

City government press releases and speeches by Mayor Daley often note the number of trees planted in recent years, which appears to be something in the range of 400,000 since his 1989 election to office. Daley's affinity for the natural environment was recognized nationally. In 1999 he received the J. Sterling Morton Award, The National Arbor Day Foundation's highest individual honor. The Foundation praised the mayor noting: "Through his GreenStreets program, he has promoted the planting of hundreds of thousands of trees and millions of flowers and perennials, reversing a trend of urban tree loss in Chicago and making the city a model for other large metropolitan areas."[26]

Other beautification projects have included the restoration of the Roosevelt Road Bridge in 1995 and the renovation of State Street in 1996. The Roosevelt Road Bridge connects the Museum Campus with the Near South Side neighborhoods and the University of Illinois at Chicago on Halsted Street. The new bridge's ornamentation includes sculptures of dolphins, as well as books and navigation instruments representing the cultural institutions of the city. Similarly, State Street was turned from an urban transit mall to an eye-catching public space following the installation of historic streetlights, wrought-iron planters, shrubs, flowers and old style signage.

Ultimately, Chicago's beautification efforts also represent a strategy to bring suburbanites back to the city. Daley has repeatedly argued that the city is more effective than the suburbs in its efforts to create outdoor spaces for its residents:

In fact many suburbanites have found the city does a better job of creating human spaces than the suburbs. It's hard to find a nice neighborhood park in our newer suburbs. You can't ride your bike to visit friends in another subdivision, and you certainly cannot walk to the regional shopping mall. But if you come to downtown Chicago on a summer weekend, you'll see thousands of people strolling past the Michigan Avenue shops, enjoying Navy Pier and the free Lincoln Park Zoo, and biking or jogging on our 18-mile lakefront path. Many of those people are suburbanites who come into the city to work during the week and to play on the weekends. It makes you wonder why they don't just move into the city to avoid all that travel time and many are doing that.[27]

It is clear that improving the city's material environment not only serves as a way to position Chicago in a changing economy of leisure and entertainment, but, also like the "City Beautiful" movement, these investments can be construed as actually helping people better adapt to the challenges of urban life. By making beautification programs a priority, Mayor Daley envisions physical improvement as a vehicle for social reform.

Occasionally, Daley has strained the cultural imagination of the greatest policy supporters. At one recent mayoral proposal designed to expand Chicago's cultural amenities Daley promoted the introduction of gondolas on the Chicago River. In June of 2000, the Mayor introduced an ordinance that would make Chicago the Midwestern version of Venice. According to the plan, gondoliers would navigate their boats through the river, singing and serenading in Italian and even performing wedding ceremonies. Ironically, the city's current pursuit of human uplift via better urban design sometimes seems to drown by the perilous swamps of overspending.

All these activities have altered Chicago's image as explained by Mayor Daley who in a recent [2005] speech at the Massachusetts Institute of Technology explained: "Visitors are often surprised at Chicago's beauty. Some of them come to Chicago expecting Carl Sandburg or Nelson Algren. Instead, they find Martha Stewart."[28]

## The Cyclical Nature of Tourism: Turning the Corner After September 11th?

In his 2000 State of the City address, Mayor Daley proudly exclaimed: "And with tourism numbers at an all time high, the rest of the world is finally discovering what we have known for a long time: Chicago is a beautiful, diverse, welcoming and culturally rich city- on a par with the greatest cities in the world."[29] A few months later, at a speech during the opening of the annual meeting of the Chicago Convention and Tourism Bureau, the Mayor proclaimed his vision, asserting that he wants Chicago to be "on the leading edge of tourism and travel."[30] By that time the city had invested enormous resources in infrastructure and had promoted itself in a way capable of realizing this vision.

*[Following the September 11 attacks, Chicago tourism experienced a decline that lasted close to three years. Recently released figures for 2004 reveal an increase in visitors and Chicago ranked as the number one business travel city, even ahead of New York. This news belies the fact that convention attendance is actually declining even with an ambitious expansion of McCormick Place due to the high costs of space and less demand for it.]*

\* \* \*

# Conclusion

It is apparent that structural changes have impacted Chicago over the last five decades. De-industrialization, population decentralization and globalization have played a critical role, leaving the urban core subjected to disinvestment, decline and widespread social problems in housing and education amongst others. Within this rapidly evolving socioeconomic environment, and fiscally strained to provide needed social services to their residents, cities increasingly identified urban tourism and its potential revenue capability as a viable response and a key economic development strategy...

The recent decision by the MPEA [Metropolitan Pier and Exposition Authority] in the Fall of 2005 to revisit the viability of Navy Pier proves highly insightful as it points to the role of agency. Even though in 2004 the tourist destination generated $42.6 million in revenues and $5.4 million in net income, the leadership knows that this success may prove short lived. The Authority is currently considering the introduction of a hotel, additional entertainment, more sit-down restaurants, and possibly a marina on the north side of the pier. According to Leticia Peralta Daviz, MPEA Chief Executive Officer, "We hope to see a framework of what Navy Pier might look like in the next 10 years. We want to keep things very fresh. An entertainment venue like Navy Pier needs to keep things fresh."[31]

This activist approach, while aiming to maintain the competitive nature of this attraction is also informed by additional considerations. Those include inter-city competition, economic pressures, expressed corporate interests desiring to join and benefit from the existing successes of this development and even political rationales. These forces are intertwined, they are making the visitor experience, and in the process contribute to the construction of the tourist industry.

The recent emergence of a new economy of leisure, amenities and quality of life considerations have similarly shifted the interplay between structure and agency as cities not only view urban tourism as an economic development tool, but also as a recruiting mechanism capable of attracting new economy entrepreneurs and workers. This trend has to be further explored as it has increased the importance of entertainment and restructured the discourse on urban development. This will allow for unique insights into the role of agency, revealing the complex relationship between this sector and related urban processes.

In the last fifteen years Chicago has made a deliberate effort to physically reorganize its lakefront and embrace the advancement of urban tourism as an economic development tool. However, the success of this strategy, hinges on a continuously concerted effort to maintain the needed organizational capacity in marketing and image building, while balancing that against the competitive desires of other cities that have also intensified their efforts to attract visitors to their locales.

# Notes

1. Judd, D. R. The Commodity Chain of global tourism. Center for Regional-og Turismeforskning, Nexø, Denmark, May 16, 2004.

2. Bancroft, H.H. The Book of the Fair. Chicago: Bancroft Company, 1893.

3. Kaiser, R. "Blazing a Trail Through Lost Chicago." Chicago Tribune. August 5, 1997.

4. McCarron, J. Downtown Unchained? The Building Book is Back. Chicago Tribune, August 11, 1997;

5. Bernstein, D. "Just a Quiet Night at Home. Crain's Chicago Business, May 3,2004.

6. Jones, C. "The Location is he Thing Chicago's Shakespeare Rep Poised for Move to Navy Pier, and Perhaps Wider Recognition. Chicago Tribune, February 1, 1998.

7. Reardon, P. "Navy Pier off US Historic List." Chicago Tribune, February 18,1992.

8. MPEA. Navy Pier Survey, June 2005; National Arbor Day Press Release,1999.

9. Shields,Y. "Chicago Plans to Issue for Park Expansion." Bond Buyer, April 2, Vol. 324, Issue 30364. 1998. Pps. 3, 6; Spirou, C. "Urban Beautification and the Construction of a New Municipal Identity in Chicago." In The New Chicago: A Social and Cultural Analysis, ed. by J. Koval, L. Bennett, F. Demissie and Bennett, M. Philadelphia: Temple University Press, 2006.

10. City of Chicago. "New Millennium Plans Unveiled to Chicago Plan Commission on March 11, 1999." Department of Transportation. March 1999.

11. Kamin, B. "Steel Appeal." Chicago Tribune, July 6, 2003.

12. City of Chicago. "Chicago's Millennium Park". Office of Tourism, May 2003; Daley, R. M. A Letter to the People of Chicago. August 20, 1998.

13. Corfman, T. "Mandarin Oriental Hotel Will Check In." Chicago Tribune, June 8, 2005.

14. Bergen, K., and Handley, J. "High-Speed High-rises Stagger Streeterville." Chicago Tribune. July 17, 2007.

15. Gallun, Alby and Hinz, G. "Navy Pier Redo in the Works." Crain's Chicago Business, October 17, 2005.

16. "Lake Shore Drive." (1995) Planning. February, Vol. 61, Issue 2, p. 42.

17. Kamin, B. "Reinventing the Lakefront: To Shape the Shoreline." Chicago Tribune, October 26, 1998.

18. Hill, J. and Borsky, D. "City Lifts Veil in Hopes for Meigs Wetlands, Botanical Gardens are Included." Chicago Tribune, July 2, 1996.

19. Kot, G. "Stunning Skyline." Chicago Tribune, June 27, 2005.

20. Spirou, C. "Die Expansion von Stadien als kulturelle Strategie der Stadtplanung und Stadterneuerung in den USA" in Das Stadion. Geschichte, Architektur, Politik, Oekonomie, ed. by M. Marschik, R. Muellner, G. Spitaler and Zinganel, M, pp. 413-445. Vienna: Turia & Kant, 2005.

21. And Spirou, C. and Bennett, L. "Revamped Stadium … New Neighborhood?" Urban Affairs Review. 37: 675-702. 2002.

22. Osnos, E. and Pearson, R. Bears, "City Says This May Be Real Deal for Soldier Field. Chicago Tribune, August 16, 2000.

23. Ford, L. "Soldier Field Landscaping Takes Shape." Chicago Tribune, April 26, 2004. Section 2, p.1

24. Spirou, C. and Bennett, L. It's Hardly Sportin': Stadiums, Neighborhoods and the New Chicago. DeKalb: Northern Illinois University Press. 2003.

25. Daley, R. M. Inaugural Address. Journal of the Proceedings, City Council, May 5, 2003.

26. Berg, S. "Chicago Shows What Can Happen When a City Strives for Beauty." Minneapolis Star-Tribune, September 10, 2000.

27. USDA Forest Service, 2003.

28. Daley, R. M. Revitalizing Chicago through Parks and Public Spaces. Keynote address to the Urban Parks Institute's "Great Parks/Great Cities" Conference, New York, NY, July 31, 2001.

29. National Arbor Day Press Release, 2000.

30. Daley, R. M.  Speech at the Chicago Greening Symposium, March 8, 2000.

31. Daley, R.M. Richard M. Daley Remarks at MIT, April 7, 2005.

32. Daley, R. M. State of the City Address. January 19, 2000.

33. Daley, R.M. Speech at the annual meeting of the Chicago Conventions and Tourism Bureau, March 24, 2000.

34. Gallun, A. and Heinz, G. City Floats Tax Hike for Loop. Crain's Chicago Business, August 29, 2005.

# Part VI

## Metropolitan Chicago

# Metropolitan Chicago

At the beginning of the twentieth century, social scientists at the University of Chicago on the city's south side, sought descriptively and "scientifically" to capture urban land-use growth patterns. The most famous was a model of concentric rings of growth. This model was used to describe Chicago at the turn of the Twentieth Century. As

**Figure 1. Concentric Rings of Growth for Chicago.**

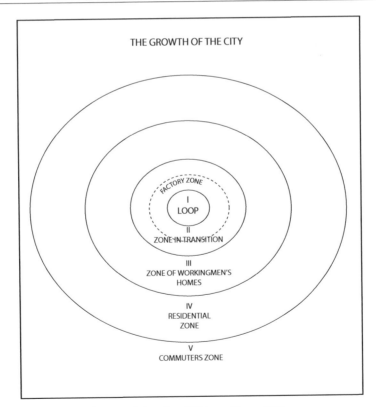

Source: Ernest Burgess from *The City*, University of Chicago Press, 1925.

depicted in Figure 1, at the center was downtown Chicago: "The Loop" named after the original loop of the Chicago River and later the Chicago Elevated Tracks. Factories and slums surrounded this downtown area in the next circle out from the Loop. Further out still were the working-class neighborhoods, residential, and commuter zones, each zone following the other.

Earnest Burgess, who developed the concentric circle model in 1928, argued that there was a correlation between the distance from the downtown area and the wealth of an area; wealthier families with the desire and means to escape the dirt, grime, and crime of the city, tended to live further away from downtown. After World War II, wealthy families moved even further away from the central city, into the emerging sprawl of the suburbs. Since 1950, more than 90 percent of growth in U.S. metropolitan areas has occurred far from central downtowns. This mass migration to the suburbs was made possible by various federal public policies, like the 1944 Serviceman's Readjustment Act and the 1956 Interstate and Defense Highways Act. As shown Figure 2, in the decades following World War II, the Chicago metropolitan region continued its unsustainable sprawl, further and further away from the city.

Although the concentric ring model was never a perfect fit, it is even less so today. Chicago is no longer a compact urban area, surrounded by wealthy and white suburbs. Chicago is now part of a much larger metropolitan region with over 12 million people, spanning three states. Today's metropolitan areas are no longer neat concentric rings of growth like rings on a tree, but rather complicated systems, more like a human body with a heart and brain still in the downtown area, and networks of arteries, veins, nerves, and appendages stretching for many miles.

**Figure 2. Developed Area, 1900-2005.**

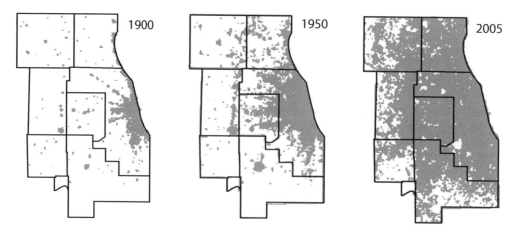

Source: U.S. Environmental Protection Agency and CMAP.

Today a new migration is taking place. As described by many of the articles in this section, a demographic inversion is occurring throughout the Chicago region. Driven out of the city by market forces and gentrification, lower-income and working-class families, along with new immigrants, are dispersing to the suburbs in search of jobs and cheaper housing. As a result, our suburbs are becoming more diverse, both racially and economically.

Poverty in Chicago is no longer confined to the inner city. As depicted in Figure 3, poverty is growing much more rapidly in Chicago's collar counties than in Cook County and the city itself. In DuPage County, one of the wealthiest counties in the United States, poverty is growing at an alarming 63.3%. Unfortunately, most suburban areas are ill prepared to deal with the increasing needs of the growing poor. Safety net programs for the poor have traditionally and more easily been provided in central cities. Public hospitals, nutrition assistance programs, childcare programs, and food banks are few and far between in sprawling suburban areas.

One of the greatest challenges facing the Chicago metropolitan region is the spatial mismatch between jobs and affordable housing. Increasingly, low and moderate income workers must move farther from their jobs to find affordable housing, incurring greater

**Figure 3. Percent Poverty Rate Growth in the Chicago Region, 1980-2006.**

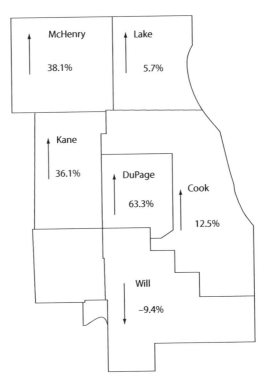

Source: Heartland Alliance. *2008 Report on Illinois Poverty: Chicago Area Snapshot.*

commuter costs. Where the metropolitan job supply is growing, there is little affordable housing; where the metropolitan job supply is decreasing, there is affordable housing.

The solution to this spatial mismatch between jobs and affordable housing is either better public transportation for reverse commuting, new low-cost housing in the suburbs, or some combination of the two. Land-use zoning policies that encourage high-density, mixed-use developments in the suburbs as opposed to single family homes on large lots are needed. Unfortunately, exclusionary zoning laws, found in many suburban communities, make it nearly impossible for affordable housing to be built. Without regional planning and agreement, there is little incentive for well-to-do suburbs to become more inclusive. Local resistance to affordable housing is a significant factor. In a 2001 Chicago Metropolis 2020 survey, only 36% of those responding thought that regional interests should prevail over local interests in housing and land-use decisions.

Created in 2006, the Chicago Metropolitan Agency for Planning (CMAP) serves as the region's official agency for comprehensive planning of land use and transportation. Although CMAP does not have taxing or enforcement powers, it has developed a regional "long-range comprehensive plan to link transportation, land use, the natural environment, economic prosperity, housing, and human and community development." Listed below is a summary of the CMAP 2040 recommendations:

- Livable Communities
- Achieve Greater Livability through Land Use and Housing
- Manage and Conserve Water and Energy Resources
- Expand and Improve Parks and Open Space
- Promote Sustainable Local Food
- Human Capital
- Improve Education and Workforce Development
- Support Economic Innovation
- Efficient Governance
- Reform State and Local Tax Policy
- Improve Access to Information
- Pursue Coordinated Investments
- Regional Mobility
- Invest Strategically in Transportation
- Increase Commitment to Public Transit
- Create a More Efficient Freight Network

Despite the efforts of CMAP and other regional organizations, politics and government in the Chicago metropolitan region remain in flux. Governmentally, the region remains fragmented with some efforts at coordination occurring but no move towards creating a regional government. As detailed in the articles that follow, mayors in suburban municipalities have come together with the mayor of Chicago in councils of government and mayoral organizations, but they have yet to reach agreement on controversial issues like affordable housing and creating a third airport.

# Planning Chicago

## By Carl Abbott

*In this article, written for the Encyclopedia of Chicago, Carl Abbott traces the history of urban planning in Chicago and the "continuing challenge… to craft political alliances and civic institutions to support physical efficiency and social equity across the entire metropolitan area."*

Everyone plans. Businesses contemplate markets and products, social service agencies seek to improve service to their clients, workers think about retirement, politicians calculate their chances for reelection. In the language of urban history and policy, however, "planning" refers to efforts to shape the physical form and distribution of activities within a city. The objects of planning are sites and systems—the neighborhoods and places within which we carry on our lives and the networks that link the parts of a metropolitan area into a functioning whole. Planning shaped everything from Pullman and Hyde Park to the Chicago park system and the web of highways that knit together the metropolitan region.

\* \* \*

Chicago's planning history offers a lesson that can be generalized to other American cities: efficiency is an easier goal than equity. Residents have found it relatively easy to agree and act on community needs that invite engineering solutions, for it has been possible to argue convincingly that canals, roads, sewers, and parks serve the entire population. Chicagoans have been less ambitious and less successful in shaping ideal communities that combine physical quality with social purpose. They have tried repeatedly to improve on the typical products of the real-estate market, but their experiments have faced often intractable issues of class and race. Success has usually required planning for narrowly defined segments of the middle class, while planning for socially inclusive communities at any large scale has built social conflict into the community fabric.

## Metropolitan Planning

In the decades around the turn of the [20th] century, a widely shared metropolitan vision coalesced around the planning of systems to integrate the sprawling Chicago region. New York and Chicago epitomized the urban crisis of fin de siècle America, whose institutions seemed to be overwhelmed by waves of European immigration, increasing polarization of wealth, and the sheer complexity and congestion of the giant city. These challenges of headlong metropolitan growth called forth similar responses in both cities. Some Americans reacted with sweeping utopian or dystopian visions of the national future. Others searched for practical technological fixes such as electric lighting, improved sanitation, or electric streetcars and subways. Still others constructed ameliorative institutions such as settlement houses and began to lay the foundations of a modern welfare state with the social and economic reforms of Progressivism. And a significant minority worked to systematize the future growth of their cities, consolidating separate local governments into vast regional cities and developing regional plans for the extension of public services.

This story began in Chicago with the park system of the late nineteenth century. Although separate South, West, and Lincoln Park commissions (1869) served the three geographic divisions of the city, their investments and improvements worked together as a unified whole. Large semi-pastoral parks in the zone of the fastest residential growth allowed the poor and middle classes to enjoy temporary respite from the city. Broad boulevards connected the parks in a great chain from Lincoln Park to Jackson Park.

The annexation of 1889 tripled the area of the city; it took in established suburban communities and vast tracts of undeveloped land and set the stage for large public expenditures for water supply and sanitation. The Sanitary District of Chicago (1889) covered 185 square miles; its impressive regional accomplishment was construction of the Sanitary and Ship Canal (1900) and the reversal of the Chicago River to carry the city's waste into the Illinois and Mississippi Rivers. Annexation also paved the way for a metropolitan vision that achieved full expression in Daniel Burnham and Edward Bennett's *Plan of Chicago* of 1909. Promoted by a civic-minded business elite and widely embraced by middle-class Chicagoans, the "Burnham Plan" was an effort to frame the market (and the work of city builders) with a regional infrastructure of rationalized railroads, new highways, and regional parks to anticipate population growth. The plan knit downtown and neighborhoods, city and suburbs and surroundings, to a distance of 60 miles. It was to be implemented with public investments that would order and constrain the private market. The plan took the regional booster vision of the nineteenth century and transformed it into a concrete form and format for shaping a vast but functional cityscape.

Economically comprehensive as well as spatially unifying, the plan envisioned a Chicago that located management functions, production, and transportation in their most appropriate places. It assumed that the city would continue to be the fountainhead of industrial employment.

* * *

The commercial-civic elite mounted a vigorous campaign to put the Burnham Plan into action. The city established a unique City Plan Commission—a miniature city parliament of 328 businessmen, politicians, and civic leaders—to monitor and promote implementation. Advocates tirelessly preached the gospel of urban efficiency with newspaper and magazine stories (575 in 1912 alone), illustrated lectures, a motion picture, and *Wacker's Manual of the Plan of Chicago,* a summary text that introduced the Burnham Plan to tens of thousands of Chicago schoolchildren.

Chicagoans acted in accord with many of Burnham's prescriptions. The city acquired lakefront land for Grant Park, a stately open space to set off and contrast with the growing skyline. Creation of the Cook County Forest Preserve system implemented another set of recommendations. So did the extension of Roosevelt Road, improvement of terminals for railroad freight and passengers, movement of harbor facilities to Lake Calumet, and widening of North Michigan Avenue to allow expansion of the downtown office core.

As growth moved beyond the city limits, civic leaders in 1923 organized the semipublic Chicago Regional Planning Association. This effort to keep alive the planning vision of the 1910s was a forum for the voluntary coordination of local government plans outside the direct control of Chicago. Involving municipalities from three states, it had substantial success in coordinating park expansion and highways. However, the growing scale of the metropolitan area also introduced the erosive problem of suburban independence and competition for growth that would dominate regional planning in the United States in remaining decades of the century.

The Burnham Plan was certainly not perfect—it spoke to social issues indirectly at best—but it did place the question of good urban form at the center of the public agenda and held up Chicago as a model for wide-ranging thought about metropolitan futures. A publication entitled *Chicago's World-Wide Influence* (1913) trumpeted the importance of Chicago planning. Burnham and Bennett had tried out their ideas in San Francisco and followed with consulting work in other cities. The *Plan of Chicago* was also a template for more "practical" comprehensive planning in the 1920s.

* * *

Since the 1920s, the civic ideal has eroded in the face of racial conflict, suburban self-suf-ficiency, industrial transition, and the daunting complexity of a huge metropolitan region. Like every other large American metropolis, Chicago has fragmented by race and place. At the same time, urban planning as a field of work began to splinter into poorly connected subfields. Advocates of public housing worked in the 1920s and 1930s for specific state and federal legislation. Proponents of improved social services became social workers and bureaucrats of the incipient welfare state. Engineers and builders of physical infrastructure concentrated on adapting a rail-based circulation system to automobiles, as with Chicago's Wacker Drive, Congress Expressway, and hundreds of miles of newly paved or widened thoroughfares. In Chicago and elsewhere, New Deal work relief programs reinforced the transmutation of comprehensive planning into a set of public works projects. City plan-ners were left to effect incremental changes in private land uses by administering zoning regulations.

Chicagoans returned to the intentional creation of "better" communities with the help of the federal government after World War II. The Housing Acts of 1949 and 1954, the bases for an urban renewal program lasting until 1974, were intended as federal-local partnerships to rescue blighted city districts with exemplary reconstruction. But the politics of planning required that new or newly improved neighborhoods be homogeneous communities for single races or classes. This generation of neighborhood planning found it possible to bridge the chasms of class or race, but not both. The results were not necessarily bad, but they were neither as comprehensive nor as socially integrative as planning idealists might have hoped.

A central postwar imperative was how to keep white Chicagoans on the South Side in a time of heavy black migration and ghetto expansion. The city in the 1950s used urban renewal to clear low-rent real estate, attract new investment in middle-class housing, and buffer large civic institutions. A key example was the city's partnership with Michael Reese Hospital and Illinois Institute of Technology to create the new neighborhoods of Lake Meadows and Prairie Shores. High-rise apartments integrated middle-class whites and middle-class African Americans while displacing an economically diversified black neigh-borhood. The city and the University of Chicago worked together on a similar makeover of Hyde Park that preserved the university and a university-oriented neighborhood while building economic fences against lower-income African Americans. Federal funds also financed arrays of public housing towers, such as the Robert Taylor Homes, to hold black Chicagoans within the established ghetto.

Oak Park since the 1960s has offered an alternative approach to middle-class integra-tion. Oak Park residents have used social engineering rather than land redevelopment to manage integration and harmonize some of the tensions of race and place. Working through private organization rather than municipal government, Oak Parkers have directly faced the problem of racial balance and quotas, marketing their town to white families and selected black families and steering other blacks to alternative communities.

The planned suburb of Park Forest (1948) tried to be inclusive by class (at least the range of the middle class). In so doing, however, it was solving a problem of the last century rather than directly addressing the issues of race and suburban isolation. The Park Forest plat reflected the best of midcentury suburban design, using superblocks to reduce the impact of automobiles and assembling the blocks into neighborhood units with neighborhood parks and schools. It also mixed single-family homes and two-story garden apartments so that upward mobility was possible within the same community. Park Forest has nonetheless gained increasing racial variety, emerging in the 1980s as another example of successful integration.

Park Forest, like Riverside, Evanston, and Pullman in the previous century, also assumed that men and women operated in separate spheres. Such communities turned inward on home and neighborhood for women and children while opening out to the workplace for men. This social vision would prove fragile as social customs changed and a majority of American women entered the workforce by the 1970s.

Chicago's South Shore neighborhood offers a twist on the Park Forest story. Efforts to replicate the Hyde Park experience of racial integration failed in the 1960s and 1970s, in part because of the contrast between middle-class whites and working-class blacks. Instead, it has gained as a broadly based African American neighborhood with the help of development efforts orchestrated by the community-oriented South Shore Bank (now ShoreBank).

In a less progressive variation on the Oak Park and South Shore examples, the private sector has increasingly controlled downtown redevelopment in the interests of business corporations and their professional and managerial employees. Through the 1960s, redevelopment initiative remained with the city because urban renewal put local governments in control of land acquisition. The University of Illinois campus in Chicago was built on lands acquired through urban renewal. In a variation on the Hyde Park / University of Chicago story, it transformed tracts originally intended for replacement housing into a pioneering public campus. As federal urban renewal funds dried up with the Housing and Community Development Act (1974) and the Reagan administration, however, the public sector lost most of its capacity to act directly. Efforts to leverage mixed-use development have met with success outside the Loop but left a gaping hole in the center of downtown during the 1990s.

Planning for regional systems, in contrast, has been more successful. Infrastructure planners can fall back on the rhetoric of technically sound proposals and sidestep direct confrontation with racial conflict. The Chicago Regional Plan Association issued *Planning for the Region of Chicago* in 1956. The Northeastern Illinois Planning Commission (NIPC) began work for a six-county region in 1957; it has issued and updated regional plans for water, open space, recreation, and land development. The 1962 plan of the Chicago Area Transportation Study (CATS) was a national model for transportation demand forecasting. CATS (now a federally recognized transportation planning organization) and NIPC have had the practical success of framing a regional road/rail system that reflects Burnham and Bennett's ideas and has kept the vast metropolis together.

Nevertheless, regional growth frameworks cannot themselves stem intraregional competition for jobs and upper-income residents. Mayor Richard M. Daley might admonish his suburban counterparts in 1997 that "we have to think of mass transit as a regional issue," point proudly to the continuing importance of downtown Chicago jobs, and convene meetings to discuss regional cooperation. Only the federal courts, however, have been able to override local isolationism on issues such as low-income housing.

## Conclusion

In the civic moment of the late nineteenth and early twentieth centuries, business interest and "civic" interest converged around the physical redesign of the metropolis. Much of the private sector was self-consciously public in rhetoric and often in reality. Middle-class women as well as men shared a vision of a reformed city that was implicitly assimilationist. The well-oiled economic machinery of the metropolis would have a place for everyone; improved housing and public services would help to integrate newcomers into the social fabric.

Even as the imposing *Plan of Chicago* was being so vigorously promoted, however, Chicago's growing black population was posing a challenge that lay outside the intellectual framework of physical planning. The congratulatory report *Ten Years Work of the Chicago Plan Commission* (1920) made no reference to the bloody race riot of the previous year. In the second half of the century, planning fractured into technical specialties and efforts to improve pieces of the metropolis—downtown, historic districts, new suburbs, and the occasional integrated neighborhood. In a time when everyone acknowledges the economic unity of city regions, the continuing challenge is to reinvigorate the civic-mindedness that has served Chicago well in the past and to craft political alliances and civic institutions to support physical efficiency and social equity across the entire metropolitan area.

# Remarks by the President at the Urban and Metropolitan Policy Roundtable on July 13, 2009

## By President Barack Obama

I went to college in LA and New York, and law school across the river from Boston, I received my greatest education on Chicago's South Side, working at the local level to bring about change in those communities and opportunities to people's lives…

And that experience also gave me an understanding of some of the challenges facing city halls all across the country. And I know that those challenges are particularly severe today because of this recession. Four in five cities have had to cut services, just when folks need it the most, and 48 states face the prospects of budget deficits in the coming fiscal year.

And that's one reason why we took swift and aggressive action in the first months of my administration to pull our economy back from the brink, including the largest and most sweeping economic recovery plan in our nation's history. If we had not taken that step, our cities would be in an even deeper hole, and state budget deficits would be nearly twice as large as they are right now, and tens of thousands of police officers and firefighters and teachers would be out of a job as we speak. And I think that all of you are aware of that.

But what's also clear is we're going to need to do more than just help our cities weather the current economic storm. We've got to figure out ways to rebuild them on a newer, firmer, stronger foundation for our future. And that requires new strategies for our cities and metropolitan areas that focus on advancing opportunity through competitive, sustainable, and inclusive growth…

Now, the first thing we need to recognize is that this is not just a time of challenge for America's cities; it's also a time of great change. Even as we've seen many of our central cities continuing to grow in recent years, we've seen their suburbs and exurbs grow roughly twice as fast—that spreads homes and jobs and businesses to a broader geographic area. And this transformation is creating new pressures and problems, of course, but it's also opening up new opportunities, because it's not just our cities that are hotbeds of innovation anymore, it's our growing metropolitan areas.

And when I spoke to the U.S. Conference of Mayors last year, I tried to hone in on this point that what I think traditionally had been seen as this divide between city and suburb, that in some ways you've seen both city and suburb now come together and recognize they can't solve their problems in isolation; they've got to be paying attention to each other. And these metropolitan areas, they're home to 85 percent of our jobs and 90 percent of our economic output.

Now, that doesn't mean investing in America comes at the expense of rural America; quite the opposite. Investing in mass transit and high-speed rail, for example, doesn't just make our downtowns more livable; it helps our regional economies grow. Investing in renewable energy doesn't just make our cities cleaner; it boosts rural areas that harness that energy. Our urban and rural communities are not independent; they are interdependent.

So what's needed now is a new, imaginative, bold vision tailored to this reality that brings opportunity to every corner of our growing metropolitan areas—a new strategy that's about Southern Florida as much as Miami; that's about Mesa and Scottsdale as much as it's about Phoenix; that's about Aurora and Boulder and Northglenn as much as about Denver.

An early step was to appoint Adolfo Carrion as our first White House Director of Urban Affairs. And his team and he share my belief that our cities need more than just a partner—they need a partner who knows that the old ways of looking at our cities just won't do. And that's why I've directed the Office of Management and Budget, the Domestic Policy Council, the National Economic Council, and the Office of Urban Affairs to conduct the first comprehensive interagency review in 30 years of how the federal government approaches and funds urban and metropolitan areas so that we can start having a concentrated, focused, strategic approach to federal efforts to revitalize our metropolitan areas.

And we're also going to take a hard look at how Washington helps or hinders our cities and metro areas—from infrastructure to transportation; from housing to energy; from sustainable development to education. And we're going to make sure federal policies aren't hostile to good ideas or best practices on the local levels. We're going to put an end to throwing money at what doesn't work—and we're going to start investing in what does work and make sure that we're encouraging that.

Now, we began to do just that with my budget proposal, which included two investments in innovative and proven strategies. I just want to mention these briefly. The first, Promise Neighborhoods, is modeled on Geoffrey Canada's successful Harlem Children's Zone. It's an all-encompassing, all-hands-on-deck effort that's turning around the lives of New York City's children, block by block. And what we want to do is to make grants available for communities in other cities to jumpstart their own neighborhood-level interventions that change the odds for our kids.

The second proposal we call Choice Neighborhoods—focuses on new ideas for housing in our cities by recognizing that different communities need different solutions. So instead of isolated and monolithic public housing projects that too often trap residents in a cycle of poverty and isolate them further, we want to invest in proven strategies that actually transform communities and enhance opportunity for residents and businesses alike.

But we also need to fundamentally change the way we look at metropolitan development. For too long, federal policy has actually encouraged sprawl and congestion and pollution, rather than quality public transportation and smart, sustainable development. And we've been keeping communities isolated when we should have been bringing them together.

And that's why we've created a new interagency partnership on sustainable communities, led by Shaun Donovan, as well as Ray LaHood and Lisa Jackson. And by working together, their agencies can make sure that when it comes to development—housing, transportation, energy efficiency—these things aren't mutually exclusive; they go hand in hand. And that means making sure that affordable housing exists in close proximity to jobs and transportation. That means encouraging shorter travel times and lower travel costs. It means safer, greener, more livable communities.

So we're off to a good start. But the truth is, that Washington can't solve all of these problems that face our cities, and frankly, I know that cities don't expect Washington to solve all these problems. Instead of waiting for Washington, a lot of cities have already gone ahead and become their own laboratories for change and innovation, some leading the world in coming up with new ways to solve the problems of our time.

So you take an example like Denver. Their metropolitan area is projected to grow by one million residents over the next 15 years or so. But rather than wait for a congestion crisis, they're already at work on plans to build and operate a public transit system up to the challenge, and to surround that system with smart new housing, retail, and office development near each stop.

Philadelphia is an example of what's been called "urban agriculture." It may sound like an oxymoron, but one proposal is trying to make a situation where fresh, local food supplies are within a short walk for most city residents, which will have a direct impact not only on the economy and on the environment, but also make an immeasurable difference in the health of Americans.

Or Kansas City. One idea there focuses on transforming a low-income community into a national model of sustainability by weatherizing homes and building a green local transit system.

Three different cities with three unique ideas for the future. And that's why they're three of the cities that members of my Cabinet and Office of Urban Affairs will visit this summer as part of a ongoing national conversation to lift up best practices from around the country, to look at innovations for the metropolitan areas of tomorrow. Forward-looking cities shouldn't be succeeding despite Washington; they should be succeeding with a hand from Washington. We want to hear directly from them, and we want to hear directly from all of you, on fresh ideas and successful solutions that you've devised, and then figure out what the federal government should do or shouldn't do to help reinvent cities and metropolitan areas for the 21st century.

So I know that this change is possible. After all, I'm from a city that knows a little something about reinventing itself. In the 19th century, after a cataclysmic fire, Chicagoans rebuilt stronger than before. In the last century, they led the world upward in steel and glass. And in this century, under my friend Mayor Daley's leadership, they're helping to lead the world forward in newer, greener, more livable ways.

Daniel Burnam said, "Make no little plans." And that's the spirit behind his bold and ambitious designs unveiled 100 years ago this month that helped transform Chicago into a world-class city. That's the same spirit which we have to approach the reinvention of all America's cities and metropolitan areas—a vision of vibrant, sustainable places that provide our children with every chance to learn and to grow, and that allow our businesses and workers the best opportunity to innovate and succeed, and that let our older Americans live out their best years in the midst of all that metropolitan life can offer. Now is the time to seize that moment of possibility, and I am absolutely confident that, starting today with this conversation, you and I together, we're going to be able to make this happen.

# The Metro Moment

## By Bruce Katz

*The following excerpts are from a 2010 commencement speech at the University of Illinois at Chicago, College of Urban Planning and Public Affairs. The speech was delivered by Bruce Katz who serves as the Director of the Metropolitan Policy Program at the Brookings Institution.*

You begin your professional career at what can only be described as a Metro Moment, in the United States and throughout the world. Metropolitan areas, cities and their surrounding suburbs, exurbs and rural communities, are the world's essential communities. These places are the engines of national prosperity. They are on the front lines of demographic transformation. They are the vehicles for environmental sustainability. They are the vanguards of innovation ... in technology, in business, in government policy, and practice.

If this is a Metro Moment, then it is also a time for individuals who are engaged in building strong cities and suburbs. Professionals who plan, design, finance, develop, retrofit, manage, implement in ways that affect the lives of metro citizens every day. Like metros, your profession is on the front lines, of a revolution in thinking and practice.

The traditional ways of specialized disciplines and siloed bureaucracies are giving way to holistic thinking and integrated solutions. This, in turn, is fuelling a burst of creativity and imagination. These are not your parents' metros and this is not your parents' urban planning profession.

So let me situate your work in the complex dynamics of metropolitan America. Broad forces have positioned metropolitan areas as the engines of national prosperity.

Thomas Friedman has famously taught us that the world is "flat." But the spatial reality of modern economies is that they concentrate intensely in a relatively small number of places. Strictly speaking, there is no single American economy, but rather a network of highly connected, hyperlinked, and economically integrated metros.

The real heart of the American economy lies in the top 100 metropolitan areas that take up only 12 percent of our land mass, but harbor two-thirds of our population and generate 75 percent of our gross domestic product. These metropolitan areas dominate the economy because they gather and strengthen the assets—innovation, human capital, and infrastructure—that drive economic growth and productivity. The Chicago metropolis, for example, is home to 67 percent of the population of Illinois, but contributes 78 percent of that state's GDP.

Metros punch above their weight. The true economic geography, here and abroad, is a metropolitan one, enveloping city and suburb, exurb and rural town. Goods, people, capital and energy flow seamlessly across the metropolitan landscape. Labor markets are metro-politan as are housing markets and commuter-sheds. Sports teams, cultural institutions, and media all exist in metropolitan space.

As we emerge from this devastating recession, metropolitan economies will undergo a radical shift. They are likely to become more export oriented, less consumption oriented. They are likely to make a slow but critical transition to lower carbon, through renewable energy sources, the manufacture of sustainable infrastructure and sustainable products, and changes in buildings and the built environment. And they are likely to be even more dependent on innovation as the catalyst for growth and more reliant on educated and skilled workers.

For today's graduates, the point is this: The U.S. economy is going through a substantial restructuring with enormous implications for every aspect of the work you are about to do. If metros are the engines of national prosperity, then they are also on the front lines of demographic transformation.

* * *

We are a growing nation. Our population exceeded 300 million back in 2006 and we are now on our way to hit 350 million around 2025. We are a diversifying nation. An incredible 83 percent of our growth this decade was driven by racial and ethnic minorities. We are an aging nation. The number of seniors and boomers exceeded 100 million this decade.

We are a nation riven by educational disparities. Whites and Asians are now more than twice as likely to hold a bachelors degree as blacks and Hispanics.

We are a nation divided by income inequities and a growing gap between rich and poor. Low wage workers saw hourly earnings decline by 8 percent this decade; high wage workers saw wages rise by 3 percent.

America's top 100 metropolitan areas are on the front lines of our nation's demographic transformation. The trends I've identified—growth, diversity, aging, educational disparities, income inequities—are happening at a faster pace, a greater scale, and a higher level of intensity in our major metropolitan areas.

Let's take diversity and immigration as an example of the leading role of metropolitan areas.

Racial and ethnic minorities accounted for an astonishing 83 percent of national population growth this decade. As a result, Hispanics now make up roughly 15 percent of the nation's population. African Americans comprise a little over 12 percent of the nation's population. Racial and ethnic minorities make up an even larger share of the population in the top 100 metros: nearly 19 percent of metro populations are Hispanic; nearly 14 percent African American.

We are well on the path to becoming a majority-minority nation and metros are leading the way. Seventeen metropolitan areas are now majority minority, compared to 14 in 2000 and just five in 1990. Thirty-one metropolitan areas have children populations that are majority minority.

The growing diversity of America owes primarily to the natural increase in racial and ethnic populations that were already present in the U.S. in 2000. But new immigrants continued to come to America this decade, accounting for roughly 30 percent of national population growth. In metro America, the pace and volume of immigration was faster, with the share of growth approaching one third. As a result, one in every six metropolitan residents is now foreign born compared to one in eight Americans in total. This share is larger than the share experienced during the other great wave of international migration in the early 20<sup>th</sup> century.

Like that earlier period, immigration is one of the most contentious issues in our nation, best illustrated by Arizona's recent actions. Yet the benefits of immigration—and diversity more broadly—are immense: New markets; new ideas; new workers to replace those that retire; new connections to emerging markets outside the U.S.

So we have a central challenge: How do we embrace diversity and adapt to being a majority–minority nation? How do we particularly focus on educating and training the future, diverse workforce of Americans, so that they can compete and succeed globally?

Metros are not only engines of prosperity and on the front lines of demographic transformation... they are also vehicles for delivering environmental sustainability. The low-carbon economy, like the export-oriented economy, will be primarily invented, financed, produced and delivered in the top 100 metros.

The investment base for the green economy is intensely concentrated; 94 percent of venture capital comes from the top 100 metro areas.

The most innovative aspects of the green economy will cluster around major, largely metro-based, research institutions. Fifteen of the 21 national labs run by the Department of Energy are located within the top 100 metropolitan areas. Making our old and new homes, office, retail, and commercial facilities energy efficient will primarily be a metropolitan act, given the heavy concentration of our population, buildings, and businesses.

As metros move forward, they will need to make some hard choices about development. Despite the resurgence of many cities and urban cores, sprawl remains alive and well in the United States, which helps explain why the U.S. has double the per capita carbon dioxide emissions of other modern economies like Germany and the United Kingdom.

During this decade, cities and high density suburbs grew a little under 5 percent while less developed counties grew at more than three times that rate. By 2008, more than 40 percent of metropolitan population lived in spread out areas, creating a distended "autoscape" in place of the traditional landscape of human habitation.

One of the most difficult challenges before us, for both environmental and economic reasons, is to move away from a sprawling, distended landscape to communities that connect jobs, housing, and transport for people and firms.

America's metros are confronting the super-sized challenges of our new global order with energy, invention, and creativity. Challenged by continuous economic restructuring, metros are finding new ways to bolster innovation whether by financing wind energy and fuel cells in struggling, industrial metros like Cleveland or by connecting new entrepreneurs to money, markets, partners, management, and other resources in prosperous metros like San Diego.

Confronted with a diverse, less educated workforce, metros are laboring to elevate human capital by preparing disadvantaged workers to excel in such global hotbeds of employment as logistics in Louisville, life sciences in the Bay Area, and health care in both.

Burdened by concentrated poverty, a new wave of housing developers are producing mixed income housing in America's poorest neighborhoods—in Pittsburgh, in Chicago, in St. Louis—as a catalyst for modernizing and improving neighborhood schools. The result is not just quality, distinctive housing but, more importantly, neighborhood schools that work and sharp improvements in student performance.

Faced with rising congestion, exploding gas prices and aging systems, metros are designing and implementing market-shaping infrastructure investments to reconfigure freeways in Milwaukee, modernize water and sewer systems in Atlanta, build out region wide transit in Denver, and install fiber optic networks in Scranton.

And, confronted with what Strobe Talbott calls the "existential threat of global warming," metros like Seattle and Chicago are taking ambitious steps to create quality, sustainable places by promoting green building, transit oriented development, urban regeneration, and renewable sources of energy.

What knits these policy efforts? It's their embrace of a new style of governance that brings together city and suburban leaders around common purpose, cuts across conventional lines of government, business, university and philanthropy and deploys systemic market and environment shaping investments and interventions.

\* \* \*

The Metro Moment has meaning and import far beyond those few of us who observe metros or build metros or govern metros. This is truly a call to this generation to build a different world of metro opportunity and possibility.

A Metro Moment requires that we act, with vision, imagination, and confidence. Will we seize the possibilities before us?

# Trading Places

## The Demographic Inversion of the American City

### By Alan Ehrenhalt

*Throughout the United States, a demographic inversion is taking place. The affluent are now choosing city life over life in the suburbs. Immigrants and those with lesser means have little choice but to settle in the suburbs. Chicago is gradually coming to resemble a traditional European city—with more of the rich living downtown and many of the poor in the suburbs.*

Thirty years ago, the mayor of Chicago was unseated by a snowstorm. A blizzard in January of 1979 dumped some 20 inches on the ground, causing, among other problems, a curtailment of transit service. The few available trains coming downtown from the northwest side filled up with middle-class white riders near the far end of the line, leaving no room for poorer people trying to board on inner-city platforms. African Americans and Hispanics blamed this on Mayor Michael Bilandic, and he lost the Democratic primary to Jane Byrne a few weeks later.

Today, this could never happen. Not because of climate change, or because the Chicago Transit Authority now runs flawlessly. It couldn't happen because the trains would fill up with minorities and immigrants on the outskirts of the city, and the passengers left stranded at the inner-city stations would be members of the affluent professional class.

\* \* \*

We are not witnessing the abandonment of the suburbs or a movement of millions of people back to the city all at once. But we are living at a moment in which the massive outward migration of the affluent that characterized the second half of the twentieth century is coming to an end. For several decades now, cities in the United States have wished for a "24/7" downtown, a place where people live as well as work, and keep the streets busy, interesting, and safe at all times of day. This is what urbanist Jane Jacobs preached in the 1960s, and it has long since become the accepted goal of urban planners. Only when significant numbers of people lived downtown, planners believed, could central cities regain their historic role as magnets for culture and as a source of identity and pride for the metropolitan areas they served. Now that's starting to happen, fueled by the changing mores of the young and by gasoline prices fast approaching $5-per-gallon. In many of its urbanized regions, an America that seemed destined for ever increasing individualization and sprawl is experimenting with new versions of community and sociability.

Why has demographic inversion begun? For one thing, the deindustrialization of the central city, for all the tragic human dislocations it caused, has eliminated many of the things that made affluent people want to move away from it. Nothing much is manufactured downtown anymore (or anywhere near it), and that means that the noise and grime that prevailed for most of the twentieth century have gone away. Manhattan may seem like a loud and gritty place now, but it is nothing like the city of tenement manufacturing, rumbling elevated trains, and horses and coal dust in the streets that confronted inhabitants in the early 1900s. Third-floor factory lofts, whether in Soho or in St. Louis, can be marketed as attractive and stylish places to live. The urban historian Robert Bruegmann goes so far as to claim that deindustrialization has, on the whole, been good for downtowns because it has permitted so many opportunities for creative reuse of the buildings. I wouldn't go quite that far, and, given the massive job losses of recent years, I doubt most of the residents of Detroit would, either. But it is true that the environmental factors that made middle-class people leave the central city for streetcar suburbs in the 1900s and for station-wagon suburbs in the 1950s do not apply any more.

Nor, in general, does the scourge of urban life in the 1970s and '80s: random street violence. True, the murder rates in cities like Chicago, Philadelphia, and Cleveland have climbed in the last few years, but this increase has been propelled in large part by gang- and drug-related violence. For the most part, middle-class people of all colors began to feel safe on the streets of urban America in the 1990s, and they still feel that way. The paralyzing fear that anyone of middle age can still recall vividly from the 1970s—that the shadowy figure passing by on a dark city street at night stands a good chance of being a mugger—is rare these days, and almost nonexistent among young people. Walk around the neighborhood of 14th and U streets in Washington, D.C. on a Saturday night, and you will find it perhaps the liveliest part of the city, at least for those under 25. This is a neighborhood where the riots of 1968 left physical scars that still have not disappeared, and where outsiders were afraid to venture for more than 30 years.

The young newcomers who have rejuvenated 14th and U believe that this recovering slum is the sort of place where they want to spend time and, increasingly, where they want to live. This is the generation that grew up watching "Seinfeld," "Friends," and "Sex and the City," mostly from the comfort of suburban sofas. We have gone from a sitcom world defined by "Leave It to Beaver" and "Father Knows Best" to one that offers a whole range of urban experiences and enticements. I do not claim that a handful of TV shows has somehow produced a new urbanist generation, but it is striking how pervasive the pro-city sensibility is within this generation, particularly among its elite. In recent years, teaching undergraduates at the University of Richmond, the majority of them from affluent suburban backgrounds, I made a point of asking where they would prefer to live in 15 years—in a suburb or in a neighborhood close to the center of the city. Few ever voted for suburban life.

I can't say that they had necessarily devoted a great deal of thought to the question: When I asked them whether they would want to live in an urban neighborhood without a car, many seemed puzzled and said no. Clearly, we are a long way from producing a generation for whom urban life and automobile ownership are mutually exclusive. In downtown Charlotte, a luxury condominium is scheduled for construction this year that will allow residents to drive their cars into a garage elevator, ride up to the floor they live on, and park right next to their front door. I have a hard time figuring out whether that is a triumph for urbanism or a defeat. But my guess is that, except in Manhattan, the carless life has yet to achieve any significant traction in the affluent new enclaves of urban America.

Not that cars and the demographic inversion aren't closely related; they are. In Atlanta, where the middle-class return to the city is occurring with more suddenness than perhaps anywhere in the United States, the most frequently cited reason is traffic. People who did not object to a 20-mile commute from the suburbs a decade ago are objecting to it now in part because the same commute takes quite a bit longer. To this, we can add the prospect of $5-per-gallon gasoline. It's impossible at this point to say with any certainty just what energy costs will do to American living patterns over the next decade. Urbanists predicted a return to the city during previous spikes in the cost of gasoline, notably during shortages in the 1970s. They were wrong. Gas prices came down, and the suburbs expanded dramatically. But today's prices at the pump are not the result of political pressures by angry sheiks in the Persian Gulf. They are the result of increased worldwide demand that is only going to continue to increase. Some suburbanites will simply stay where they are and accept the cost. But many will decide to stop paying $100 every few days for a tank of gasoline that will allow them to commute 40 or 50 miles a day, round-trip.

Ultimately, though, the current inversion is less the result of middle-aged people changing their minds than of young adults expressing different values, habits, and living preferences than their parents. The demographic changes that have taken place in America over the past generation—the increased propensity to remain single, the rise of cohabitation, the much later age at first marriage for those who do marry, the smaller size of families for those who have children, and, at the other end, the rapidly growing number of healthy and active adults in their sixties, seventies, and eighties—have combined virtually all of the significant elements that make a demographic inversion not only possible but likely. We are moving toward a society in which millions of people with substantial earning power or ample savings can live wherever they want, and many will choose central cities over distant suburbs. As they do this, others will find themselves forced to live in less desirable places—now defined as those further from the center of the metropolis. And, as this happens, suburbs that never dreamed of being entry points for immigrants will have to cope with new realities. It should come as no surprise that the most intense arguments about hiring and educating the undocumented have occurred in the relatively distant reaches of American suburbia, such as Prince William County, Virginia.

The reality of demographic inversion strikes me every time I return to Chicago, the city in which I was born and grew up. My grandfather arrived there in 1889, found his way to the Near West Side, and opened a tailor shop that remained in business for 50 years. During that time, the neighborhood was a compact and somewhat culturally isolated enclave of Jewish and Italian families. (It was also the location of Hull House and the original home of the Chicago Cubs.) The building that housed my grandfather's store was torn down in the 1960s when the University of Illinois built its Chicago campus in the neighborhood. The street corner where the store stood now houses part of the university science complex.

The UIC campus is, to my eyes, one of the ugliest in America. But I have made my peace with that. What interests me is what is going on all around that neighborhood, now called University Village. For a while after the school was built, its environs were a sort of residential no-man's-land, dangerous at night and unattractive to the young academics who taught there. Today, assistant professors at UIC generally don't live there either, but for a different reason: They can't afford it. Demand for the townhouses and condominiums on the Near West Side has priced junior faculty out of the market. One can walk a couple of blocks down the street from where my grandfather's shop once stood and order a steak for $24.

You might respond that there is nothing especially noteworthy in this. A college setting, liberal academics, houses close to the city's cultural attractions: That's garden-variety gentrification. What else would you expect?

If you feel that way, you might want to ride an elevated train going northwest, to the lesser-known Logan Square, a few miles beyond the Loop. Whatever Logan Square might be, it is not downtown chic. It is a moderately close-in nineteenth-century neighborhood with a history fairly typical for a city that A.J. Liebling once called "an endless succession of factory-town main streets." Logan Square was developed primarily by Scandinavian manufacturers, who lived on the tree-lined boulevards while their workers, many of them Polish, rented the cottages on the side streets. By the 1970s, nearly all the Poles had decamped for suburbia, and they were replaced by an influx of Puerto Ricans. The area became a haven for gangs and gang violence, and most of the retail shopping that held the community together disappeared.

Logan Square is still not the safest neighborhood in Chicago. There are armed robberies and some killings on its western fringe, and, even on the quiet residential streets, mothers tell their children to be home before dark. But that hasn't prevented Logan Square from changing dramatically again—not over the past generation, or the past decade, but in the past five years. The big stone houses built by the factory owners on Logan Boulevard are selling for nearly $1 million, despite the housing recession. The restaurant that sits on the square itself sells goat cheese quesadillas and fettuccine with octopus, and attracts long lines of customers who drive in from the suburbs on weekend evenings. To describe what has happened virtually overnight in Logan Square as gentrification is to miss the point. Chicago, like much of America, is rearranging itself, and the result is an entire metropolitan area that looks considerably different from what it looked like when this decade started.

Of course, demographic inversion cannot be a one-way street. If some people are coming inside, some people have to be going out. And so they are—in Chicago as in much of the rest of the country. During the past ten years, with relatively little fanfare and surprisingly little press attention, the great high-rise public housing projects that defined squalor in urban America for half a century have essentially disappeared. In Chicago, the infamous Robert Taylor Homes are gone, and the equally infamous Cabrini-Green is all but gone. This has meant the removal of tens of thousands of people, who have taken their Section 8 federal housing subsidies and moved to struggling African American neighborhoods elsewhere in the city. Some have moved to the city's southern suburbs—small suburbs such as Dixmoor, Robbins, and Harvey, which have been among the poorest communities in metropolitan Chicago. At the same time, tens of thousands of immigrants are coming to Chicago every year, mostly from various parts of Latin America. Where are they settling? Not in University Village. Some in Logan Square, but fewer every year. They are living in suburban or exurban territory that, until a decade ago, was almost exclusively English-speaking, middle-class, and white.

There are responsible critics who look at all this and see a lot being made out of very little. They argue that, in absolute numbers, the return to the urban center remains a minor demographic event. They have a point. In most metropolitan areas, in the first few years of the twenty-first century, many more people have moved to the suburbs than have moved downtown. A city of half a million that can report a downtown residential population of 25,000—5 percent of the total—can claim that it is doing relatively well....

Even if the vast majority of cities never see a downtown residential boom of massive proportions—there is no doubt that a demographic inversion, in which the rich are moving inside and the poor are moving outside, is taking place. The crucial issue is not the number of people living downtown, although that matters. The crucial issue is who they are, and the ways in which urban life is changing as a result.

What would a post-inversion American city look like? In the most extreme scenario, it would look like many of the European capitals of the 1890s. Take Vienna, for example. In the mid-nineteenth century, the medieval wall that had surrounded the city's central core for hundreds of years was torn down. In its place there appeared the Ringstrasse, the circle of fashionable boulevards where opera was sung and plays performed, where rich merchants and minor noblemen lived in spacious apartments, where gentlemen and ladies promenaded in the evening under the gaslights, where Freud, Mahler, and their friends held long conversations about death over coffee and pastry in sidewalk cafes. By contrast, if you were part of the servant class, odds were you lived far beyond the center, in a neighborhood called Ottakring, a concentration of more than 30, 000 cramped one- and two-bedroom apartments, whose residents—largely immigrant Czechs, Slovaks, and Slovenes—endured a long horse-car ride to get to work in the heart of the city.

* * *

[Finally, there is] the vision of Jane Jacobs, who idealized the Greenwich Village of the 1950s and the casual everyday relationships that made living there comfortable, stimulating, and safe. Much of what Jacobs loved and wrote about will not reappear: The era of the mom-and-pop grocer, the shoemaker, and the candy store has ended for good. We live in a big-box, big-chain century. But I think the youthful urban elites of the twenty-first-century are looking in some sense for the things Jacobs valued, whether they have heard of her or not. They are drawn to the densely packed urban life that they saw on television and found vastly more interesting than the cul-de-sac world they grew up in. And, by and large, I believe central cities will give it to them. Not only that, but much of suburbia, in an effort to stay afloat, will seek to urbanize itself to some extent. That reinvention is already taking place: Look at all the car-created suburbs built in the 1970s and '80s that have created "town centers" in the past five years, with sidewalks and as much of a street grid as they can manage to impose on a faded strip-mall landscape. None of these retrofit efforts look much like a real city. But they are a clue to the direction in which we are heading.

In the 1990s, a flurry of academics and journalists (me among them) wrote books lamenting the decline of community and predicting that it would reappear in some fashion in the new century. I think that is beginning to happen now in the downtowns of America, and I believe, for all its imperfections and inequalities, that the demographic inversion ultimately will do more good than harm. We will never return—nor would most of us want to return—to the close-knit but frequently constricting form of community life that prevailed 50 years ago. But, as we rearrange ourselves in and around many of our big cities, we are groping toward the new communities of the twenty-first century.

# Poverty in DuPage County

## By Barbara Rose

*The number of suburban poor is growing in metropolitan areas across the country. In DuPage County, which is one of the most affluent counties in the country, over 56,000 residents live at or below the poverty level. One in every five households in DuPage County has an annual income below $35,000. Although suburban poverty is less concentrated, and therefore less visible, than in the more blighted areas of Chicago—it is here and it is growing. As poverty disperses to the suburbs, policymakers must recognize that the interests of suburbanites and city dwellers are no longer diametrically opposed.*

A tourism guide depicts DuPage County, eight miles west of Chicago, as "the magnificent miles," a playground of upscale hotels and shopping centers, manicured golf courses and pristine prairie paths. One of the nation's wealthiest counties—with a median household income exceeding $77,000 a year—it's a place where leafy older neighborhoods and historic downtowns alternate with new tracts of super-sized houses, landscaped corporate campuses and clusters of boxy industrial buildings.

By all appearances, John Moore, a corporate finance and strategy professional, enjoys the good life in a new subdivision on the western edge of the county, where homes sold for $490,000 when his was built in 2006. But appearances are deceiving. Two years ago, Moore lost his six-figure job at an international software company. He has nearly exhausted his savings paying his mortgage. Unable to find work or to sell his home in a market glutted with foreclosures, he visits food pantries to stock his fancy four-year-old kitchen. He gets medical care through a network that donates services to the low-income uninsured.

The same network helps Francisca, who asked that her last name be withheld. Francisca lives with her husband Julio and their four teenage sons in a two-bedroom apartment less than a mile from Village Hall in Addison. Julio makes $8.50 per hour working seven days a week, sometimes two shifts a day, cleaning warehouses, a church and a movie theater. Francisca tried to supplement the family's meager income by buying discounted goods in Chicago and selling them to her neighbors at a profit. But lately, because of the bad economy, her customers can't afford to pay for the winter coats they bought on installment.

In Glen Ellyn, where the median household income is nearly $90,000, Laura Davidson gets home from an overnight shift at Target to her family's ground-floor apartment in time to take a two-hour nap before getting her six-year-old off to school. She will get another chance to sleep when her toddler naps at noon. Their middle-class life crumbled after her husband, a 31-year-old machinist, became disabled. Even with food stamps and help from charities, they aren't making it.

These are not the comfortable lifestyles that lure families to the suburbs. Yet venture into any corner of DuPage County's 334 square miles and you discover people in need. They include the newly impoverished, hit by illness or unemployment or both, and the marginally employed, whose payday-to-payday struggle gets harder in bad times.

The number of suburban poor is growing in metropolitan areas across the country. Their neighborhoods little resemble the graffiti-scarred pockets of hopelessness common to big cities; but their situation is no less debilitating. The suburban poor subsist, often all but invisible to the more-fortunate majority, in high-cost areas where their income doesn't begin to cover basic needs.

"DuPage County has changed," says Rita Gonzalez, a member of the DuPage County Board. "The demographics have changed. People's financial situations have changed." Today, nearly 6 percent of DuPage's population of 930,000 lives below the federal poverty level of $22,050 for a family of four. A much larger segment struggles to make ends meet. These so-called "working poor" live at twice the poverty level, a common proxy for low income.

Together with poverty-level residents, they make up 15.8 percent of the county's population, or about one in six residents. Their number grew steadily even during the boom years of the 1990s, more than doubling to about 145,000 by 2008.

"It's a challenge to leadership to take the demographic shift that's been going on for decades and make sure it is a positive for our community," says Candace King, executive director of DuPage Federation on Human Services Reform, an umbrella group that coordinates responses to families in need.

## A Study in Contrasts

The changes in DuPage mirror powerful trends across the country, where poor families in search of jobs and affordable rents move farther from city centers, even as affluent empty nesters and young professionals gravitate downtown. The United States marked a watershed in 2005 when the number of poor living in suburbs outnumbered those in cities for the first time, according to a Brookings Institution study of 100 metropolitan areas. Urban poverty is more concentrated; but in absolute numbers, the suburban poor population is larger.

"We are more of a suburban nation. Our suburbs are growing faster than the cities," says Elizabeth Kneebone, a Brookings Institution senior analyst. "As that population has grown, it also has diversified."

The result is sharp contrasts. In central Wheaton, across the street from luxury condominiums, people wait in line at a nonprofit for free food and clothing. In Lisle during evening rush hour, men and women with backpacks and rolling suitcases cross a busy six-lane highway on foot, making their way from a bus stop to an overnight shelter in a church. A meat market in Addison features goat legs for $2.79 per pound within a short drive from a Lombard butcher selling boneless prime rib for $12.99 per pound.

In a suburban land of plenty, the poor remain isolated and often overlooked. Immigrants such as Francisca, who came from Mexico 13 years ago to join her husband in Bensenville, increasingly bypass the city to settle in the suburbs, where they often find little support to help them assimilate.

Today, immigrants and low-income families displaced from gentrifying city neighborhoods crowd into older suburban apartments and tract homes. At the same time, many of the manufacturing jobs that once helped newcomers get a financial foothold have disappeared, replaced by low-paying service work. More recently, the collapse of the real estate market eliminated hundreds of local construction jobs.

Fernando Ibarra is feeling the impact. He stood shivering in line on a chilly evening last October, a clean-shaven 28-year-old in a gray sweatshirt, waiting for a food pantry to open at People's Resource Center in downtown Wheaton. A bricklayer and union member, he and his brothers found good-paying jobs when they moved to West Chicago from Mexico six years ago, but the work dried up two years ago. Now he struggles to support his wife and two-year-old daughter on an $11 hourly wage assembling cabinetry. Of the construction market, he says simply, "It's bad."

Poverty rates inevitably increase during downturns, but suburban areas paid a heavier toll during this recession than in previous ones. Among the hardest hit are communities on the metropolitan fringe, where the torrid building boom fueled a false prosperity.

"Suburbs are feeling the brunt," Kneebone says. "This downturn is only going to contribute to the suburbanization of poverty. Many areas are unprepared. There's less of a safety net in these communities."

In DuPage, both public and private providers of social services are feeling the strain. "All of the agencies are feeling a little bit overwhelmed," says Joan Rickard, human services manager at DuPage County Community Services.

## "I don't know where we would be"

At the nonprofit People's Resource Center, a 35-year-old multiservice agency that operates one of the county's largest food pantries, demand surged by nearly 30 percent in the second half of 2009 compared with the same period a year earlier. The pantry distributed nearly 21,000 grocery carts of food. Recipients are allowed one visit per month.

"It's the most dramatic increase in our history," says Development Director Karen Hill. "We're seeing a lot of families that have never had to use a food pantry before, people who never in a million years thought they'd use a food pantry."

"They're desperately looking for any service," says Food Services Director Melissa Travis. "We all have this image there's this huge welfare state." But many struggling people, she adds, "don't qualify for any kind of government help. They can't afford medical insurance, medicine for their kids, mortgage payments. They come in here much more stressed, much more afraid."

Many of the pantry's patrons are unemployed. But 56 percent report at least one family member working. They were getting by until their hours got cut or, like Ibarra, they were forced to take lower-paying jobs.

On the evening when Ibarra stood in line, the waiting area filled to standing room only with dozens of people, each with a different story. An Iraqi family had fled Baghdad's violence for Wheaton. A 62-year-old Wood Dale woman quit her job to care for her frail husband. A mother of three could no longer make ends meet on her factory wages. A shy Sudanese refugee from Carol Stream lost her job as a nursing assistant.

Among the first-time visitors was Paula Marcum, a single mom with four children who works as an assistant facilities manager for a local bank. "Things have gotten a little tight," says the Warrenville resident, explaining that she fell behind in her rent when a roommate moved out without warning.

Davidson, the Target employee, began visiting the pantry last year when she and her disabled husband, George, exhausted their savings. In better times, their combined household income had inched above $60,000. Then she was laid off from her job as an administrative assistant and her husband's health deteriorated. The Social Security Administration denied him permanent disability payments for a degenerative spine condition that has left him unable to work or even to care reliably for their youngest, an active curly-haired blond toddler, Zachary.

\* \* \*

## "At this point I need miracles"

Access DuPage member Estella Rodriguez, 61, spends part of her days keeping the linoleum floors shining in the spotless basement apartment she shares with her husband in Glendale Heights. They pay rent to a family that owns the split-level house, where an American flag decal decorates the front door. She also takes an English class at the College of DuPage and looks for work. Her husband, who is treated for cancer by Access DuPage, earns $7.75 per hour as a commercial mover. (The minimum wage in Illinois is $8.25 per hour.)

A grandmother now, Rodriguez raised two sons alone while working in an airplane-parts factory after emigrating from Mexico to California in 1985. One son is a registered nurse; the other works in medical records. "I'm very happy about my sons; they have a good life," she says. "I love America."

For Francisca's four teenage sons, a similar upwardly mobile path seems less certain. Isolated from support that could help her improve her prospects, she encounters barriers even when she tries to access basic safety-net services at the food pantry near her apartment in Addison.

On one visit to the pantry, Francisca brought one of her sons—a polite and fluently bilingual high school senior—to help her communicate in English. The pantry's paid coordinator sent the pair away to get copies of their birth certificates, a requirement to be placed on a list for holiday baskets. When they returned with the copies, he asked them for a letter proving the family's need. When she returned with the letter, hoping to take home food, he allowed her to take some bread off a front table, then motioned her to an exit.

On a cold evening in Francisca's small living room, an image of Mary Magdalene flickered on a votive candle. Her family turned on the kitchen's oven to warm the apartment. She recalled a time when both she and Julio were sick and unable to work, when the family ate for a week on $34 they had saved for emergencies.

Then Julio spoke about his dream of a better future for his sons: good jobs, a home. What would it take to realize his dream? "At this point I need miracles," he says.

# The Metropolitan Mayors Caucus

## Institution Building in a Political Fragmented Metropolitan Region

### By Bonnie Lindstrom

*The Mayors Caucus began as a forum to foster cooperation among the munici-palities in the Chicago metropolitan region. This article presents a case study of the development of the Mayors Caucus as a new institution established to overcome the region's extreme government fragmentation and decades of city-suburban hostility. The article concludes with the argument that "in the twenty-first century, developing new capacities to solve regional problems will depend on developing new institutional arrangements, on a shared vision of the region's challenges, and on strong leadership."*

In *Exploring Ad Hoc Regionalism* (2002), Douglas Porter and Allan Wallis argue that the nation is in a time of invention and experiment aimed to develop governance capacity to address regional challenges.[1] They suggest that one of the ways to develop governance capacity is to enhance existing institutional arrangements such as councils of governments (COGs). The Metropolitan Mayors Caucus is an example of one new institutional arrange-ment that emerged from the Chicago metropolitan region's suburban COGs.

The Mayors Caucus was established so that the mayors in the six-county region could work together on issues of mutual concern. When first established, the Mayors Caucus established an agenda and set up task forces to address issues specific to their municipali-ties. After it was formally designated a nonprofit organization, the Mayors Caucus joined the region's civic and nonprofit advocacy organizations in ad hoc coalitions to promote its

Bonnie Lindstrom, Excerpts from: "The Metropolitan Mayors Caucus: Institution Building in a Political Fragmented Metropolitan Region," *Urban Affairs Review*, vol. 46, no. 1, pp. 37-45, 47-62. Copyright © 2010 by Sage Publications. Reprinted with permission.

regional agenda. This is a case study of how Chicago's suburban COGs developed into the Mayors Caucus and the impact the caucus has had on regional governance.

\* \* \*

## Political Fragmentation

The Chicago metropolitan region is one of the most politically fragmented in the nation. The six counties in northeastern Illinois (Cook, DuPage, Kane, Lake, McHenry, and Will) are the core of the Chicago metropolitan region. By 2010, the metropolitan region had over 1,200 units of local government, composed of 273 municipalities (including the city of Chicago); county and township governments, special purpose districts,[2] and joint action water agencies.[3] The political fragmentation is the result of Illinois laws that limit municipal indebtedness and revenues, encouraging the creation of special purpose districts with their own bonding power and taxing authority.[4]

The political fragmentation is also the result of a historic city-suburban hostility dating to the late nineteenth century. From 1870 to 1893, the city of Chicago expanded from 35 square miles to approximately 185 square miles by annexing adjacent townships whose residents voted to join the city to be able to utilize city services, primarily Lake Michigan water. Chicago's rapid annexation of its adjacent townships, the possible threat that the city would cut off Lake Michigan water, and the influx of immigrants from Southern and Eastern Europe to work in Chicago's heavy industries contributed to suburban distrust of Chicago before World War I. After World War II, the city of Chicago experienced the in-migration of African-Americans from the South and White flight from city neighborhoods. Chicago Democrat-suburban Republican competition for control of the Illinois General Assembly intensified the city-suburban hostility in the 1980s and 1990s.

\* \* \*

## Metropolitan Mayors Caucus

Given a political culture of local autonomy and a historic pattern of city-suburban hostility, what explains the establishment of a new regional institution such as the Metropolitan Mayors Caucus in 1997? The primary answer is that the mayor of Chicago and the leaders of the suburban COGs agreed to work together based on their awareness that they shared the same concerns on maintaining the region's economic vitality and promoting sustainable development. Their willingness to cooperate was also based on the successes of the suburban COGs. Beginning in the 1950s, mayors in different subregions had begun meeting to find ways to cooperate to meet the challenges they faced. These informal meetings set the pattern for the development of the nine suburban COGs that agreed to join with Mayor Richard M. Daley and the city of Chicago to work toward resolving their common challenges.

\* \* \*

## Coalition Partners

[F]or its initiatives on housing, education funding reform, freight rail and ground transportation, and regional growth, the Mayors Caucus needed coalition partners to achieve its goals.

In the 1980s, the region's business leadership [represented by civic organizations] became actively engaged in a regional dialogue on how to remain competitive in a global economy. The Commercial Club of Chicago, whose members included the CEOs of the major corporations in the region, established the Civic Committee to pursue policies that would improve education and workforce development in Chicago and make Chicago and the region more attractive for new businesses. The two major regional initiatives of the Civic Committee were the establishment of World Business Chicago, a public-private partnership with Chicago, and adding new runways at O'Hare International Airport.

After the Civic Committee issued a report calling for the region to unite to solve its transportation, education, and inequitable tax problems, the committee established Chicago Metropolis 2020 to pursue this agenda.[16] The Civic Committee and Chicago Metropolis 2020 were joined by two other civic organizations: the Chicago land Chamber of Commerce and the Metropolitan Planning Council (MPC).

The civic organizations were joined in their initiatives by public-interest advocacy organizations originally founded to promote an agenda of social justice and reinvestment in lower-income Chicago neighborhoods. Concerned about job creation on the exurban fringe at the expense of inner-city poverty and job loss, Business and Professional People for the Public Interest and the Center for Neighborhood Technology have agendas supporting sustainable regional development. Financed by national advocacy organizations (e.g., the Sierra Club and the American Lung Foundation), national foundations, and Chicago's business community, the advocacy organizations use their legal and technical expertise to mobilize public opinion and challenge regional institutional decision making.

### From Republican to Democratic Hegemony

During the 1990s, the Republican leadership in the General Assembly, James "Pate" Philip and Lee Daniels, were both from DuPage County, the most Republican county in Illinois. Pate Philip was the president of the Illinois Senate throughout the 1990s. Lee Daniels was the house speaker for two years and minority leader for the other eight. The two leaders promoted a partisan legislative agenda that favored the Republican suburbs over Chicago interests. Pate Philip, in particular, articulated a political philosophy strongly antagonistic to Chicago and its minority residents.

The sweep by Democrats in the 2002 election altered the balance of political power in the state. For the first time in 26 years, the Democrats controlled the Governorship and had a majority in both houses of the Illinois General Assembly.

The Democratic leadership in the General Assembly, Emil Jones and Michael Madigan, represented south and southwest Cook suburbs and neighborhoods in south and southwest Chicago. Political power had moved from the economically prosperous suburbs in northwest Cook and northeast DuPage Counties to the city of Chicago and the suburbs in south and southwest Cook County. With a Democratic majority in the Illinois General Assembly and a newly elected Democratic governor, members of the legislature supported the new measures proposed by the civic organizations, advocacy groups, and the Mayors Caucus.

## Regional Cooperation

The Mayors Caucus and the civic organizations worked cooperatively on policies in which they had a common agenda. All of the civic organizations, including the Chicagoland Chamber of Commerce, supported Mayor Daley's initiatives for regional economic development. The Civic Committee, Chicago Metropolis 2020, and the Mayors Caucus supported initiatives on surface transportation and freight rail. The Mayors Caucus worked with Chicago Metropolis 2020 and the MPC on initiatives to increase the supply of affordable housing in the region and to promote sustainable development.

### *World Business Chicago and the CREATE Program*

The city of Chicago, Chicago Metropolis 2020, and the Chicagoland Chamber of Commerce established World Business Chicago as a public-private partnership to attract new and retain existing businesses. Founded in 1998 as an outgrowth of an initiative of the Civic Committee of the Commercial Club of Chicago, World Business Chicago's mission is to heighten the region's profile as a destination for global investment and talent. The organization is chaired by Chicago Mayor Richard M. Daley, and the city funds more than half of World Business Chicago's $3.2 million annual operating budget.

Since 1974, the mayors had worked cooperatively in each suburban council of mayors to prioritize their allocation of surface transportation funds. The federal legislative priorities of the Mayors Caucus for 2005 reflected this long-standing involvement in regional transportation issues. The Mayors Caucus strongly supported the reauthorization of federal funding for transit, highway, and safety programs. In addition, they recommended funding support for the Chicago Region Environmental and Transportation Efficiency Project (CREATE), a public-private partnership proposed by Mayor Richard M. Daley to resolve the freight rail gridlock in the region.

### *Housing*

In the late 1990s, the major civic organizations and planning agencies began working with local governments and state housing officials to address the region's serious housing-jobs mismatch and the lack of affordable housing. The MPC had issued "For Rent: Housing Options in the Chicago Region" in 1999. The report, funded by HUD, detailed the affordable housing crisis in the Chicago region. The problems identified were increasing housing costs, increasing traffic congestion, and a decreasing supply of rental housing.

\* \* \*

Working with the MPC, the first housing initiatives of the caucus were to develop a set of housing endorsement criteria designed "to promote housing and mixed-use developments that meet community needs while also addressing broader regional sensible growth goals."[17] The caucus approved the nonbinding Housing Action Agenda on February 28, 2002.

In 2005, the Mayors Caucus and the MPC produced *Welcome Home: Housing Our Community,* a DVD narrated by Bill Kurtis, for distribution to the region's mayors and village officials. Its Housing Committee also worked with Chicago Metropolis 2020 on "Homes for a Changing Region" to promote a range of housing possibilities for the region's growing and diverse populations. There have been two additional reports. The Mayors Caucus's Housing Committee, the Chicago Metropolitan Agency for Planning (CMAP), the Illinois Housing Council, and the MPC published a series of workbooks for local officials and community leaders. The publications and workbooks were designed to inform local mayors and village boards of the possibilities available to them in improving their housing stock and meeting the needs for affordable housing and housing for seniors and persons with disabilities.

Many of the suburbs have moved beyond a nonbinding acceptance of the housing endorsement criteria proposed in 2002 in planning for transit-oriented development in their downtowns. In 2009, the Housing Committee and the MPC worked with interjurisdictional housing collaboratives in south and west Cook County to find solutions to the foreclosed and vacant properties in their areas.

## Regional Conflict

Regional cooperation broke down when the Mayors Caucus and the civic leadership addressed three critical transportation issues: expanding regional airport capacity, restructuring the region's two planning agencies, and restructuring and refinancing the RTA. These three issues were of critical importance to the business community. When the Mayors Caucus was established, the mayors knew that there was no consensus among its membership on the question of expanding airport capacity and so initially agreed to keep the issue off the table. In 2001 they established a Regional Air Capacity Task Force to discuss the issues of expanding O'Hare and building a third airport. Not only was the question of how to restructure the two planning agencies and the RTA not on its agenda, but also the membership of the Mayors Caucus was unhappy with legislation initially proposed by the civic community.

### Expanding Regional Airport Capacity

One of the most contentious issues in regional decision making was whether to add new runways at O'Hare International Airport or build a new regional airport in southeast Will County on a greenfield site near Peotone. Throughout the 1990s, proposals to add new runways at O'Hare were stopped by a coalition of Republicans from DuPage County and suburbs adjacent to the airport. The suburbs adjacent to O'Hare in northwest Cook and northeast DuPage counties had established the Suburban O'Hare Commission (SOC) in 1981. They were financially supported by the DuPage County Board. In the 1990s, the suburbs in SOC formed a coalition with the South Suburban Mayors and Managers Association to push for the new Peotone airport. The mayors in the South Suburban Mayors and Managers Association were proactive in promoting the Peotone airport as a way to revitalize the south Cook suburbs that had suffered from deindustrialization in the 1960s and 1970s.

By the late 1990s, expanding O'Hare had become the top priority for the regional business community. The Civic Committee of the Commercial Club took the lead in pressing for expanded capacity at O'Hare. Mayor Richard M. Daley and the airline industry supported adding new runways. The Cook County Board never took a position regarding new runways at O'Hare, nor did the Metropolitan Planning Commission (MPC).

Consistent with its mandate, the Mayors Caucus took no official position on expanding O'Hare International Airport. The Regional Air Capacity Task Force provided the opportunity for participants to present their positions and listen to other positions. The task force was not asked to find a consensus or make recommendations on the issue. The Mayors Caucus, representing SOC municipalities vehemently opposed to any expansion of O'Hare Airport as well as those municipalities strongly in favor, remained neutral. The Mayors Caucus also remained neutral on the equally contentious question of building the Peotone airport.

\* \* \*

### *The Northeastern Illinois Regional Transportation Task Force*

After Democrats won the governorship and control of the Illinois General Assembly in 2002, the region's business community pressed for a resolution of the contentious issues regarding restructuring the region's transportation and land-use agencies. In late 2003 the Illinois General Assembly established the Northeastern Illinois Regional Transportation Task Force chaired by Congressman Lipinski (D-Chicago) to make recommendations regarding whether restructuring the transportation agencies into a single agency was viable.

\* \* \*

### *The Chicago Metropolitan Agency for Planning*

The Regional Transportation Task Force resolutions were sent to the Illinois General Assembly. The Mayors Caucus began its own hearings over the summer to determine whether it would be best to reinvent the two planning agencies or merge them. Their recommendations would then be submitted to the General Assembly. The Mayors Caucus established a CATS/NIPC Coordinating Committee composed of the officers of the two agencies with oversight by the caucus and the region's county board chairmen. The recommendations of the coordinating committee were to have an oversight board for the two agencies, but the agencies themselves would still have final authority over any plans they submitted to the oversight board. The mayors would maintain control over land-use and zoning issues and would continue to control the local surface transportation allocation projects through the Councils of Mayors process.

In 2005, after consultation with all of the stakeholders, legislation was introduced to consolidate the two agencies. In May, the Illinois General Assembly unanimously approved the legislation (110-0). The Regional Planning Board was established as a municipal corporation with a I5-member board. The Mayors Caucus coordinated the transition of CATS and NIPC into the Regional Planning Board with funding assistance from the MacArthur Foundation.

The membership of the Regional Planning Board, renamed the Chicago Metropolitan Agency for Planning (CMAP), reflects the new political and population balance of the region. One-third of its members represent Chicago, one-third of its members represent suburban Cook County, and one-third of its members represent the collar counties. The mayors of the suburban regional councils continue to control their allocation of surface transportation funding. The policy-making boards of NIPC and CATS are committees of CMAP. CATS retains its federal designation as the MPO for the region. The new agency would have no authority over the local zoning, land-use, and annexation decisions made by the region's municipalities.

For the first time, the Chicago metropolitan region has a planning agency whose decision-making board is appointed by elected officials in the region. The oversight board is entirely composed of members selected by the county board presidents and the mayors, giving regional stakeholders, including the county board chairmen, the final say in the decisions.

* * *

## Analysis

The Mayors Caucus has proven successful in advancing its policy agenda and working with state legislators and government agencies to achieve its goals. As a regional stakeholder, the Mayors Caucus has worked with the civic organizations in ad hoc coalitions in regional task forces. The mayors knew when they established the caucus that they would not have a consensus on the question of how to expand airport capacity. The question of restructuring NIPC and CATS and restructuring and refinancing the RTA, however, presented new challenges for a caucus based on consensus building.

### *Mayors Caucus: Membership Agenda*

The region's mayors originally agreed to work together on initiatives dealing with global competitiveness, noncompliance with the Clean Air Act standards on ozone, electric deregulation, and regional economic development. "The Greenest Region Compact" of Metropolitan Chicago states their continuing focus:

> We, the undersigned Mayors will strive to improve the environment in the Chicago region by taking actions in our own operations and communities. Through our leadership we will demonstrate the economic and social viability of sustainable and environmentally-friendly practices.[23]

Their original priorities have expanded. The Critical Infrastructure Committee, begun because of the earlier problems with Commonwealth Edison, now has expanded to ensure the protection of natural gas, potable water, and telecommunications as well as electric power. The most recent initiative in providing information and technical services to the membership is the task force on service delivery for police and fire services. The task force made recommendations to assist the Mayors Caucus members in analyzing and evaluating their opportunities to reduce their public safety costs.[24]

The legislative agenda of the Mayors Caucus similarly centers on those items that the membership supports: unfunded personnel and pension mandates, the cable and video competition law, protecting state-shared revenues, and protecting the Chicago region's share of state transportation funding. The education reform legislation remains one of the Mayors Caucus's main legislative objectives.

### Refinancing the RTA and the STAR Line

The Mayors Caucus did not reach a consensus on increasing the sales tax in the collar counties. One tension underlying the proposal to increase the sales tax in the collar counties was that there was no agreement between the mayors from the south and southwest Cook suburbs and those from the northwest Cook and collar counties. The Republican members of the General Assembly had sent a letter to Congressman Lipinski as chair of the Task Force arguing that

> "an attempt to restructure our transportation governance system may *jeopardize the collaborative balance that exists between the City of Chicago and the rapidly developing suburban region .... The governance system is balanced regionally and politically."*

Their argument was based on the historic hostility between the city of Chicago and the Republican suburbs. The flaw in their argument was that restructuring and refinancing the RTA was no longer a simple city-suburban issue. In the new regional context, the RTA, and Metra in particular, had become identified with transportation policies that advantaged northwest Cook, DuPage, and Will County residents and seriously disadvantaged residents in the south and southwest Cook suburbs.

One of the most contentious issues was Metra's planned Suburban Transit Access Route (STAR) line. The proposed STAR line would run from Joliet north to Hoffman Estates and then in the median strip of Interstate 90 to O'Hare International Airport, using the Elgin, Joliet & Eastern railroad line. When the RTA supported Metra's proposed $1 billion suburb-to-suburb commuter rail system, the municipalities in the South Suburban Mayors and Managers Association were outraged.

In a letter to Metra Chairman Jeff Ladd, the South Suburban Mayors and Managers Association argued that the new STAR line would "perpetuate the economic disparity between the northern region of the metropolitan area and the south suburbs."[25] Rep. Jesse Jackson Jr. (D-2nd) who represents the suburbs in south Cook County argued that the STAR line would mainly serve a White area rich in jobs and not dependent on transit. The needs of his constituents, minority populations with long commutes to jobs in the northwest suburbs or downtown, were ignored.

In an interview with the Daily Southtown, Metra's chairman Jeff Ladd responded to the criticism that Metra was unconcerned about the commuter rail needs of the south and southwest suburbs. He said, "Metra is not a social service agency...and it is not looking to solve the unemployment issue. What good does it do to start a rail service that nobody rides?"[26]

His argument ignored the fact that the Metra Electric Line to the south suburbs has the 4th highest ridership of the lines.[27]

The other contentious issue was Metra's serious neglect of the Electric Line itself. Commuters complained of unfair ticketing practices, the lack of on-train restrooms, and poorly maintained stations. The Randolph Street terminal, gutted in 1996 for planned restoration, had not been repaired. After a series of hearings were held, Metra ordered new cars with on-train restrooms, removed the turnstiles, upgraded its stations, and completed the Randolph Street terminal.

### Restructuring and Refinancing the RTA

The conflict surrounding the recommendations of the Northeastern Illinois Transportation Task Force to merge NIPC and CATS and restructure and refinance the RTA highlights the historical support in the region for the benefits of fragmented government. The statements made by Republican mayors, who did not represent the Mayors Caucus, against consolidating the planning agencies, centralized transportation planning, and making the governor more responsible for the agencies reflect a long-standing opposition to the establishment of a regional government. The opposition to any restructuring of the transportation system also represented the opposition of those mayors on the task force from the collar counties to any reduction in their de facto control of Metra, Pace, and the RTA.

The resolutions proposed by the Northeastern Illinois Regional Transportation Task Force reflected the changing sociodemographic and political landscape in the region. The Republicans on the task force attempted to categorize the resolutions as exemplifying the older city-suburban split and a Democratic power grab. Labeling the outcome of the task force as a city-suburb conflict or a Democratic power grab deliberately obscured the critical fact that the task force proposed a shift to address the inequities in service to the inner-ring suburbs and suburbs in south and southwest Cook.

One of the underlying concerns of the Republican legislators was that any attempt to merge NIPC and CATS and restructure the RTA would create new bureaucracies and "[usurp] the authority granted to local units of governments in Article VII of the Illinois Constitution." Their concerns regarding the merger of NIPC and CATS into CMAP and the restructuring of the RTA have proven unfounded. The region's political culture remains based on local government autonomy and a reluctance to establish autonomous public authorities.

Two years after the legislation was passed to restructure and refinance the Regional Transportation Authority, the reforms specified in the legislation had not been implemented. The RTA had not changed the older, formula-based process for allocating funding between the CTA and Metra nor had the RTA initiated a universal fare card linking all three transit agencies. The CTA and Pace have established an integrated fare system utilizing credit and debit cards and tickets from fare vending machines. Metra, continuing with its own system of paper tickets that conductors punch individually, initiated its own system of online ticket sales in 2009. Anticipation that restructuring and refinancing the RTA would lead to a "seamless" regional transportation system that would coordinate fare collection and services has not been achieved. The failure to implement the reforms legislated by the Illinois General Assembly underscores how difficult it is to change an institution when individual members have already established territory and historic patterns of interaction.

## Institution Building and Regional Governance

In his analysis of the emergence of global city regions, Allen J. Scott argues that a new form of governance has emerged, involving a set of complex institutional responses in reaction to the emerging global-local system.[28] He argues that the development of a policy agenda committed to institution building is critical for regional stability and economic growth. These institutions are needed to overcome the fragmentation characteristic of local governments and to work toward collective decision-making. In *Regions and the World Economy*, Scott underscores that as global city regions develop more capacity for collective decision making, intraregional conflict will emerge.[29] Both greater intraregional collaboration and increased intraregional conflict have occurred in the Chicago metropolitan region.

The formation of the Metropolitan Mayors Caucus was the way to overcome the extreme government fragmentation and decades of city-suburban hostility. The Mayors Caucus serves as a regional forum and a regional stakeholder. Its institutional antecedents were the suburban councils of mayors, the suburban COGs, and the intralocal agreements for service delivery negotiated by the municipalities. The catalyst for Mayor Daley's overture to the suburban COGs was the potential consequences of noncompliance with the Clean Air Act on the economic well-being of the region and the quality of life of its residents. The success of the Mayors Caucus with Commonwealth Edison and the Clean Air Campaign firmly established the caucus as a new institution representing the region's mayors.

In the twenty-first century, developing new capacities to solve regional problems will depend on developing new institutional arrangements, on a shared vision of the region's challenges, and on strong leadership. Denver's Metro Mayors Caucus, a cooperative alliance of the 39 mayors in the Denver metropolitan region, has the same commitment to decision making by consensus as Chicago's Mayors Caucus. Its agenda is focused on those issues of greatest importance to the Denver metropolitan region: growth management, multimodal transportation, affordable housing, and intergovernmental cooperation. The Pittsburgh Renaissance is the result of the organizational capacity of a public-private partnership (the Allegheny Conference on Community Development) and the enduring commitment of the region's corporate elite to expand and diversify the regional economy.[30]

Los Angeles and New York City face different challenges. Both global city regions have multiple governments with independent financial resources. The conflict over restructuring and refinancing the RTA highlights the problems in restructuring a public authority with its legally established funding formulas and institutionalized patterns of interaction.

Global city regions with entrenched public authorities and strong county governments may have more difficulty in developing a vision and a consensus on how to achieve that vision. Metropolitan New York City spans three states and has three public transportation authorities. The Port Authority of New York and New Jersey as the regional planning agency has not been able to overcome the intense economic rivalry among the political jurisdictions in the tristate area.[31] Metropolitan Los Angeles has strong city and county governments with little incentive to develop coordinated regional policies.[32]

Regional governance is not regional government. Regionalism, to cite Savitch and Vogel, is "an incremental and evolutionary process."[33] Regional governance in the twenty-first century is also an incremental and evolutionary process, one that necessitates building new institutional capacity for collective decision making.

# Notes

1. Porter, D. R., and A. D. Wallis. 2002. *Exploring Ad Hot Regionalism.* Cambridge, MA: Lincoln Institute of Land Policy.
2. These special purpose districts include park and recreation districts, school districts, fire protection districts, mosquito abatement districts, sewage districts, water supply districts, drainage districts, cemetery districts, irrigation and water conservation districts, and soil conservation districts.
3. This pattern is statewide. The state of Illinois has more units of local taxing bodies than any other state (Lawrence 2009).
4. Ford, J. 1980. Intergovernmentalism and regional governance in the 1980s. Paper presented at the Conference on Illinois Government and Politics, Springfield.
5. Intergovernmental agreements are in use in all 50 states. Atkins (1997) asserts that intergovernmental agreements are the preferred administrative structure for cooperation by local governments. They by definition are the most limited forms of governance in that they leave intact the authority of each individual jurisdiction.
6. The system of water provision by Chicago to its suburbs established the pattern for the sale of water in the- region. The suburbs purchasing water from Chicago in turn sell water to adjacent suburbs. Other municipalities with riparian rights on Lake Michigan have constructed water works for their residents and sell lake water to municipalities farther west.
7. Intergovernmental Cooperation Act 220, effective October 1, 1973.
8. These associations include municipal joint action water agencies, municipal joint action agencies for waste disposal, and local economic development commissions.
9. Bums, N. 1994. *The formation of American local governments: Private values in public institutions.* New York: Oxford Univ. Press.
10. The intralocal cooperation in the collar counties include radio dispatch centers, police and fire mutual aid, joint paramedic services, building code enforcement services, and solid waste and water agencies.
11. Fiske, B., ed. 1989. *Key to governmen in Chicago and suburban Cook County.* Chicago: Univ. of Chicago Press.

12. Wandling, R. 2001. Illinois. In *Home rule in America: A fifty-state handbook,* edited by D. Krane, P. N. Rigos, and M. B. Hill, Jr., 128-138. Washington, DC: CQ Press.

13. Hoene, C., M. Baldassare, and M. Shires. 2002. "The development of counties-as municipal governments: A case study of Los Angeles County in the twenty-first century." *Urban Affairs Review* 37 (4): 575-591.

14. Metra directly operates seven of the lines and contracts with two freight carriers to run four others. The carriers use their employees and own or control the rights of way.

15. Civic Federation of Chicago. 2003. A desktop guide to state revenue sources: A report to the education funding reform task force of the Metropolitan Mayors Caucus.

16. Chicago Metropolis 2020 and the Metropolitan Mayors Caucus. 2002. Recommendations for developing attainable workforce housing in the Chicago region. Chicago.

17. Metropolitan Mayors Caucus. 2002. Housing action agenda. Chicago.

18. See Gove and Nowlan (1996) and Lindstrom (2002).

19. Each county sent one".-representative. Cook County, with two-thirds of the region's population, had only one representative. In addition, only one mayor from the region was on its board.

20. Savitch, H. V, and R. K. Vogel, eds. 1996. *Regional politics: America in a post-city age.* Thousand Oaks, CA: Sage.

21. Metropolitan Mayors Caucus. 1998. Review of metropolis project recommendations. November. Chicago.

22. The funding allocation formula was established in 1983.

23. Metropolitan Mayors Caucus. 2009b. Greenest region compact of metropolitan Chicago. Chicago.

24. Metropolitan Mayors Caucus. 2009c. Service delivery task force first report to the full caucus. December 14. Chicago.

25. Diversity, Inc. 2003. Letter to Jeffrey Ladd, Metra Chairman.

26. *Daily Southtown.* 2003. Time for new blood on Metra board. June 12.

27. Metra. 2009. Ridership reports-System facts. http://metrarail.com/metralenlhome/about_metraplanningrecords reports/ridership report.

28. Scott, A. 1. 2000. Global city-regions: Economic planning and policy dilemmas in a neoliberal world. In *Urban-suburban interdependencies,* edited by R. Greenstein and W. Wiewel, 119-40. Cambridge, MA: Lincoln Institute *of* Land Policy.

29. Scott, A J. 1998. *Regions and the world economy: The coming shape of global production, competition, and political order.* Oxford, UK: Oxford Univ. Press.

30. Jezierski, L. 1996. Pittsburgh: Partnerships in a regional city_ In *Regional politics: America in a post-city age,* edited by H. V. Savitch and R. K. Vogel, 159-81. Thousand Oaks, CA: Sage.

31. Berg, B., and P. Kantor. 1996. New York: The politics of conflict and avoidance. In *Regional politics: America in a post-city age,* edited by H. V. Savitch and R. K. Vogel, 25-50. Thousand Oaks, CA: Sage.

32. Saltzstein, A. L. 1996. Los Angeles: Politics without governance. In *Regional politics: America in a post-city age,* edited by H. V Savitch and R. K. Vogel, 51-71. Thousand Oaks, CA: Sage.

33. Savitch, H. V, and R. K. Vogel, eds. 1996. *Regional politics: America in a post-city age.* Thousand Oaks, CA: Sage.p. 294.

# Part VII

## A New Chicago

# A New Chicago

To borrow the words of a Biblical prophet, "without a vision, a people perish; with vision, faith, and commitment, a people flourish." In past decades Chicago has faced major crises as old social, economic, and political systems have partially collapsed and have partially been reformed. The Old Chicago is passing away so a New Chicago can be born.

The two terms of Mayor Harold Washington were a watershed, a major turning point. But he left an uncompleted reform agenda for us to implement. Some reforms have been adopted under Mayor Richard M. Daley, but the list of reforms needed under the new mayor, Rahm Emanuel and a new city council elected in 2011, remains very long. Racial and political machine forces continue to reassert themselves in the city council, in elections, and in local governments throughout the metropolitan region. The political future of Chicago is still to be determined.

Nationally, the 2008 and 2010 elections have brought changes in Washington. President Obama has promised more positive urban policies, but the new Congress elected in 2010 has as its top priority cutting deficit spending. If there is to be improvement in our metropolitan region, we will probably have to depend upon ourselves.

We are still recovering from the Great Recession that began in 2008. In the years immediately ahead, we must strengthen our local economy and fortify our role in the global economy. To do this, we must compete as a metropolitan region; while we have many advantages, which include our diverse economy, we have yet to develop a coherent focus in either the private or public sectors.

Ultimately, our vision of our city's future must transcend the machine/reform and Republican/Democrat divisions of local and national politics. Our vision must transcend city and suburban divisions and public and private sector divides. Our vision of a New Chicago must be drawn from deeper wellsprings. We need to reassert the biblical vision of a just city in which old inequities, hatreds, and injustices are dissolved.

Let us work to create a New Chicago characterized by joy rather than by suffering. Let us cut our high rate of infant mortality and improve the health of everyone. Let the homeless be housed, the hungry fed, and the unemployed and underemployed provided meaningful and rewarding work. Let crime, which has characterized our city for so long, be eliminated. Let everyone walk freely on our streets unafraid. Let traditional hatreds as well as racial, religious, and sexual discrimination disappear.

Let our metropolitan region be an example of how to resolve the problems that now plague our planet. Let us end pollution and create a more energy-efficient green city. Let us order our economy and our education system so that the underclass is fully integrated into society. No more shall we be a metropolitan region that is half rich and half poor.

The struggle for the future of Chicago and our region occurs at many levels. It takes place in elections that dominate the political arena. It takes place in governmental struggles to implement reforms. It occurs in the marketplace as new firms arise, as old companies create new products, and as some enterprises die. It takes place in each of our neighborhoods and communities. It requires a sustained commitment by many individuals to create a new and more just Chicago.

We are engaged in a struggle of hope against despair. It is our task to uphold the vision of a New Chicago and to convince Chicagoans and their leaders to embrace it. This is a task for a lifetime, as the final article attests.

# How Long Is Your Anger?

## By Mary Scott Simpson

*In this article, Mary Scott Simpson argues that we have not sustained our anger at an unjust political system. Instead we have turned "toward acceptance of the failures of our political system" and turned "toward private amusements and away from public action."*

One of my favorite moments in modern drama occurs in Bertolt Brecht's *Mother Courage.* The title character waits with a young soldier outside an army officer's tent; both are there to protest unjust treatment by an army captain. Courage listens with scant patience to the tirade of the young soldier (he won't "stand for injustice"), then asks: "But how long? How long won't you stand for injustice? One Hour? Two?" She sings for him "The Song of the Great Capitulation," an account of the series of small failures, accommodations, compromises through which she has come "to march in lockstep with the rest." At last she advises him, "You should stay here with your sword drawn if you're set on it and your anger is big enough ... but if your anger is a short one, you'd better go." And then she takes her own advice. She leaves, "I've thought better of it. I'm not complaining."

I think of this scene often as I consider the turns of events in the city and the country over the past few years—turnings toward acceptance of the failures of our political system, turnings toward private amusements and away from public action. "Curses," I say to myself, "that was a most remarkably short anger." And I'm inclined to think that more than just a cause or two may be lost in the shuffle. For me, cultivating a long anger and, thus, keeping faith with that belief in democracy which, when offended, gives rise to anger has come to be a matter of personal and cultural survival.

Courage, like many another Brechtian protagonists, knows both that she is given to lapses in virtue and that the system that surrounds her nudges her toward those lapses: it makes survival so desperate an undertaking that only the advantaged few can afford sustained virtue. I, too, see the system that surrounds us as one reason why so many, once angry, have thought better of it and aren't complaining. Our trouble, however, is not so much a matter of survival amid scarcity as it is a matter of surviving plenitude.

As a people we are governed by a restless urge to consume—food, clothes, gadgets, relationships, news, ideologies, causes. I regularly find myself awash in impressions: a whirl of polyester, electric woks, sunshine laws, punk rock, T-groups, protein diets; boycotts, catastrophes and intimations of apocalypse. The buzz is ubiquitous. In such circumstances, to sustain anger, to sustain a thought requires Promethean powers of concentration.

Our system teaches us to live like those pigeons that congregate on El platforms—scurrying frantically from one bright flash to the next, hoping for grain and finding (worse luck) discarded gum wrappers. Allowing ourselves to follow that pattern has consequences for our character—individually and corporately. It means, at least, that we may be allowing the erosion of some capacities that make us human: the capacity for fidelity, for instance, to other persons, to our own beliefs, to carefully considered goals. I wonder, too, what we do to our capacity for hard thought when we subject our minds daily to the impressionistic patterns of the six o'clock news: fragments and facts, uninterrupted, unexamined. And I wonder what difference it will someday make that we consistently prefer intense, ephemeral pleasures to the others—longer, slower, substantial satisfactions that come from solving problems, making things, keeping promises.

These are habits we can't afford to lose.

Choosing a goal (the political reformation of Chicago, for instance), then pursuing it steadily—testing, refining ourselves and our ideas through experience: these things take years, not months of our time. But those who give themselves to that long endeavor learn that there are goods of a personal sort to be taken from it—growth in skill and understanding, certainly, but perhaps even more important, the sense that one has said, "Here I stand," and meant it to a world that is forever telling us, "Move along, there."

To sustain one's anger is to secure one's humanity.